I0817566

The Oak and the Larch

ALSO BY SOPHIE PINKHAM

Black Square: Adventures in Post-Soviet Ukraine

The Oak and the Larch

A Forest History of Russia and Its Empires

SOPHIE PINKHAM

W. W. NORTON & COMPANY

Independent Publishers Since 1923

Printed in the United States of America
First Edition

For information about special discounts for bulk purchases, please contact
W. W. Norton Special Sales at specialsales@wwnorton.com or 800-233-4830

Manufacturing by Lake Book Manufacturing
Maps by handmademaps.com
Book design by Chris Welch
Production manager: Devon Zahn

ISBN 978-1-324-03668-5

W. W. Norton & Company, Inc.
500 Fifth Avenue, New York, NY 10110
www.wwnorton.com

W. W. Norton & Company Ltd.
15 Carlisle Street, London W1D 3BS

Authorized EU representative: EAS, Mustamäe tee 50, 10621 Tallinn, Estonia

1 2 3 4 5 6 7 8 9 0

In memory of my father,

Henry C. Pinkham,

inveterate reader and planter of trees

Contents

A Note on Transliteration xi

Introduction 1

CHAPTER 1: A Fortress in the Taiga 13

CHAPTER 2: The Golden Horde and the Tree of Life 28

CHAPTER 3: The Emperor's Fleet 45

CHAPTER 4: Subduing the Sublime 58

CHAPTER 5: Clear Glade and Murmuring Forest 72

CHAPTER 6: Prince, Peasant, Tungus, Yakut 89

CHAPTER 7: Tigers Listen to Water Talk 101

CHAPTER 8: Cutting Orchards and Moving Mountains 116

CHAPTER 9: Electricity and Resurrection 129

CHAPTER 10: Young Oaks 141

CHAPTER 11: Stalin and the Wood Goblin 155

CHAPTER 12: The Tsar-Larch and the Flood 171

CHAPTER 13: Arks and Anarchists 186

CHAPTER 14: Militiamen 202

CHAPTER 15: Bears, Wolves, and Archipelagoes 219

EPILOGUE: Last Stand on the Ugra 239

Acknowledgments 247

Notes 251

Index 271

A Note on Transliteration

Transliteration—in this case, the conversion of non-Latin scripts into the Latin alphabet—is a chronic headache for anyone writing about the Slavic lands. I have chosen a path of willful, mindful inconsistency in my transliterations. My choices are oriented largely around intelligibility and ease of reading. For most Russian words, I use a simplified version of the Library of Congress transliteration system. But popular transliteration is often inconsistent, and transliteration systems vary over time and across countries. Where there is another, more widely recognized transliteration of a name, or when I am aware of a person's preferred transliteration of their own name, I use that one: for instance, Tolstoy instead of Tolstoi. In endnotes, I use the Library of Congress system without adaptation—soft signs, hard signs, and all.

The difficulties of transliteration mount when one is dealing with multiple countries and languages, since each has its own variants of the same names and its own set of transliteration rules. The plot thickens further when one is writing about a long span of history. Many places, for instance, have different names depending on which source language one uses. One well-known example is Ukraine's capital city. "Kiev" is the standard transliteration of the city's Russian name. "Kyiv" is the Ukrainian version. It took a war with Russia for the spelling to be changed in the English-language media. For obvious reasons, I use the Ukrainian spelling here. But this raises the question of what to call Kyivan/Kievan Rus, the first East Slavic state. The conventional spelling is Kievan Rus. But for consistency with "Kyiv" and because Rus is, in my view, as much Ukrainian as Russian, I use a Ukrainian spelling for this and several other Ukrainian place names. Likewise, for the person previously known as Genghis Khan, I use the spelling preferred in Mongolia: Chinggis Khan. It is only respectful. Such choices may seem anachronistic to some readers. In my view, they reflect our evolving understanding of the historiography of diverse, multilingual northern Eurasia.

The Oak and the Larch

Introduction

Russia has more trees than there are stars in our galaxy. From the Baltic to the Pacific, from the Arctic to the steppes of Central Asia, Russia's forests account for nearly one-fifth of the world's forest cover. It is not surprising, then, that the forest lies at the heart of Russian culture and history. One prominent Soviet writer observed in the 1950s that the forest greeted the Russian at his birth, when it provided the wood for his cradle, and that it "attended him through all the stages of his life."[1] When he died, the forest offered a cross to mark his grave. Throughout Russian history, the forest has been at the heart of national identity, a symbol of what is good and what must be preserved, the last bulwark against annihilation.

But Russians have long had a deeply contradictory attitude to the forest, blending respect and affection with neglect and even hostility. This ambivalence is characteristic of a place that has long been torn between east and west, city and country, proletariat and peasantry, past and future. It is a tension that spans Russia's vast territory, whose tree population is as diverse as its peoples and its sense of self. *The Oak and the Larch* tells the story of the northern Eurasian forests, which have, over the centuries, been part of the domain of Chinggis Khan's Golden Horde, the Russian Empire, the Soviet Union, and now the Russian Federation and other states that emerged from the USSR.

The two trees of the title are sylvan symbols of the poles of Russian geography, climate, and culture. Russian fairytales often feature oaks:

sacred, towering, and mighty, attributed with righteous authority and healing powers. Reigning over the deciduous forests of European Russia, the oak is a symbol of the earliest rise of Muscovy. Its wood built the ships of Peter the Great's imperial fleet, which made Russia a great power in the eighteenth century. But in the expanse east of the Ural Mountains, conifers hold sway. The larch, which can live for a thousand years, stands for the northern forest, the taiga. This biome comprises much of Siberia, the vast territory of northern Asia that Russia began colonizing in the sixteenth century. The taiga was wild and unmapped, a realm of mortal danger but also the source of luxurious furs that traversed the globe and made Russia rich.

Many of the places explored in this book were captured by Russia only in the last few centuries—within the lifetime of a middle-aged larch. The accidents of history have given Russia control of a large and extraordinarily diverse share of the world's forests, from taiga to deciduous forest to pine barrens to temperate rainforests to wetlands. Russia's imperial expansion has encompassed a huge range of ethnicities, languages, religions, and approaches to nature. For both people and trees, the story of northern Eurasia's forests is about much more than Russia. Some of the most important tales these forests tell are about Siberia, one-third of Asia's landmass; Ukraine, Belarus, and Poland; the North Caucasus; and Central Asia.

Most accounts of Russian history start in Kyivan Rus, the first East Slavic state, and move north to central Russia before expanding into Siberia. This book breaks with that tradition by beginning with the story of Siberia's forests and the people who inhabited them thousands of years before Russians set foot in northern Asia. We move west with Chinggis Khan, who emerged from the forest of northern Mongolia; his Golden Horde went on to conquer much of Eurasia, leaving an indelible mark on Russian society. From the days of Kyivan Rus to the present, the forest has played a central role in Russia's imperial expansion, and resistance to this expansion. Russian victory in the North Caucasus was predicated on the destruction of forests that gave cover to Chechens and Avars who waged one of the fiercest guerrilla wars of the century. The swampy forests of Belarus and northern Ukraine, meanwhile, were a nearly ungovernable space where centralized powers struggled to exert full control, even in the twentieth century. When the Nazis invaded, the region's woods were a crucial hiding place for Soviet partisans who helped win the Second World War.

The dizzying scale and variety of the northern Eurasian forests have granted them an exceptional multiplicity of stories and meanings. Long after western Europe had felled a large proportion of its trees, the Russian Empire still had more forests than it could map. Forest myths and sacred trees figure in many cultures.[2] Mythology and religion do not stop at national boundaries; they began long before national boundaries existed. Yet in its centrality and manifold meanings, the forest has given rise to some of the most vexing questions of Russian political and cultural history: questions about power, identity, responsibility, and agency. Is the forest to be feared or respected? Does the forest protect people, or is it people's responsibility to protect the forest? Can humans design their future by manipulating the nonhuman world, or are they at the mercy of forces larger than themselves? The societies and peoples inhabiting Russia and its empires have oscillated wildly in their responses, which have ranged from creeds of submission to fantasies of mastery.

Writers have very often been the ones formulating and answering these questions. In Russia, novelists and poets have a long history as forest defenders—and as agents of empire, shaping ideas of national identity. For centuries, the distinctly Russian combination of censorship and veneration of literature pushed political and scientific debates into belles lettres. With its power to leap across boundaries of time, space, and identity, meanwhile, literature is an ideal dwelling place for new visions of society and nature. This is why writers have pride of place in this book. The 2022 invasion of Ukraine has caused reconsideration of Russia's cultural legacy, with some arguing that all Russian cultural achievements are sullied by the war crimes committed under Putin. What is needed is not dismissal but a deeper kind of consideration, and inclusion of the many realms of identity and experience that have been pushed aside by conventional narratives that assume the primacy of ethnic Russians. The story of the forest offers a new vantage point from which to understand the history and culture of the Russian Empire, the Soviet Union, and now the Russian Federation. By looking at Russia from the forest's perspective, we can gain new understanding of the nature of Russian power, Russian nationalism, Russian imperialism, and Russia's ideas of itself.

According to a Slavic legend, at the beginning of time two oak trees stood in a vast blue sea, awaiting the creation of earth and sky. Pagan Slavs worshipped at the feet of oaks in sacred glades, dedicating the trees to the god of thunder.[3] In fairytales, the forest stretched up into heaven; one Russian folk saying describes "a forest so tall it makes a hole in the sky." The oldest written histories of the Eastern Slavs—the tribes who later became Belarusians, Russians, and Ukrainians—describe newly founded Kyiv, capital of Rus, as surrounded by a great pine forest teeming with wild beasts, prey for hunters.[4] After the Mongols sacked Kyiv in 1240, the center of East Slavic power shifted north to the densely forested lands around the upper Volga River. Russian chroniclers of the thirteenth and fourteenth centuries often wrote about "the wooded land" rather than naming any specific location. The forest was their home. In Russian icons of the sixteenth and seventeenth centuries, heaven was a stand of trees.[5]

As the Slavs expanded their territory, forest areas provided a natural fortress from which to launch attacks on the enemy tribes who inhabited the windswept Eurasian steppe. In the late sixteenth century, the newly dominant principality of Muscovy started making the *zaseki*, a line of arboreal fortifications to protect against nomad raids.* Long belts of trees were cut and laid out, their branches sharpened so

* This practice, also seen in the Roman Empire and western Europe, is known in English as an abatis.

that they formed a spiky line to stop invaders on horseback. The forest was militarized. This practice turned magical in Russian fairytales, where the hero often throws a comb that changes into a thick forest to protect him from pursuers.

The forest also held danger. The greatest rival to humans was the bear, "abbot of the forest." He competed with humans for precious honey. According to legend, the bear had once been a man who was denied the bread and salt traditionally offered to guests as a sign of friendship. In revenge for this slight, he took on a frightening new shape and made the forest his stronghold, defending it against the species to which he had once belonged.[6] Enemy soldiers often found refuge in the woods, a place where death was always lurking.

An early chronicle of Kyivan Rus describes forest dwellers as "magicians," or as existing like "wild beasts"—in other words, as pagans.[7] In those days, history was written by monks. As the Slavs embraced Orthodox Christianity, the forest became the repository of pre-Christian beliefs and mystical practices. The Christian church wished to extirpate the spirits and rituals that hid among the dense trees, but these endured in the form of superstition and fairytales—often told during tree felling, when whole villages camped deep in the woods and passed the evenings telling stories around a fire.[8] In folklore, the ruler of the forest was Baba Yaga, the dreadful, fascinating witch who lived in an ambulatory hut on chicken legs. Baba Yaga loved to devour children and maidens, but at other times she took pity on those cast into the forest, giving them magical gifts. Guardian of a portal to the underworld, she ruled a bountiful forest where a hero could be transformed. Baba Yaga is probably a deformed version of a mother goddess from pre-Christian tradition. Stories about her are remnants of old initiation rites that marked the passage from childhood to adulthood, with symbolic death and rebirth achieved through a trip into the forest.[9] The Virgin Mary was imported; Baba Yaga, in her forest hut, is the true mother of Russian culture.

Another folkloric character, the *leshii*, or wood goblin, embodied both the forest's power of protection and its potential menace.

Like Baba Yaga, he is a remnant of pre-Christian beliefs, and he has all the resentment of a defrocked deity. The *leshii* was sometimes called the "forest tsar," "forest master," or even "forest official," in a tongue-in-cheek acknowledgment of nonhuman forms of sovereignty over natural spaces. Those who walked in the *leshii*'s realm had to play by his rules. Russian peasants knew that the spirit of the woods had to be appeased or avoided, lest he wreak havoc on human endeavors. Modern-minded people denounced this idea as backward; today, as human error causes a cascade of natural disasters, it seems wise.

As Russian agriculture expanded, the forest became an enemy. Backbreaking work was needed to fell and burn trees to make way for cultivated fields. A peasant family would often repeat this process several times, exhausting one field and going on to slash and burn the next plot of forest. The woods were home to wolves, bears, and unclean spirits, not a nurturing home but a dark past. As Slavs ventured east in search of the taiga's precious furs, Christian missionaries in Siberia wielded their axes against the sacred trees of animist natives.

In the push and pull of Russian expansion, the forest often served as a refuge. When Russian colonists marched east into Siberia, many Indigenous peoples retreated into the taiga. So did escaped serfs, bandits, and religious dissidents. The Romanov dynasty consolidated its power over the Russian Orthodox Church in the seventeenth century, but a small group of schismatics, known as Old Believers, fled for the depths of the forest, where they preserved their old ways in sanctified isolation. Siberia's remote forests and mountains became a paradoxical place of liberty and penal servitude. Old Believers bartered with fugitives, and political exiles documented the traditions of Indigenous people who still lived as hunter-fisher-gatherers and herders. Convicts sent to Siberia in the nineteenth century often absconded from their hard labor during the warmer months, when the call of the cuckoo bird, "General Kukushka," roused them to escape into the forest. They liked to declare, "The prison is my father, and the taiga is my mother."[10]

The Siberian taiga seemed infinite. But by the nineteenth century, some of Russia's most gifted writers feared for Russia's heartland forests, which were too quickly being turned into timber. This concern was allied with opposition to serfdom, one of Russia's greatest moral blights. In 1852, Ivan Turgenev published a book of stories that celebrated the Russian countryside, lamented the high-speed felling of its forests, and portrayed serfs and peasants with dignity and compassion. At a time when many members of the Russian aristocracy viewed serfs as less than human, the book caused a sensation. It is credited with helping to bring about the emancipation of 1861. But the process of emancipation and associated land reforms accelerated deforestation, which became so severe that it affected rivers and precipitation. There were public debates about how to "emancipate" the woods and save them from the ravages of the market. The forest's plight was taken up by Lev Tolstoy. As a young man, he participated in the military deforestation of the Caucasus; his experience in the army helped make him a writer, a pacifist, and a lifelong planter of trees. He used the proceeds from *War and Peace* to reforest his estate in central Russia, recycling books back into woods.

Tolstoy was one of a growing number of Russians who dreamed of an end to private property. In his uncompromising pacifism, however, he was an outlier in an age of mounting political violence. When the Bolsheviks executed the last tsar and his family in 1918, the royal bodies were left in unmarked graves in a forest outside Ekaterinburg. As the Russian Empire descended into civil war between revolutionaries and counterrevolutionaries, Reds and Whites, the countryside was caught in between. Peasants calling themselves the Green Armies resisted the requisition of their grain and waged an antigovernment insurgency from their lairs in the forest. In Siberia, the descendants of settlers and prisoners united with Indigenous peoples to resist Bolshevik rule; partisan armies dissolved into the taiga and then struck at unexpected moments, fending off Soviet control for years.

For those who fled the revolution, the forest and its inhabitants became emblems of exile. In Vladimir Nabokov's first published story, "The Wood-Sprite," a dreamy young man is visited by a "bony and implausible" creature who perches on an armchair "like a crow on a tree stump." The sound of the creature's rustling voice recalls all that the young émigré has lost.[11] Russia's black fir forests and white birches have been felled or burned; the *leshii* fled the country after finding a forest glade full of dead bodies. Published in 1921 in a Berlin newspaper for Russian émigrés, "The Wood-Sprite" expresses Nabokov's own grief and anger at being driven out of Russia by the revolution.

Having vanquished their opponents, the Bolsheviks set out to bend nature to human will in their attempt to build a new world. This project entailed a refashioning of time itself: In the 1920s and 1930s, revolutionary time was imagined as entirely linear, accelerating like a train hurtling along a track. Any belief in the old logic of nature, and any pity for casualties, was counterrevolutionary. The passage from one season to the next, the familiar cycles of buds and blossoms, fading flowers and falling leaves, were no longer valid. But Stalin proved nostalgic for the old shelter of the *zaseka*. After the Second World War, he devised a scheme to plant immense walls of forest that would shield Russian cities and fields from the wild winds of the Central Asian steppe. Acorns became tools of ideology. Most of the trees that were planted died.

The Soviet approach to time and nature had disastrous results for humans and ecosystems alike, but survivors and witnesses learned from the trauma. As early as the 1950s, before much of the world cared about climate change, Soviet environmentalist writers recognized that breaking with the cycles of nature could destroy the forest, as well as other biomes, and upend the foundations of society. Tempered in the fire of the Soviet experiment, Soviet writers of the forest were prescient in their understanding of climate change and forest destruction. They saw that loss of the forest meant the loss of one of Russia's most important refuges, its source of material and spiritual nourishment. To safeguard Russia's national spirit, they believed that it was essential to protect its forests.

As the Soviet Union thawed, the *leshii* became a symbol of environmental degradation but also of the forest's resilience, and even its potential for retaliation. In his 1959 short story "Tenants," the dissident writer Andrei Sinyavsky imagined a communal apartment populated by a *leshii* and other creatures of Russian folklore made refugees by Soviet industrialization. Sinyavsky suggested that as people polluted the environment, the spirits of the forest would reemerge in unexpected places, with ruinous results. Nature would have its revenge, the forest's murmur becoming a roar of righteous fury. Sinyavsky soon ended up in a prison camp felling trees.

It was fitting that the Soviet Union died in the forest. On December 8, 1991, Boris Yeltsin of Russia, Stanislav Shushkevich of Belarus, and Leonid Kravchuk of Ukraine met at a hunting lodge in the primeval forest of western Belarus and agreed to dissolve the Soviet Union. The accord sank Mikhail Gorbachev's efforts to keep the union together, and he stepped down as president of the USSR a few weeks later. No longer anchored by an empire, Russia was adrift. Some Russians searched for reassurance, as well as berries and mushrooms, in the forest—and depended on garden plots for food as supply chains and currency collapsed. Environmental activists fought to protect forests from the new threats of privatization and global capitalism as Russia's trees were offered to the highest bidder.

In the Russian Federation, trees have not lost their connection to Russia's history of conquest and military might. Some of the most advanced weapons of war bear the names of trees. The Russian Navy's prime nuclear-powered submarine is called the Ash Tree (*Yasen*), while the Strategic Rocket Forces field an intercontinental ballistic missile called the White Poplar (*Topol*). In November 2024, the Russians fired a new hypersonic intermediate-range ballistic missile called the Hazel Tree (*Oreshnik*) at a factory in the Ukrainian city of Dnipro. Ukraine, meanwhile, has developed a "Baba Yaga" combat drone: a bomb-dropping forest witch.

Under Putin, pro-regime writers are warrior-ideologues defining the "national idea"—and sometimes finding it in the forest. At the same time, the country is awash in fantasies of quitting corrupt civilization for a self-sufficient life in the woods. Some Russian citizens have escaped conscription to the war in Ukraine by disappearing into the forest, a time-honored tradition. At a moment of exceptional fragmentation, when much of the Russian liberal and leftist intelligentsia has fled the country, the image of the forest continues to bind together disparate factions.

And yet Russia's forests are shrinking. From 2001 to 2023, Russia, the largest country in the world by area, lost about 11 percent of its tree cover.[12] Russia is warming at more than twice the average global speed: One result is a dramatic increase in forest fires. The world's newspaper readers have been shocked in recent years to learn that even Siberia—the land of permafrost and nine-month winters, shoulder-deep snow and rare tigers—is aflame. Wildfires are a natural phenomenon in the taiga, but warmer, drier conditions have made them more severe and more frequent. In 2021, Siberia's forests were ravaged by the biggest wildfires in Russia's history, larger than those in all the rest of the world combined.[13] An area of forest twice the size of Ireland was burned. For the first time ever recorded, smoke reached the North Pole. In 2022, smoke from Russian wildfires reached California.[14] In 2024, wildfires swept Siberia and the Russian Far East; the burned area was 50 percent larger than that of the previous year's fires.[15] While Russia was focused on the war in Ukraine and its consequences, its own landscape was transformed. As permafrost and glaciers melt, as forests and peat bogs burn, Russia is faced with profound questions about its future identity.

The dream of subjugating nature is deeply embedded in many societies, especially Christian ones. In the Book of Genesis, God tells Adam and Eve to "fill the earth and subdue it," naming them rulers of all living things. Advancing technology gave humanity ever more effective ways of subordinating the earth to human needs and desires. But today many of us are remembering that we are not above or outside the nonhuman world, and never will be. Here the forest history of Russia and its empires offers a certain comfort, a new way of seeing. Faced with an exceptionally harsh climate and centuries of political repression and upheaval, inhabitants of northern Eurasia cultivated a resilience that has much to teach us as the planet enters a new age of political and climatic extremes. These forest dwellers never forgot what it was like to live at the mercy of nature. Through their stories, we can learn not only about the bounty, beauty, and refuge offered by the forest but also about how to survive in hard times.

In Anton Chekhov's last play, a felled cherry orchard stands for the death of the old social order. The fate of the vast northern Eurasian forests will help determine the future climate of the whole world. Recent battles fought in the charred forests of Ukraine have shaped European history and international geopolitics. As in a fairytale, the forest is the threshold between the worlds of the living and the dead, between arrogant new gods and disgruntled old ones. The story of these forests is a testament to human cruelty, shortsightedness, and vain ambition. But it is also a tale of resilience and of the power of art.

CHAPTER 1

A Fortress in the Taiga

A man rows a canoe along a broad, glassy river. As he approaches the sandy shore, he fires two shots from his rifle. Villagers rush to greet him and his honored guest: a bear. The hunter has already opened the bear's coat in the forest and removed its shoes and gloves. In other words, he has skinned it. Women and children kiss the animal's pelt, stroke its staring face, and implore it not to frighten them when they pick berries in the forest. The bear is lowered into a specially prepared house adorned with its favorite tree, a young Siberian pine. Now men sing songs of Torum, the forest's god and the bear's father. The soul of Torum's son must be returned home with due pomp, so that he will not trouble the people who killed him. "Out of wood," the men sing, "a gallant new man was created." Like bears, humans depend on the forest for their existence.[1]

The people celebrating this ritual are Khanty who live near the Agan River, in northwestern Siberia. Their ancestors arrived in the region by 500 CE, long before a Slav ever set foot there. The bear's arrival was captured in *Sons of Torum*, a 1989 film by an Estonian writer and filmmaker named Lennart Meri. In 1941, at age twelve, Meri had been exiled to the Volga River region after Stalin annexed Estonia.[2] He later became fascinated by Uralic languages like Khanty and Mansi, which are related to Hungarian and, more distantly, to Finnish and Estonian. The members of this far-flung linguistic family shared more than vocabulary; they were united by a history of domination by Russia. *Sons of Torum* is an ode to survival and return. Meri became the second president of newly independent Estonia in 1992, bringing the memory of Siberia's forests to the highest rungs of Estonia's government. In 2006, he was buried in Tallinn's Forest Cemetery, where Estonian luminaries rest eternally among the trees.

The Khanty bear ceremony survived encounters first with imperial Russian missionaries and colonizers, then with forced Soviet modernization, collectivization, and executions. Some of the earliest information about Khanty religious traditions comes from Russian priests who sent their reports to the archbishop of Siberia to alert him to the problem of continued paganism.[3] In the latter half of the nineteenth century, ethnographers became fascinated by the bear ceremony. Finnish and Hungarian visitors were particularly attracted by the linguistic link to their own languages. It was mind-boggling to think that one branch of the same population had ended up in the baroque palaces of Budapest while another had remained hunter-fisher-gatherers in the remote northern forests.

The strange kinship had a whiff of alternative history: What would have happened if Hungarians had never adopted agriculture, never become owners of grand estates, never built cities? Well into the twentieth century, the Khanty relied for their survival on their reindeer herds and on the gifts of the forest and rivers: berries and pine nuts, dried and smoked fish, frozen meat, dried birds. Their forest lifeway still resembled societies that existed across northern Eurasia for millennia. Once upon a time, the people living in this area were at the vanguard of human development.

A few hundred kilometers northwest of the river where Meri filmed, a sandy elevated spit overlooks the vast expanse of the West Siberian plain. Whorls of Siberian pine, spruce, and larch cede to brown, squelching swamp. This stretch of forest is the last before the beginning of Arctic tundra to the north. It is traced with wide, slow rivers, still the principal routes of transport for the Khanty and other Indigenous people—by boat in summer, and in winter, along the ice. White moss, food for reindeer, foams on the ground beneath the trees.

This remote expanse of taiga hardly seems like a cradle of human innovation. Today, it sits squarely in the middle of nowhere. Yet it contains one of the oldest-known fortified settlements in the world. The Amnya site, named for the nearby river of that name, has astonished the archaeology world and helped overturn assumptions about how societies progress over time, changing from peaceful hunter-gatherer communities to agrarian societies characterized by private property, social inequality, and warfare. Radiocarbon dating published in 2023 shows that the fortifications were built eight thousand years ago—almost five thousand years earlier than researchers had thought such settlements were first established in the region, and many centuries before the appearance of similar forts in Europe. The tiny, wooded citadel is the northernmost Stone Age stronghold anywhere in Eurasia. It survived in part because the area's forest, too cold and swampy for agriculture, has never been plowed. Up to the present day, the Indigenous people living nearby have refrained from building over the visible house pits. According to their traditional cosmology, digging is dangerous, because it risks disturbing the spirits of the lower world.[4]

This fortified settlement, and numerous similar, more recent promontory forts in the Ob River region, offer a tantalizing riddle for archaeologists. Why did Neolithic people need forts in the first place? What were these fortifications meant to protect, at a time long before trade? And how did Neolithic hunter-fisher-gatherers manage to construct this monumental architecture so deep in the northern forest, in a place that even today is seventeen hours by car from the nearest major Russian city?

There is clearly something exceptional about the Ob River basin. The area shows evidence of continuous habitation since the Neolithic period. A former riverbed nearby, abandoned by the larger rivercourse and reduced to a dead-end lake, provides one clue. This area is known even today for its abundant fish. It is home to pike, perch, and whitefish, as well as exotic, fatty northern fish of the salmonid family: tender, silvery muksun, white-fleshed nelma, and the hucho taimen, which makes for delectable "taiga sushi," as Henny Piezonka, a German archaeologist studying the Amnya site, described it. With its blue-green head and luminous, sunset-colored tail, the taimen is so big that Chinese and Mongolian legends render it as a kind of sea monster. The so-called river wolf or river tiger is known to prey on rats, ducks, and muskrats, though it usually hunts other fish. It can grow to be up to six feet long and one hundred pounds, and it can live for fifty-five years. The taimen makes the Amnya site look modern: It has existed for fifty million years.[5]

Archaeologists suspect that the Amnya settlement was built to store and protect the bounty caught in this relict lake, which is a perfect place to fish using a weir, an underwater fence. The Khanty and Selkup, another Indigenous group in the area, still fish using weirs—as Piezonka put it, "technology perfected eight thousand years ago." *Sons of Torum* shows how Khanty men strip pine roots with their knives and teeth, smoothing them until they are supple as leather. The roots are used to bind wooden laths, forming a screen to trap fish in a lake after they swim in during the spring. In the autumn, when it becomes cold enough to preserve them, the fish can be pulled out of the water without the aid of lines or nets.

Such piscine bounty demanded new ways of living. A weir cannot be abandoned for a season. It requires year-round maintenance, as well as protection from enemies and wild animals such as bears. A weir could make the difference between a well-fed winter and death by starvation. This explains why nomadic or seminomadic hunter-gatherers chose to build a fortress on the riverbank and commit to settling down. The strong but flexible roots of the Siberian pine, woven into a weir, bound them to a single place.

The Neolithic hunter-fisher-gatherers lived relatively well. Like the Khanty as late as the twentieth century, they hunted forest animals and ate preserved fish in winter; in spring, they turned to migratory birds arriving from the south; in autumn, they caught fish and elk migrating from the other side of the Ural Mountains. The beginning of the Neolithic period was the moment when people began to use ceramic vessels as well as wooden ones, and this area near the Amnya is the first place in the region where pottery has been found. Before ceramics, containers were made of birch bark, which can be used for baking but cannot be held over an open flame. Clay pottery made it possible to simmer, a process essential to making fish oil or fish glue, and to store food safely over long periods. (The local Indigenous people still make fish glue from pike bones.) The taiga's long stretches of subzero weather, meanwhile, allowed the Neolithic people to freeze meat and oils.

The accumulation of precious food opened new possibilities for social organization. Inequality resulted, as did property rights and collective projects such as the construction of the fort.[6] And there was war. Fish oil and fish meal, easy to store and transport but requiring much labor in its acquisition and preparation, was an appealing target for raiders. The Amnya complex shows evidence of the first stone arrowheads in the region, contemporaneous with the emergence of fortified settlements. Archaeologists suggest that they were used for war rather than hunting. This warfare may have been a product not only of competition for existing resources but also of prehistoric climate change. Around 6200–6050 BCE, the climate cooled, causing population movements and prompting hunter-gatherers around northern Eurasia to mark their territory in novel ways; hunter-gatherers in Russian Karelia, at the border of present-day Finland, began to use formal cemeteries.

Away from their fortified home, the taiga dwellers built small structures and made offerings, depositing stone arrowheads and pottery decorated with the sculpted heads of birds and animals. The worshippers set the structures alight and then heaped them with soil, pouring out vivid red ochre to close the ceremony. As the ritual was repeated, red hills grew; they contain animal bones, antlers, and human skulls. The hills prefigure the burial mounds of the Scythian warrior-nomads of Siberia as well as the festive bonfires of the pagan Slavs—a tradition that continues even today.

The Amnya site's rustling, wet expanse of trees and swamp has yielded a new understanding of human progress. The establishment of agriculture is still widely considered to be an essential step on the road to social "complexity": accumulation, private property, social hierarchies, economic inequality, military conquest. The Neolithic Amnya fort shows that warfare and surplus economies can be sustained for millennia without agriculture, and that hunter-fisher-gatherers, who have often been imagined as primitive and peaceful, may have been more warlike and more sophisticated than scientific tradition had assumed. Even in the 2020s, the Siberian forest murmurs with startling secrets. It is a treasure chest, a hiding place, a fortress. The dream of living in absolute freedom in the woods, following a lifestyle not so different from that of hunter-fisher-gatherers, recurs again and again in Russian history—which has a habit of relapsing into the distant past.

In the prehistoric period, the taiga's fish determined the course of human civilization. During the medieval era, it was the taiga's furs that would reshape Eurasian economies and societies. During that period, fortifications around the Ob River served as safe storage points for the precious sable pelts collected by Indigenous hunters—Khanty, Mansi, Selkup, and Nenets—who sold them to traders or surrendered them as tribute. The mysterious northern forests of Siberia and northern Russia were renowned throughout medieval Eurasia as the source of furs that were traded as far as China, Italy, and North Africa, coveted by monarchs and aristocrats, traders and warlords. Archaeologists have found Persian Sassanid silver, ornate Byzantine vessels, and Chinese coins at forts in the Ob River basin, which was a spur of the Silk Road.[7]

Fur first became fashionable in the Islamic world. In the tenth century, Arab rulers and European kings wore dresses made of black and red fox fur. The very best fur, the most gorgeous pelts in the purest tints, came from northern European Russia and from northwestern Siberia, which became known to the Islamic world as "the land of darkness." By the eleventh century, Europe's monarchs, lords and ladies were draping themselves in sable, ermine, and "vair," squirrel fur sewn into heraldic patterns. Later, they trimmed their brightly colored woolen clothes in gray and white "minever," another name for squirrel. The fashion caught on among merchants and craftsmen. In 1327 England restricted fur-wearing to royalty and people of "high birth with incomes over 100 pounds per annum." The effort failed, and upwardly mobile English people continued to deck their ambition in animal pelts.[8]

As western Europe hacked down its forests to make way for agriculture, its taste for fur only grew. The most desirable gray-blue and white winter squirrel pelts, favorites of Henry III and Edward I of England, came from Scandinavia and northern Russia. The Siberian forests, still nearly untouched, were a treasure trove. Fur could be exchanged for silver, fine woolen textiles, salt, and other luxury goods. It could even be a tool of diplomacy, sent to foreign rulers as a gesture of goodwill. For centuries, furs were by far the most valuable commodity coming from the dark northern lands, and one of the most valuable luxury goods circulating in Eurasia. The fur trading network reached as far as Spain, North Africa, China, and India. Once small groups of hunter-gatherers had fought over fish meal in the taiga; now states and armies across Eurasia competed for fur.

Controlling the fur trade depended on controlling the people who knew best how to trap the elusive sable, ermine, squirrel, and other creatures. But who were these expert hunters? Thanks to the fur trade, the peoples of the northern Eurasian forests were vaguely known as far away as Central Asia and China. The first accounts of the people dwelling on the southern edges of Siberia are from Chinese chronicles rather than Russian ones. The word *taiga* (the stress comes on the final "a"), synonymous with Siberia's forests today, is not a Russian word but a Turkic name that comes from these earlier encounters with the forest peoples.

The forest and its inhabitants sparked the imagination of the era's travel writers, who did not restrain their fancy. The twelfth-century

Muslim traveler Abū Hāmid described one of the Islamic world's first fur sources: "On the sea is an area of darkness, known under the name Iura." The people of Iura (a name for the Indigenous people of western Siberia) have no war and no animals for transportation, "only huge trees and forests in which there is a lot of honey, and they have a lot of sables."[9] The forest provides for all their needs. In the summer the sun does not set for forty days, and in the winter the night lasts for forty days—a nightmare for Muslims, whose religious practices depend on more regular cycles. Most striking is Abū Hāmid's description of Iura's trade:

> The merchants say that the land of darkness is not far from them and that the people of Iura go to this land of darkness and enter it with torches and find there a large tree not unlike a large village, and in it is a large animal, which, they say, is a bird. They bring goods with them, and each merchant puts his property down in a separate place, makes his sign on it and goes away. Then after a while they return and find goods that are needed in their country. And each man finds some of those things near his own goods; if he agrees, then he takes them; if not, he gathers his own things and leaves the others and no exchange takes place. And they do not know from whom they are buying these goods.[10]

The single large tree, with its single bird inhabitant, represents the huge, frightening treasure chest of the taiga. It yields its riches only to the initiated, who trade their furs through a string of mysterious middlemen. The process is opaque enough to seem mythical.

The Eastern Slavs, too, imagined the fur-collecting peoples of the north as creatures from a fairytale. In the Primary Chronicle of 1096, the writer recounts a story told to him by a certain Giuriata Rogovich of Novgorod. According to Rogovich, the Iugra (an alternate version of "Iura"), Indigenous people of northwestern Siberia, described mountains that reached from the heavens to the sea. From the mountains, the Iugra said, could be heard the sound of voices, people cutting their way out of the rock. Though their language was incomprehensible, it was somehow evident that the people in the mountain were asking for more iron. In exchange, they would trade furs to the Iugra. But most of the year, the route to these mysterious mountain dwellers was impassable thanks to forest, snow, and precipices.

Beneath its fabulously improbable surface, this medieval game of telephone likely contains several kernels of truth. Travelers of the period exaggerated all their tales of unfamiliar peoples. But by telling this story, the Iugra may have been discouraging the Slavs from establishing direct contact with their trading partners, or from attempting to extract the forest's riches themselves.[11] The Iugra had good reason to protect their status as middlemen, which brought profit and safety. For several centuries, they would succeed in preserving their land of darkness from the incursions of Russian colonizers.

The city-state of Novgorod was an early seat of Slavic power, existing from the ninth to the fifteenth centuries. At its peak, it stretched from the Baltics to the Urals. Its capital city was built with the wood of the surrounding forests. Oak, lime, and elm were used for the most valuable structures; the more abundant pine, spruce, and birch served for everything else.[12] Novgorod was a forest transmuted into a society, a kingdom of woodworking. It grew rich from its forests, where precious furs were so abundant that medieval visitors to Novgorod reported silky-coated animals falling from the sky. The Novgorodians were the first Slavic people to conquer the northern forest west of the Urals. Beginning in the eleventh century, they forced the Komi, natives of northeastern European Russia who are distantly related to the Hungarians, Finns, and Estonians, to bring them fur tribute. Now the native hunters were not traders exchanging pelts for weapons, metals, and other goods, as in the fanciful tales about the Iura/Iugra, but subjects paying tax to Slavic lords.

A fifteenth-century account of an exploratory trip into Siberia by Novgorodian merchants in search of fur, "On unknown men in the eastern land," describes the peoples encountered along the way. These sketches are outlandish and clearly fanciful, drawing on a long-standing tradition of European myths about semihuman tribes.[13] The first group are described as cannibals who serve their own children as a welcome meal for the visiting merchants. But other descriptions can be read as a kind of magical ethnography. One group lives in the sea for a month every year as its people shed their old skins and grow new ones—perhaps a reference to the practice of wearing fish leather, common among northern peoples, and to seasonal migration. Another tribe is mouthless. Its mute members eat by putting food under their caps and chewing with their shoulders—a highly embroidered version of a people who speak a language unintelligible to the merchants or their interpreters. Another group dies for two months every winter, then returns to life. This is simply hibernation: a merging of humans with bears. The historian Janet Martin has pointed out that this story was not pure invention: The locations of the peoples described and the indication of who had sable were accurate.[14] Ethnography began as a means of gathering information essential to trade and war. In the northern forests, fur was the center of every story, the logic that shaped every intercultural interaction.

According to Khanty cosmology, the bear, the son of Torum, was a creature of the upper realm. Torum banished him to the forest for bad behavior. Human visitors to the Siberian taiga often saw it as a place of exile—or of escape. This included anthropologists and ethnographers. In the nineteenth century, many Russian scholars of Indigenous culture were intellectuals who had been banished to Siberia for political reasons. Unwilling to let their energies go to waste, they devoted themselves to documenting and analyzing the traditions and languages of the many peoples of Siberia, which comprise Uralic, Tungusic, Paleosiberian, Turkic, Mongolic, and other subgroups. Ethnography continued to thrive in the early Soviet Union, which was intent on mapping and understanding Indigenous peoples in order to reshape them into modern Soviet subjects.

In the 1920s, the intrepid Russian scholar Raisa Mitusova became the first ethnographer to study the area between the lower Nadym River and the upper Tromagan, Agan, and Pur Rivers, a region inhabited by the Khanty, Selkup, and Nenets, the northern neighbors of the Khanty. As the daughter of a Novgorod noblewoman and the young widow of a White Army officer—a biography that marked her as a potential "enemy of the people"—she may have known that the taiga was the safest place for her. She spent months migrating with the nomadic forest Nenets. She often slept outdoors with them; her hosts spread a piece of canvas on the snow and covered it with deerskins, then heaped her with the fur coats she had collected for her ethnographic museum. She learned both Nenets and Khanty on her own, and soon came to be respected by the two communities.

When Mitusova visited the Khanty of the Agan River, she found that centuries of contact with Russian missionaries and traders had had little effect; they were still almost untouched by Russian culture. Though they were considered Christian for official purposes, they continued to practice their traditional forms of worship. Mitusova was particularly intrigued by the bear ceremony, part of which she managed to attend and record. Her research was put to an end by Stalin's purges: She was arrested on spurious conspiracy charges and shot in 1937. But the materials she collected survived, a priceless testament to the cultures of the forest and tundra.[15]

The forest and the snow were not deep enough to protect Mitusova; neither was the forest dense enough to save the northwestern Siberians. Soviet collectivization extended to Indigenous people, including hunter-fisher-gatherers and herders like the Khanty and Nenets. According to Soviet logic, oceans, rivers, and forests could be treated like factories, and their output of whales, seals, fish, and wood could be ramped up the same way output could be increased in a modern steel plant.[16] Reindeer were seized and sent to the area's new collective farm, and opponents of collectivization were exiled. The Khanty were concentrated in "national settlements," to promote a supposedly more civilized way of life; this forced settlement destroyed traditional patterns of subsistence and thus Khanty independence from the state.[17] Children were taken from their families and put in Soviet boarding schools.

Nomads and seminomads like the Khanty were much more likely than sedentary populations to rebel against the Soviets; it was easier for them to pack up and leave a territory, taking their reindeer and other possessions with them. Shamans led the rebellions. After years of mounting tension over collectivization and the forced schooling of children, the Soviets offended Khanty and Nenets religious practice by forcing them to fish in a sacred lake. After unsuccessful attempts at negotiation, the Khanty took Soviet emissaries hostage and sacrificed them in a ritual killing on the lake's frozen surface.

According to the Khanty writer Eremei Aipin, the rebels built defensive structures on the frozen lake and poured water over them, making an ice fortress—a tactic the Khanty had refined many centuries ago, and one that may have been used by prehistoric dwellers of earthen fortresses like the one at the Amnya site. The insurrectionists managed to defeat the first Soviet detachment, but reinforcements arrived and bombed the ice fortress from above. Some rebels were killed or captured; others scattered to the east or to the northern tundra. The Soviet secret police pursued rebels by plane across tundra and forest for eight months. Those captured, among them twenty-nine shamans, were executed.[18] This was a final, painful chapter in the conquest of Siberia.

One of the groups described by the fifteenth-century Novgorodian travelers knew the way to an underground city where trade occurred in absolute silence. Ethnographers and anthropologists have since documented the Khanty belief in silence as a gesture of respect to the other creatures and spirits with whom they share the forest. In a 2013 documentary film, Khanty linguist Agrafena Pesikova explained that for the Khanty, silence and unobtrusiveness are paramount. Khanty strive not to be seen or heard in the forest, not to leave a trace of themselves. Rather than worshipping the spirits of a place, the Khanty try not to trouble them.

"You shouldn't disturb the beings living around you," Pesikova explained. "Neither animals nor spirits, neither gods nor devils are to be disturbed. They live for themselves and we live for ourselves." It is a philosophy of tactful coexistence, without a sense of absolute evil or absolute good.[19] In Khanty tradition there is no concept of "wilderness" or "nature." There is no division between the forest and inhabited space, because the forest is itself fully inhabited. Territorial relationships are always being negotiated and renegotiated. Good manners are as imperative in a forest glade as they would be in the home of a friend—more important, because in the forest bad manners can spell fatal misfortune.

As we will see in the next chapters, this ethos is profoundly different from the Russian Orthodox Christian worldview, which maintained a Manichean sense of good and evil and called on Russians to subdue nature as God had commanded. Agents of the Russian Empire and then the Soviet Union subscribed to the idea, still prevalent today, of linear progress from "primitive" hunter-gatherers to "complex" sedentary societies. The recently uncovered prehistory of northwestern Siberia challenges this narrative; the Neolithic people at Amnya and later the Khanty, Mansi, Selkup, and Nenets proved that sophistication was possible without agriculture or a sedentary way of life. The history of Siberia's conquest is another reminder of the heights achieved by nomadic societies. The first empire builders to lay claim to Siberia were not the settled Slavs but the Mongols, who were seduced by the riches of the taiga.

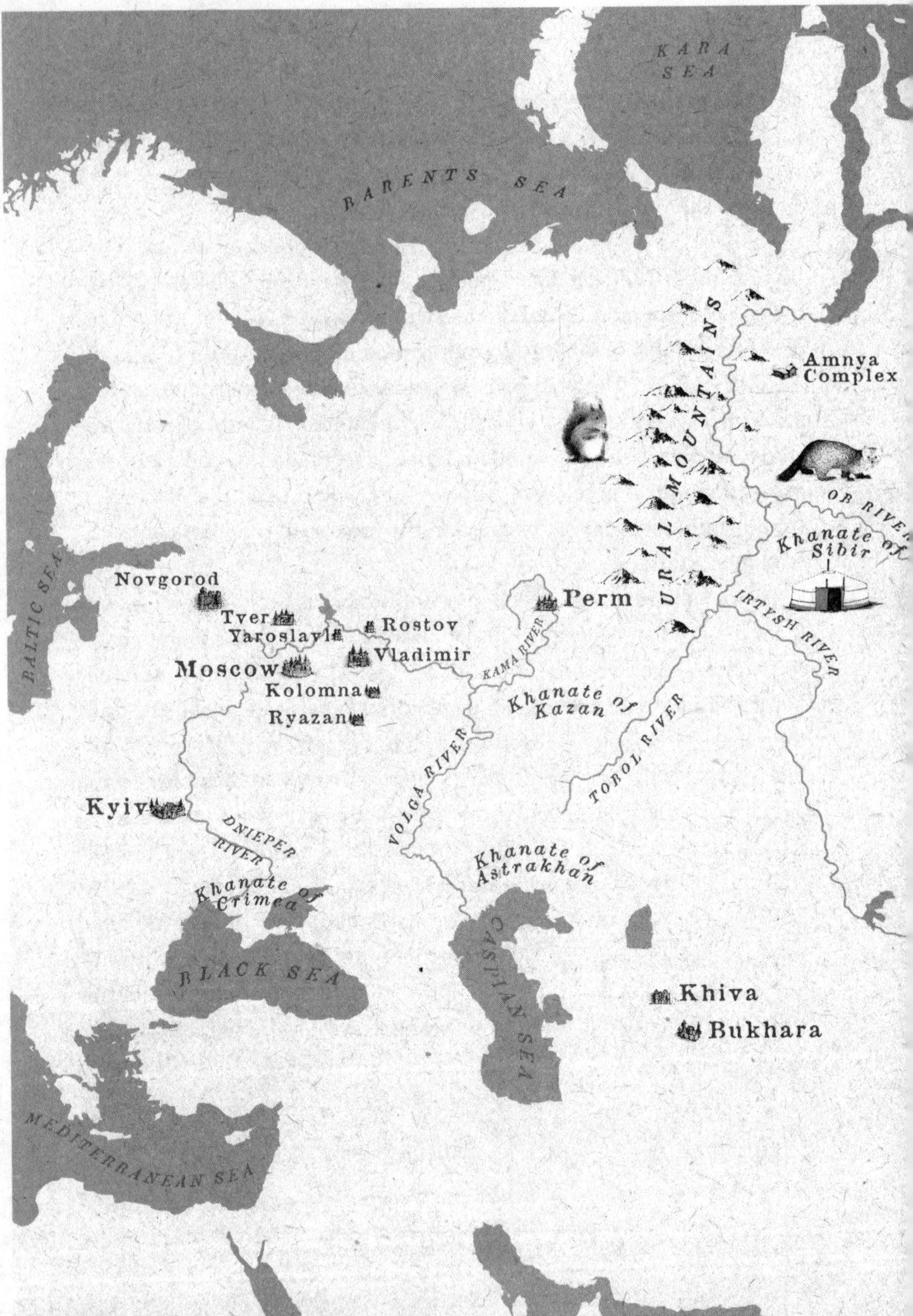

KARA SEA
BARENTS SEA
URAL MOUNTAINS
Amnya Complex
OB RIVER
Khanate of Sibir
IRTYSH RIVER
BALTIC SEA
Novgorod
Tver
Yaroslavl
Rostov
Vladimir
Moscow
Kolomna
Ryazan
Perm
KAMA RIVER
Khanate of Kazan
TOBOL RIVER
VOLGA RIVER
Kyiv
DNIEPER RIVER
Khanate of Crimea
Khanate of Astrakhan
BLACK SEA
CASPIAN SEA
Khiva
Bukhara
MEDITERRANEAN SEA

THE GOLDEN HORDE *and the* CONQUEST *of* SIBERIA

CHAPTER 2

The Golden Horde and the Tree of Life

In the beginning there was a blue-gray wolf, and a fallow doe who was his wife. They crossed the sea, or perhaps only Lake Baikal, and they settled at the source of the Onon River, where steppe and forested mountains meet. The wolf and the deer had a son, and their son had a son. A boy was born: Yesugei Ba'atur. He became a Mongol chief. One day he was hunting with falcons along the river when he encountered a member of the Merkit, a rival tribe. This Merkit was accompanied by a beautiful young girl. Yesugei stole her.[1] Soon she bore a son, who arrived clutching a clot of blood as big as a knucklebone.

This son, called Temujin, was born among forest people who hunted foxes, wolves, deer, and forest antelopes. They lived in small tents made of wool and bark, rather than in felt yurts like the steppe herders, and they traveled by reindeer or by ski, the fastest way to move without the help of an animal.[2] One of these forest people brought baby Temujin sable swaddling from the sacred crescent of Burkhan Khaldun, the mountain that rose from the green sea of forest and marked the beginning of the northern lands—Siberia.

When Temujin was only nine years old, enemies killed his father. Another tribe took power, food grew scarce, and Temujin and his family were driven back into the depths of the forest, alone. His mother fed her sons on forest crab apples and bird cherries, burnet and silverweed roots, wild garlic, onion, leek, and lily bulbs. But hiding was not enough. Emissaries of the rival tribe arrived to kill Temujin and his brothers. The small family barricaded themselves in the forest, pulling out trees and fashioning a palisade.

The attackers demanded Temujin, the eldest brother. He mounted his horse and fled deeper into the forest, taking refuge in a thicket so dense that his enemies could not penetrate it. When hunger flushed him out at last, his enemies took him. But clever Temujin soon escaped again, floating down the Onon River, which flowed from Burkhan Khaldun. He returned to the forest, to his own people and to the holy mountain. According to the *Secret History of the Mongols*, the thirteenth-century Mongolian account of the life of Chinggis Khan, "the swallowing quagmires and the tangled woods made so impenetrable a forest that a glutted snake could not creep in."[3] The sacred mountain and its forest had saved Temujin. He gave thanks to the mountain for rescuing him, and he resolved to make sacrifices to it every day.

Temujin grew in strength, and soon he defeated the Merkit. At an assembly near the sources of the Onon River, nine tribes submitted to him. He raised a standard adorned with the tails of nine horses with pure white hair. Now Temujin acquired a new name: Chinggis Khan. Over the next decades his armies would ride victorious all the way across Eurasia. The supreme ruler of the steppe, founder of the largest empire in human history, had come from the forest.

Chinggis Khan and his sons extended their realm across the territory of forty modern countries. The boundaries of their conquest reached from Poland to Korea and from Egypt to Vietnam. They galloped for decades across what would later become the Russian Empire, transforming the region's economies, culture, and language. Eurasia was easy prey for the Mongols because of its long stretch of steppe, a broad swath of grassland reaching from Manchuria to Hungary that was hardly disrupted by mountains or sea. On this natural highway, master horsemen could reach historical velocity, traversing continents in record time. They inspired panic by their mere approach.

The Mongols were not interested in converting others to their religion, imposing their language, or forcing them to conform to Mongol social mores. They were interested in profit. Before attacking, the Mongols offered a deal. If a ruler agreed to pay tax, he could avoid having his city pillaged and its population massacred. This was usually the only hope of survival for the stationary Slavs, anchored in place by their wooden towns and piles of possessions. Russian cities stood little chance against the unfamiliar Mongol siege engines, against onslaughts that seemed to come out of thin air. The Mongols routinely defeated principalities with armies much larger than theirs. When local rulers heard the Mongols were coming, many did not even wait to catch a glimpse of them. They simply fled in terror.

Often the greatest resistance to Mongol conquest was offered not by humans but by the landscape. The Mongols could only cross swampy land when it was frozen; during a thaw, their troops and siege engines sank into the muddy ground, immobilized, and their horses struggled to find food. The Mongols were nearly omnipotent as long as they were galloping across the steppe. But as soon as they struck forest or bog (not to mention sea), they were ordinary men. This is why forests and swamps became one of the best defenses against the Horde, and one of the best refuges for those fleeing the invaders.

The Kipchaks, another group of Turkic nomads, fended off the Mongols by making themselves a moving target. In the thirteenth century, the Kipchak leader Bashman succeeded in rebuffing the Mongols on the lower Volga River. The forest was a key part of his tactics. According to the Persian historian Juvayni, who had an unsympathetic perspective on Bashman,

> Having no lair or hiding-place to serve as base, [Bashman] betook himself every day and night to a different spot. And because of his dog-like nature he would strike wolf-like on every side and make off with something. Gradually his evil grew worse and he wrought greater mischief; and wherever the [Mongol] army sought him they could not find him since he had departed

> elsewhere and hidden his tracks. Most of his refuges and hiding places were on the banks of the [Volga]. Here he would lie concealed in the forests, from which he would spring out like a jackal, seize hold of something and hide himself once again.[4]

Other tribes joined Bashman's cause, obstructing the Mongols' desired land route from their steppe capital, Karakorum, to the European steppe. It took twenty years of fighting for the indefatigable Mongols to take control of the Kipchak steppes and the Volga-Ural area.[5]

In December 1237, Mongols conquered the Russian city of Ryazan, which is about two hundred kilometers southeast of Moscow. Next they took Moscow and the nearby cities of Vladimir and Kolomna. The grand prince of Vladimir escaped into the woods near the Oka River, but the forest was not dense enough to save him: The Mongols surprised him there and decapitated him. Then they took Rostov, Yaroslavl, and Tver. In the winter of 1240–1241, the prince of Kyiv fled to the kingdom of Hungary with his family and noblemen. With no leaders to organize its defense, Kyiv, with its magnificent cathedral at the top of a wooded hill above the Dnieper River, fell quickly to the invaders. The Mongols continued west across Ukraine, easily taking Galicia, whose prince had also fled. The states of medieval Rus—whose center was Kyiv—became Mongol vassals. Only Novgorod, the kingdom of wood, saved itself. In 1257, its judicious prince, Alexander Nevsky, chose to avoid war by appeasing the Mongol lords, paying the required tax. But it was Moscow, nestled in its northern forest, that was destined to become the next center of East Slavic power.

The Russian chronicles kept during this time offer only a fragmentary picture of an unstable era of invasion and pillage. The epoch of the "Mongol-Tatar yoke" came to be enshrined in Russian national memory as a kind of martyrdom. With few written sources describing this period, it is a territory that invites imagining. Many Russian artists have answered the call. One of the greatest works of Russian twentieth-century film, Andrei Tarkovsky's 1966 *Andrei Rublev*, brings alive a moment when Russia lived in fear of invasion, and Christian monks crossed paths in the forest with pagan nature-worshippers.

In one of the most harrowing episodes of *Andrei Rublev*, Tatars—the imprecise Russian name for Mongols and their allies and successors—raid and massacre the city of Vladimir. (They are allies of the grand duke's jealous younger brother.) The scene takes place in the early fifteenth century. Tarkovsky's Tatars are always laughing, their voices full of cruelty; the Russians in the film have a surprised, balletic look as they die in motion. The villagers hide in the city's church, watching helplessly as the Tatars hammer down the door. Tarkovsky gives a miraculous delicacy to even the most violent, frightening scenes, as when a monk is tortured so that he will tell the attackers where to find the city's gold. Snow falls into the burned, pillaged church. Human walls are a pitiful defense against the vastness of what lies beyond.

Andrei Rublev is set in rainy central Russia, a flat expanse that is devoid of sacred mountains like Burkhan Khaldun but serves, in its own way, as a constant reminder of the insignificance of man. Tarkovsky shows us a moment in history when Christianity in Russia was half-hearted, nature entirely unconquered. Undisciplined rivers meander; naked pagans wade into the water, torches alight. Andrei Rublev, a monk and the greatest of Russian icon painters, catches sight of the twilight pagan ritual and cannot resist following. Soft-bodied, bare-breasted young women with streaming fair hair are half *rusalka*, forest mermaids inviting him to lie down on the riverbank and forget about God. In the morning, when he returns to the other monks and they ask where he has been, he answers, "These forests are impenetrable. The local people like it." Pagan ritual, animal love, the ancient worship of water and fire, reside in the forest. The artist must see them, even if he has promised himself to the Christian god.

Tarkovsky's film, like Russia itself, is anchored by trees. They are symbols of hope and dual representatives of paganism—the tree and nature worship seen throughout Indo-European cultures—and Chris-

Andrei Rublev and a nature worshipper *Mosfilm*

tianity, as in the trees of Eden or the Lebanese cedars of the Bible. In the film's astonishing opening sequence, a peasant flies away from a church in a primitive hot-air balloon, bobbing over the fields. But ascent is only one way of breaking free. One can also sink into land and water, bask in the fertile earth. A bold young boy, orphaned by the plague, undertakes the fashioning of an enormous church bell. As he digs the casting pit for the bell, he pursues a root that crosses the fresh hole, pulling until he realizes that it belongs to a flowering tree. He stops digging and gazes up at its pale flowers, as if admiring the work of a fellow artisan. We see the tree from his perspective; then we see him; and then the camera begins to float up, so that at last we see him and his fellow diggers from the tree's perspective. The men are very small, deep in the ground.

Rain stipples the river and thrills the leaves. Every interior scene is accompanied by an outward gaze, the vastness of nature framed through a window or a door. Andrei Rublev wants to paint for God, but his gaze cannot be confined to the stark white walls of the new church he is asked to decorate, or to the dim interiors of a peasant hut. His eye is always drawn outward. When he describes his own version of the Passion of Christ, he is walking in the forest with his teacher and his apprentice, Foma, who cleans a paintbrush in the forest stream, the pigment joining the flow of water. Andrei's thought and vocation grow in the light-filled forest, Christianity fed by animism, Tarkovsky's camera lingering on the intricate network of roots that rise on the shore of the stream. There is no desire here to transcend or deny earth: The earth is itself sublime, birthing the tree crowns of heaven.

The surviving icons painted by the real-life Andrei Rublev do not picture trees. In the manner of the age, they focus on human figures—saints, the Virgin Mary, Jesus—placed against a divinely golden background. Tarkovsky's cinematic iconography of divine trees reflects a later phase of Russian art, when trees began to appear in icons depicting the paradise lost by Adam and Eve. Over time, trees came to be associated not only with Eden but also with heaven and the Russian land; the Holy Mother defended both, as if they were synonymous. God's presence shone from Russia's forest. In one famous icon, a "bright place" reserved for saints is full of foliage. In colorful maps of the countryside around Moscow, the luminous trees of paradise pour out onto earth. Trees were God's gift to the Russians.[6]

Despite the brutal scenes of invasion and pillage in Tarkovsky's film, by the early fifteenth century the Slavs were no longer vassals of an almighty Horde. The Mongols had been weakened by the plague, internal conflict, and trading problems. Now the principality of Muscovy (centered in Moscow), which had grown richer under Mongol rule, sought to lay claim to the far-reaching trading networks established by the Mongols and to consolidate its political power. Muscovy competed with other Slavic principalities for dominion over the Uralic (Finno-Ugric) Indigenous peoples, such as the Khanty, Mansi, and Komi, of the northern Urals. For the Slavs, as for the Mongols and their successor states, the Indigenous peoples were of importance primarily as sources of fur tribute.

After several centuries of highly lucrative trapping, that fur had become harder to find. The Novgorodians, who had once had so much fur that it was said to fall from the sky, were forced to venture northeast to locate more fur-bearing animals and new trappers to catch them. In the process, Novgorod came into increasing conflict with Muscovy. The Muscovites added a religious flavor to their foray into the forests: Their monks and missionaries sought communion with God, holy solitude, and new converts in the northern taiga. In the fourteenth century, the Orthodox missionary Stefan, first bishop of Perm, worked to convert the Komi people of northeastern European Russia and assert Muscovy's claim to their land over Novgorod's. He cut down the Komi's sacred birch trees. In iconography—he was sainted for his efforts—he is sometimes shown wielding an axe. Russian trees were symbols of paradise, but the Komi birches were false idols.

In the second half of the fifteenth century, Ivan III of Muscovy, also known as Ivan the Great, united the Slavic principalities, taking control even of mighty Novgorod. Ivan was the first self-styled caesar, or tsar, of Russia, his imperial insignia the double-headed eagle looking west and east. For him, Moscow was a "Third Rome," and he lived in dread that it might fall to barbarians or infidels, as Rome and Constantinople had done. But he was unconcerned by the animism that still coursed through Russia's forests and rivers. The Muscovites felt that their presence was enough to prove the Christian sanctity of the land. Long accustomed to intermingling with peoples of different faiths, languages, and ethnicities, Muscovites were content to inscribe the names of native inhabitants in their new maps and to fill their coffers with the proceeds from the fur tribute the natives provided.

By now the Horde had been reduced to a clutch of independent khanates: Kazan, due east of Moscow, at a strategic point where the

Volga River meets the Kama River, with serried forests teeming with fox, marten, and sable; Astrakhan, southeast of Moscow, where the Volga meets the Caspian Sea; and, east of the Ural Mountains, the Khanate of Sibir, which gave Siberia its name. But the Tatar khans still saw Muscovy's grand princes as their vassals, raiding them as they pleased. Muscovy wanted its freedom, and unfettered access to the riches of the eastern and northern forests. The Mongols had rushed west; now it was Muscovy's turn to hurry eastward.

The capricious, repressive, and often homicidal Ivan IV, better known as Ivan the Terrible (his name in Russian can also be translated as "Ivan the Awesome"), conquered Kazan in 1552 and Astrakhan in 1556. He now had full control of the Volga, an essential means of transportation and trade, and dominion over the land that stretched from the Volga to the Urals, the boundary of Siberia. Muscovy founded several towns around the mouth of the Ob River and demanded tribute from the Indigenous Uralic people, including the Khanty, who lived there.

That left only the Khanate of Sibir, farther east, on the Irtysh River, the long, twirling tributary of the Ob that stretches from a spot near the Neolithic Amnya fort all the way to Mongolia. The 1636 Yesipov Chronicle, which recounts the conquest of Siberia, offers an almost mythical portrait of distant, seductive territory: "Between these kingdoms of Russia and the Siberian land there lies a mountain range of exceeding great height, so as to reach with some of its peaks up to the clouds of heaven; for thus has it been set up by God's decrees, like the fortified wall of a city."[7] The Ural Mountains, the natural boundary between Europe and Asia, were not terribly high, but their dense forest cover made them hard to cross; their deep valleys were tricks, leading to arboreal dead ends.

The chronicle longingly enumerates the many "wild beasts" that dwell among the pines, "some fit for consumption by men, others for adornment and vestments." Deer, elk, and hare are "clean" meats, good to eat, and the fox, the sable, the beaver, the wolverine, and the squirrel are precious commodities, meriting the conquest of a continent. The

Siberia of the Yesipov Chronicle bears no resemblance to the cold, forbidding cliché of the Western imagination. It is pleasing to the senses, with "an abundance of sweet-singing birds," and "even more an abundance of various flowering grasses." The chronicle's rivers are especially enchanting: "It is wonderful, indeed, how by God's decrees there are rivers there; the water wore away hard rock, and there are vast and most beautiful rivers, and in them the freshest waters and an abundance of various fishes. Where these waters issue there are forests fruitful for harvesting and most extensive grazing lands for cattle."[8] This was a New World for the Russians, a Garden of Eden, bounded by the Urals and blessed with a miraculous bounty of things to eat, drink, wear, and sell—all granted by God, and set to the tune of songbirds. It is notable, of course, that no human inhabitants are mentioned in this preliminary description. They come later, after the enumeration of the Siberian rivers. The native peoples were an afterthought—though also the key to making this Eden a lucrative one.

Sibir was a forest kingdom: Its name most likely comes from the Mongol word *shibir*, which means "dense forest on a marsh."[9] According to one legend, Sibir's first monarch was Tatar Khan, the first person to come to Siberia. The Russians perceived Sibir as a mysterious region ruled by Turkic nomads: They called it the "Yurt of Sibir," echoing a Mongol term.[10] Indeed, Sibir was the world's northernmost Mongol state; after the Golden Horde elite adopted Islam as their religion in the early fourteenth century, it also became the world's northernmost Muslim-ruled state. Sibir's Turkic rulers had left pastoralist life on the steppe to build towns in the forest; they had settled down. But many of the khanate's subjects were animist hunter-gatherers of the northern forests, distant relatives of the Hungarians, Estonians, and Finns: the Khanty, Mansi, Cheremis (Mari), and Selkup. These forest peoples were forced to pay fur tribute and fight in Sibir's armies.

Sibir was an important hub for the trade in northern furs, a point on the caravan route from Kazan to the dazzling merchant towns of Bukhara and Khiva, in what is now Uzbekistan. It had a powerful allure for the tsar and for the Stroganov family, which had grown

A map of Siberia from the Remezov Chronicle

rich from iron and copper mines in the Urals and the Russian north, and from saltworks and traded fur. Already the de facto rulers of the eastern outskirts of the Russian tsar's land, the Stroganovs aimed to expand their territory and thus increase their fortune. (They would remain one of the richest and most powerful Russian families for centuries.) In a 1558 charter, the tsar granted Grigory Stroganov privileges over the lands along the river Kama: "empty lands, dense forests, wild streams and lakes, empty islands and pools." He justified the charter by explaining, "Until now no ploughing has been done and no dwellings built there, and no kind of dues have come from there to my royal treasury." To the agrarian eye, any land that appeared empty and unprofitable was ripe for the taking. Still, it was obvious that this process would involve conflict. The tsar granted Stroganov's request for the right to build a military outpost "for defense against the Nagay people [descendants of the Mongols] and other hordes, and to fell the forest along the streams up to their headwaters and around the lakes, and to plough the cleared land, and to build dwellings."[11] Fortunately for the forests, at the time there were far too few Russians to make more than a small dent in the vast stretches of trees.

The Stroganovs hired a Cossack marauder called Yermak Timofeevich to fight Khan Kuchum, the ruler of Sibir. The Cossacks were a group comprised of outlaws, escaped peasants, and nomads of the steppe, distinguished by their expert horsemanship, military prowess, and brutal unruliness. Yermak is said to have been "courageous and shrewd, and humane, and well-favored and endowed with every kind of wisdom, with a flat face, black of beard and with curly hair, of medium stature, thickset and broad-shouldered."[12] Take this description with a grain of salt: Its source, the Remezov Chronicle, is a hagiographical Cossack work written a century after Yermak's death. Before his employment with the Stroganovs, Yermak had been a pirate on the Caspian Sea and Volga River; it is said that he even plundered the royal treasury. The tsar had sent soldiers to kill him and his men, but Yermak fled east, where he found safety on Stroganov territory. He had escaped a gruesome death: Volga pirates were usually impaled and set to drift downriver on rafts, screaming in agony as they died. The Stroganovs put the lucky Yermak to use conquering Sibir.

The khanate's capital city sat at the juncture of the Irtysh and Tobol Rivers. When the Cossacks (who may have been accompanied by Tatars) arrived at the city, Kuchum ordered his men to cut down trees to build a wooden barricade along the Irtysh, with the logs pointing toward the enemy. The mounted Siberian warriors fell on the Russians with spears and arrows; the Russians replied with musket and cannon fire. Despite the mismatch in weaponry, there were many casualties on both sides. Before battle, Yermak's men are said to have seen the white waters of the river and been "seized with doubt." Kuchum's men were as numerous at the river's mouth "as mountains and forests, as countless as sands," while Yermak's troops took heavy losses.[13] But after a series of battles, Khan Kuchum fled. Yermak and his Cossacks merrily looted the city's hoard of precious metals, stone, and pelts. In the chronicles their pillaging would be reimagined as a sacred battle undertaken on behalf of the Christian god.

In October the Khanty princes, who had been conscripted to fight for Sibir, abandoned Khan Kuchum, retreating on horseback to their wooded homeland. One chronicle observes that "it is their custom to flee and disappear when our people come." The next day, God supposedly sent a messenger telling Kuchum to flee as well, and the Mansi, another of the conscripted forest peoples, fled homeward, "beyond impassable swamps and lakes," and "took refuge with their families in inaccessible places to remain undiscovered . . . to this day a man on skis can see in the overgrown swamps and lakes earth-walls in front and behind."[14] In other words, the native Siberians retreated to the safety of forest forts like the one at Amnya. One by one, the chronicle says, Yermak drove his enemies into the dense fir forests and marshes. As the woods and swamps had been the surest protection against the Horde, now they became the best refuge from Russian domination. Yermak sent the tsar 2,400 sable, 2,000 beaver, and 800 black fox pelts, announcing that he had taken Sibir and made its natives tribute-paying subjects of the tsar.[15]

In 1584 or 1585, Khan Kuchum struck back. On a dark night with heavy rain, his men pounced on the sleeping Cossacks. Yermak drowned while trying to flee to his boat. According to one version of the story, he was unable to climb in because he was wearing two royal coats of mail that weighed him down. A young Tatar found his body floating in the pure Siberian water of the Irtysh River. In the

Remezov Chronicle, the Cossack hagiography, Yermak's body displays the miraculous qualities of a saint's. His blood flows free and red even after his death, and white birds circle his body without descending. Some of the Siberians take this as a suggestion that they ought to convert to Christianity. They call Yermak a god and bury him under "a spreading pine tree." On days of commemoration of the dead, a pillar of fire is said to appear above his grave.[16] In this version of the story, the dark eastern forests are dazzled by divine light, the sacred trees brought to Jesus.

Deprived of their leader and insufficiently inspired by these miracles, the Cossacks fled back to Russia. Khan Kuchum took back his capital city, but he was soon deposed by internal enemies. As winter drew near, Ivan the Terrible sent new troops to reinforce the Cossacks in Siberia. The chronicles describe how a group of Khanty attacked a Russian stronghold. They placed their idol under a nearby birch tree and made offerings for victory. When the Cossacks fired their cannon, the shot shattered the birch tree and the idol along with it. The terrified Khanty, who had never encountered firearms, fled.[17] The historical accuracy of this story is questionable, but its symbolic significance for the Russians is clear: They were shattering the old animism of the forest people, as Stefan of Perm had felled Komi sacred trees two centuries before. The prize of this iconoclasm was Siberia.

In reality, the success was not so swift or sweeping. The Khanate of Sibir fell and its territories were incorporated into Russia, but it was a long, slow process. The Indigenous peoples of the region put up a fierce resistance, sometimes attacking from long distances and in great numbers. A group of Mansi crossed the daunting Urals to attack a Russian fort, and a group of some two thousand Khanty warriors fought a Cossack detachment. On the lower Taz River, the Nenets won in battle against forces led by the Russian prince Miron Shakhovskoi.[18] A Russian garrison on the Yenisei River was massacred by Buryats (relatives of the Mongols) in 1634 and again in 1640. A Cossack expedition had to fight its way down the Lena River, known for the particular abundance of furs on its forested banks.[19] In the tundra of the northwest, reindeer hunters raided Russian caravans; the Russian fort of Okhotsk, on the Pacific, was under siege by the Tungus for more than thirty years in the late seventeenth century.[20] Attacks by Indigenous populations were sometimes fierce enough to force the Russians to abandon whole settlements.

Official instructions from Moscow ordered Russian emissaries in Siberia to collect tribute with kindness rather than cruelty whenever possible: Conflict disrupted commerce, and commerce was the primary purpose of expansion into Siberia. The Russians attempted to cultivate a faithful elite among the Indigenous peoples, hoping that these would supervise the collection of tribute in exchange for special privileges. Some of these newly minted Indigenous princes were even integrated into the Siberian nobility.[21] (In the years of the Mongol-Tatar yoke and after, many Tatar murzas, or noblemen, were also assimilated.) But for the most part, Indigenous peoples simply rejected this new system of authority. Tribute collectors often had to offer hunters banquets and gifts in exchange for pelts. While the Cossacks maintained the fiction that they were collecting tribute from subdued subjects of the tsar, the natives understood the process as a trade. The Cossack offerings were seductive: According to Tungus legend, as soon as two warriors tasted sugar, they threw away their bows and started to eat.[22] Alcohol, tobacco, firearms, and metal knives, axes, and traps also exerted great powers of persuasion. Where friendly tactics failed, the Cossacks turned to hostage-taking, beatings, torture, rape, and massacres.[23]

Lasting control of Siberia would require settlement, a daunting task in an area so large and with such a harsh climate. One of the most important problems was the great expense and logistical difficulty of importing food into a region where large swaths of terrain were impassable for much of the year. Russian cultivation of farmland began in western Siberia, between the Urals and the Yenisei River, where there was fertile soil and a relatively hospitable climate. In theory, settlement was only permitted on "empty lands": The government recognized the importance of allowing Indigenous peoples to continue occupying their own territories, since they were the ones supplying precious furs. But in practice, the Russian settlers—peasants and exiles—quickly came into conflict with the local peoples, who needed the land for herding and hunting. Law-abiding natives filed legal complaints; though cases were sometimes ruled in their favor, in practice the Russian settlers continued to encroach on their hunting and fishing grounds. Worst of all, Russian settlers burned down the forest to make farmland.[24]

As in the Americas, smallpox killed a large part of the Indigenous Siberian population in the 1600s. The weakened communities often attempted to flee from Russian oppression. The eastern Siberian taiga and the forested tundra west of the Lena River were bountiful and almost untouched, with a seemingly unlimited supply of waterfowl and fish, as well as wild reindeer. But the Cossacks found the refugees even deep in the taiga, and threatened them with prison or torture if they did not produce more furs. By then many of the fur-bearing animals in the forest had been killed off by the ravenous demands of the fur trade. Many Indigenous people had to buy furs to offer the state as tribute, often trading away essential items—even food staples—in desperation. Meanwhile, Indigenous women were carried off by male settlers who were desperate for wives. The old ways of life began to crumble under this pressure, and the populations of many of the forest peoples dwindled.[25]

The Russians soon realized that settlement and rapid deforestation had made precious fur much scarcer. The whole reason to conquer Siberia had been for its furs, and now the supply was in peril. In 1683, the Siberian Office sent the Yakutsk governors an order that no more forest was to be cut or burned on sable-hunting territory, on pain of death.[26] Siberia's forests had a reprieve. Over the next centuries, their depths would serve as protection for the Indigenous peoples who had survived the first wave of conquest, and for Russians who sought refuge from their own empire.

WESTERN RUSSIA

WHITE SEA
Arkhangelsk
KARELIA
BALTIC SEA
URAL MOUNTAINS
St. Petersburg
Novgorod
Perm
Bubonitsy
Khimki Forest
Vladimir
KLYAZMA RIVER
Kazan
Moscow
UGRA RIVER
Kaluga
OKA RIVER
Nizhny Novgorod
KAMA RIVER
POLESIA
Belovezha Forest
YASNAYA POLYANA
Oryol
Voronezh
CHORNOBYL ZONE OF EXCLUSION
VOLGA RIVER
Kyiv
DON RIVER
Zhytomyr
IRPIN RIVER
DNIEPER RIVER
Severodonetsk
Kakhovka Dam
Taganrog
Astrakhan
SEA of AZOV
CRIMEA
CASPIAN SEA
TEREK RIVER
BLACK SEA
Pyatigorsk
CAUCASUS MOUNTAINS

CHAPTER 3

The Emperor's Fleet

Great stillness reigned in the forest,
and I heard the green leaves dream,
I heard the dream of the bark from which
boats, ships, and sails will arise.

—Adam Zagajewski, "In May,"
translated by Renata Gorczynski

In Białowieża Forest, which spans the border of present-day Poland and Belarus, soaring pines testify to three centuries of growth. Oaks can live for six hundred years, their bark as textured as an epic poem, shaggy and fragrant with moss. Toadstools sprout from tree trunks like bookshelves. Fallen trees lie until they have been used and absorbed by birds, fungi, insects, and bacteria; here, a tree can spend a quarter of its life decomposing.[1] Some fallen trees are caught by neighbors, so that their bases gape aslant from the forest floor. Their uprooting makes damp and hospitable holes in the ground. Ash trees grow so tall that their crowns are lost in the canopy. Crooked, dynamic hornbeams cannot be made into furniture, houses, or ships. But their gnarled trunks and limbs form holes that are precious to birds and other creatures, who use them for shelter and for drinking water.

Białowieża is a border, a buffer, a prize. Before the 1917 revolution, the forest was part of imperial Russia's bulwark against its western enemies. In 1991, the USSR was quietly dissolved in its grandest hunting lodge; before that fateful meeting, Białowieża marked the western boundary of the Soviet Union. In the 2020s, it became notorious as a point of entry to the EU for migrants. It is a place where allegiances blur. *Białowieża* is the forest's Polish name; in Russian it is called *Belovezhskaia Pushcha* and in Belarusian *Biełaviežskaja pušča*, but it has existed since long before any of those nations or languages. *Pushcha* means "thick forest"; it comes from an Old Slavic word that means "desolate place," which is to say a place without human residents. The heart of Białowieża has had continuous tree cover for 11,750 years.

This makes the primeval forest an irreplaceable store of biological knowledge. Its long arboreal memory counters the region's blood-stained history of frequent conquest, rupture, and forced forgetting. Trees in this type of forest evolve much more slowly than shorter-lived organisms. A tree that grows in the same place for half a millennium, casting its foliage on the ground annually, creates a world under its branches. The forest is not an assemblage of trees but a complex network of organisms with trees at their center. A tree's evolution is intertwined with that of animals, plants, insects, and fungi, some of which disperse only a few hundred meters over the course of their lives. Part of what makes a primeval forest special is the simple fact that dead trees are not removed, so that they can nourish other forms of life as they decompose. About half the species in Białowieża rely on decaying wood.[2] Trees have an afterlife in the forest, where nothing really dies.[3]

Once upon a time, this forest was merely a small part of the green expanse that covered much of Europe. But about three thousand years ago, humans began cutting the forest down. Farmers needed more and more land to feed the continent, and people needed more timber for fuel, buildings, fences, and ships. Europe's forest cover bottomed out around 1850.[4] (Some farmland has since become forest again, but the resulting woods are young, with short memories.) Białowieża was a rare survivor of this continent-wide deforestation because it was a treasured hunting ground for the nobility. In the fourteenth century, it was the property of the Lithuanian grand dukes—the last Europeans to convert to Christianity, famous for their tree worship—until the Polish king took control in 1385. The name *Białowieża* means "white tower," for the white wooden hunting lodge built in the forest by one of the Lithuanian grand dukes. No one has ever plowed this marshy land, which, like the northwestern Siberian taiga, safeguards the traces of ancient settlements.

In the medieval period, it was against the law to settle in Białowieża, to poach, or to cut down trees without permission, but the forest was the livelihood of the region's peasants and they could not be deprived of all its goods. Villagers and royal foresters were granted the right to make hay, strip the bark of lime trees to make fiber for weaving, and collect firewood, mushrooms, nuts, berries, and herbs, which were used for medicine and as charms. The local people were also allowed to continue to keep wild bees in the forest in the traditional way, by carving holes into Scots pines and other trees. Some beehives were built high above the ground, like a treehouse, with a platform beneath the hives. The beekeepers could reach the hives with a ladder, but brown bears—the nemesis of forest beekeepers—could not. Spikes at the base of the tree waited to impale any bear who managed to clamber up and then fell. One drawing made in 1780 shows a bear who has managed to climb over the platform and devour the honey, but gotten stuck there. A ring of peasants is shooting at him, executing the honey thief.

For monarchs and nobles, the reason for the forest was hunting—not commercial trapping, as in Siberia, but performative kills that glorified the hunter. A royal guard protected the woods, making sure that the ruler and his entourage could find animals when they wanted them. Hunting in the wild was dangerous and uncertain. A king might be killed or injured, or he might return home scandalously empty-handed. To avoid this, the Lithuanian grand dukes created a system of "hunting gardens," fenced-in areas of forest from which animals had no means of escape. While the Siberian taiga offered seemingly limitless opportunities for retreat, the hunting garden was tightly circumscribed: a stage. Before the royal hunters arrived, "beaters" would push animals into the fenced-in area and close the gates. Within the larger enclosure, a system of nets and fences further eased the king's task, channeling the frightened animals to their death.[5]

The most highly valued creature in the forest was the European bison, also known as the wisent. Curly-headed and humpbacked, it looks like a monument; much later, it would be featured on the first currency of independent Belarus. But before then, Białowieża, its bison, Belarus, and much of Poland would be gathered into Russia's growing empire. As Russian power expanded from the forests to the steppe to the sea, Russian rulers turned Białowieża's old-growth oaks into warships.

The Polish-Lithuanian Commonwealth, a union of the Kingdom of Poland and Lithuania, was Russia's most important rival from the end of the fifteenth century until the reign of Peter the Great, who took the throne in 1682. The tide turned in Russia's favor in the middle of the seventeenth century, when the Zaporozhian Host, the Cossack state in central Ukraine, placed itself under Russian protection. This marked the beginning of Russia's almost inexorable expansion. In 1680, it covered 5.8 million square miles and had a population of only seven million. By 1825, Russia's empire would encompass 18.5 million square miles, with a population of forty million. About a third of this population growth was due to foreign territories that were annexed or conquered.[6]

Russia's transformation over this period would have been unimaginable without the towering, eccentric figure of Peter the Great, who ruled until 1725. He was the first to declare Russia an empire. Where his medieval predecessors had pushed east to Siberia, Peter looked west. From childhood, he was obsessed with western European technologies and ways of living. He dreamed of establishing Russia not only as a great modern military and economic power but also as an authentically European, enlightened culture. In pursuit of this project, he recruited the venerable forests of his expanding empire.

Many biographers have located Peter's passion for the west in childhood trauma. At ten, Peter witnessed the murder and dismemberment of several members of his family at the hands of the Streltsy, the tsar's infantry, during a succession crisis at the Kremlin. This was the beginning of a lifelong hatred for Moscow and the old Muscovite ways. Sidelined by his half sister, Sophia, who had taken control of the government, the precocious boy spent his adolescence in the countryside outside Moscow, playing war games.

It was during this period that the child of bosky central Russia became obsessed with the sea, which signified for him both freedom and power. After catching a glimpse of a miniature English warship stored in a warehouse, he enlisted two Dutch seamen living in Russia, Franz Timmerman and Karsten Brandt, to teach him how to build and sail such crafts. He had met them in Moscow's "German Suburb," the neighborhood where all foreigners were required to live. There he mingled with Dutch, German, Scottish, and Swiss merchants, sailors, engineers, and soldiers, many of whom would later become members of his boisterous retinue. The Dutchmen restored the tiny warship to usable condition, and it became a talisman of Peter's ambition to conquer the seas and make Russia a European power. He used his *botik*, a diminutive term of the Dutch word for "boat," for ceremonies. (It has been preserved to this day.) The bishop of Pskov, who was also a poet, said, "Who will not say that this small dinghy was to the fleet as the seed is to the tree? From that seed there grew this great, marvelous, winged, weapon-bearing tree."[7]

In June 1693, Peter traveled to his country's only port, Arkhangelsk. He was the first tsar to visit the remote northern city, where he joyfully inspected the foreign ships in the harbor. Since the sixteenth century, Dutch ships had sailed to Arkhangelsk with salt, oil, wine, and other products for sale, returning with Russia's forest furs, flax, caviar, and timber. Britain, too, was an essential buyer for Russian wood as well as pelts.[8] Until recently, furs had been by far the most important export from the Russian forests. But with western woods being felled at high speed, Russia's forests came to be coveted for their timber as well. This trade was made possible by new international networks that could transport far bulkier goods than sable and squirrel.

But Peter's focus was less on trade than on the boats themselves, and the people who manned them. During a second trip the next year, he sailed in a yacht he had ordered built for him over the winter. He set out for Solovetsky Monastery, on an island in the White Sea. The party almost drowned after an abrupt change in weather. When they reached their destination at last, Peter ordered a wooden cross inscribed in Dutch, his new favorite language, to commemorate his miraculous survival. He had become obsessed with the Dutch Republic of the United Provinces, the richest and in many ways the most sophisticated country in Europe. Russia was not alone in being profoundly shaped by the Dutch, whose influence extended all the way across the Atlantic, to North America.

Determined to create a Russian fleet, Peter established a shipyard in Voronezh, on the upper Don River, in a forest belt safe from the Crimean Tatars who still made regular raids into Russian territory. From there the Russian fleet would be able to sail south to the Azov Sea. After he won control of the Turkish garrison of Azov, he built a harbor nearby at Taganrog—the city where Chekhov would be born almost two centuries later. Peter sent fifty Russians, most from noble families, to Holland and England to learn how to build and sail ships. Next, a "Great Embassy" of 250 Russians was to travel to western Europe for eighteen months. Peter would be among them, traveling incognito—an absurd proposition for any monarch, but especially one who stood 6'7" and suffered severe facial spasms. His intention was to spend several months in the famous shipyards of Zaandam, near Amsterdam, learning firsthand how to build a ship.

To his great disappointment, he was soon recognized in Zaandam despite his Dutch workman's costume. Tormented by crowds of gaping Hollanders, he fled to Amsterdam after only a few days. There the city's burgomaster arranged for him to work in the closed shipyard of the Dutch East Indies Company, where he helped build a frigate. He departed next for England, where the bishop of Salisbury remarked that the Russian tsar seemed "designed by nature rather to be a ship-carpenter than a great prince."[9] During his months in western Europe,

Peter succeeded in recruiting large numbers of Dutch and English shipwrights and seamen to come to Russia.

Peter's passion for the sea and western Europe would transform Russia's attitude to its forests. His *botik* was the seed of his fleet, but his fleet demanded the planting of acorns and the protection of trees. To ensure supplies of wood for his ships, he established Russia's first broad forest protections, banning felling near rivers or the cutting of oak, maple, elm, larch, and pine above a certain size. In 1709, his government found a large primeval oak forest south of Voronezh. The average age of the trees was estimated to be 400 to 450 years. Peter nicknamed it the "Golden Jungle of Russia," and gave it an official name that, like *botik*, was a playful mix of a Dutch noun (here, *schip*) and a Russian suffix. This oak grove was to be called "Shipov," "of ships." Gone were the days when the empire's subjects could use oak for axles and wheels. Cutting down even a single oak was punishable by death.[10] Those who poached timber from protected woods were fined, and corrupt forest managers were punished with slit nostrils and hard labor.[11] For the first time, large areas of Russian forest were dedicated to the needs of the state.

Two-century-old oak was the preferred wood for the hulls of warships: It was exceptionally hard and resistant to fire. Larch and pine were used for smaller or less important vessels; century-old pines were also used for masts. It took four to ten thousand oaks to make a warship.[12] This meant that Peter needed far more oaks than he could find in his "Golden Jungle." The Baltics, so conveniently close to rivers and seas, were still rich in old-growth deciduous forests—northern versions of Białowieża. Once Peter and his allies wrested control of the Baltics from Sweden during the Great Northern War of 1700–1721, Russia had access not only to lucrative European markets but also to Baltic oaks.[13] Conquest brought more materials with which to expand the navy that helped make conquest possible. Napoleon would later battle the British for access to this same variety of Baltic wood, which he needed for his fleet; the Russians built a new Baltic fortress to keep him out.

As he expanded his fleet and his empire, Peter hoped not only to preserve old forests for rational use but also to fill steppe areas with new forests. He had supposedly attempted to plant oak trees "with his majestic right hand" near Taganrog after taking it from the Ottomans. A few years later he ordered a planting of oak and other trees on the steppe "in the way forests were planted in Europe."[14] Forests were no longer merely a natural feature of the Russian landscape. Following the western European example, they were to be planted, inventoried, monitored, and maintained according to the tenets of the new science of forestry. For Peter, dignified, well-managed, productive forests were a sign of western enlightenment—the antithesis of the medieval, eastern past he sought to cast off.

The first European innovations in forest management had come from the Sun King, Louis XIV, forty years Peter's senior, and his finance minister Jean-Baptiste Colbert. Recognizing the dangers of excessive cutting, Louis and Colbert made it illegal to fell any trees in royal forests. They also devised a system by which sections of forests were cut on a schedule that allowed for regeneration. But German forestry soon overtook the French approach, with a highly scientific system that maximized salable timber, notably very tall, straight trees that were suitable for ships' masts. The German approach emphasized homogeneity and strict conformity to a single standard, though that standard changed over time. The desire for simplicity and order led to a vigorous suppression of biodiversity, with "forests" consisting of orderly rows of a single species, plus whatever independent undergrowth managed to sprout up in the interstices.[15]

Peter's father, Tsar Alexis, had established hunting preserves near Moscow and Murmansk, but they followed the same medieval logic as Białowieża's hunting gardens: Game was to be protected for the enjoyment of the monarch. The good of the country or of the forest itself had no place in such reasoning. Peter has been called "Russia's first forester" because of his imposition of scientific measures. In his quest to maximize the number of long, strong masts and durable hulls for his new navy, Peter emulated Germany's innovative forestry techniques. With his characteristic enthusiasm for imported experts, he brought in German foresters to guide him as he created the first Russian forest bureau in 1696. Russian forestry positions bore German titles, and most positions of responsibility were held by Germans until the mid-nineteenth century.[16]

On the cultural front, Peter ordered both men and women living in towns to adopt western European dress and forced men to shave off their beards, which were seen as a sign of wild Russianness. After a period of resistance, the nobles became avid in their imitation of western European culture. They spoke French at home, learned French dances, wrote Russian versions of French odes, and studied German science and philosophy. Everything associated with Russian peasants, Russian folklore, and even the Russian language was backward, something to be reformed, abolished, or avoided rather than celebrated. The capital moved from Moscow to the pastel-painted canal city of St. Petersburg, which Peter had modeled on the orderly, enlightened cities of western Europe and built using Dutch state-of-the-art canal and dike technology. Medieval cities like Novgorod and Moscow had been made of wood, often lovingly carved. St. Petersburg rose in brick and mortar, its granite and marble palaces and churches built by Italian and German architects. Nothing could bear less resemblance to the forest—or to the wild steppe. The medieval past was to be repressed like a shameful family secret.

Peter's regime of coerced enlightenment brought dramatic changes in Russia's treatment of its non-Christian populations. The many peoples of the Urals and beyond were no longer mere sources of fur tribute. Peter expected them to become "civilized": to be baptized and to learn to read and write. The Khanty and Mansi were the primary targets of the baptism campaign, but the Mansi fought off the first expedition that arrived to make them Christians. In 1710, an angry Peter ordered the Siberian metropolitan to "find their seductive false gods-idols and burn them with fire and ax them, and destroy their heathen temples." Resistance was to be punishable by death.[17] Returning with reinforcements, the metropolitan destroyed idols and baptized the Khanty and Mansi in large numbers; those who complied received tin crosses, Russian clothes, waivers from their tribute-giving, and pardons for minor crimes. There was still resistance, but by 1720 the metropolitan claimed forty thousand conversions. The new Christians were monitored and disciplined by priests sent to the taiga as punishment for violations of church rules.

With his passion for scientific classification and cabinets of curiosities, Peter sent German scientists to study Siberia's flora, fauna, natural history, geography, peoples, language, and anything else worthy of note. Many of the scholars reported with horror on the low level of "civilization" they found among the Siberians, from hygiene to treatment of women. Visitors made such remarks about the settlers and their descendants as well as about the natives: Over time, the two groups had intermarried and intermingled.[18] Native clothes and practices were better suited to the harsh climate. Peter had ordered even Russian Siberians to shave and adopt German dress, but he reversed the order after just a year.[19] Indeed, many of Peter's reforms proved impossible to implement. His ambitious efforts to centralize management of rivers and forests failed, too: Many of his decrees were never put into action. Aspirations to German-style efficiency could not make it far in a territory as huge and as sparsely populated as Russia.

Catherine the Great, a German princess turned Russian empress, continued to prioritize the protection and cultivation of oaks for the navy. With her affection for the French philosophes, she was not one to order nostril-slittings or to impose the death penalty for the cutting of a tree, but she maintained strict rules on which trees could be cut down or used for sled runners. Violators were fined or flogged.[20] She was appalled by the waste of good timber, which was routinely left to rot in the rain and snow because of bad organization and a lack of storage structures. In a handwritten note from 1772, when she was waging war on the Ottomans, she reflected that "nowhere do we sin as much as in the matter of the woods. Our forests are neglected; we do not have people competent in these matters; once a tree is cut, it is cared for as little as when it is standing. I have long said that it is necessary to reward landowners who will take care of their forests and then sell them to the Admiralty [the navy] for felling."[21]

The empress adopted a new tactic: In keeping with her campaign to introduce the idea of private property in Russia, she privatized the forests. A 1782 manifesto abolished the restrictions on shipbuilding wood and other forest protections that Peter had put in place. Catherine viewed them as harmful to the economic interests of her subjects, and without a compelling benefit for the navy. Hoping to develop the timber market, she had faith that the nobility would take care of the forest across generations. In fact, she had little choice. More than half a century after Peter's death, the state was still not capable of managing Russia's vast territories. Even Catherine's privatization was hard to implement. For decades, there was uncertainty about which forests were private and which belonged to the state. Forests on state lands were often considered common property, and common lands were the first to be cut.[22]

At the same time, Catherine made efforts to promote Russian forestry and to grow new forests, as Peter had done. After she had won control of New Russia, in what is now southern and eastern Ukraine, and Crimea, Catherine embarked on a 1787 journey through the territories, a royal parade that lasted six months. For her, power was inherently theatrical; one could not rule without spectacle. She had named her lover, Grigorii Potemkin, viceroy of New Russia (Novorossiya), the area that is now the southern mainland of Ukraine. For her procession, he arranged fireworks and erected fake villages, essentially stage sets, to line her route. (This is the origin of the expression "Potemkin villages.") Forests, too, were part of Catherine's aesthetic vision, and as stage manager it was Potemkin's job to provide them. He imported oaks from central Russia to plant in Crimea, but oaks grew slowly, and often with difficulty. While the new forests took root, it was strictly forbidden to cut down trees in these territories; even the rich had to warm themselves over basins filled with alcohol and set alight.[23]

Ordinary people wanted trees, too. From the end of the eighteenth century onward, Russian and northern Ukrainian settlers to New Russia, as well as German and Mennonite settlers brought in by Catherine, pined for the familiar forests they had relied on for centuries. Orderly rows of trees were associated with European civilization. Inspired by German theories about the almost infinite utility of forests, which were imagined even to mitigate earthquakes, settlers felt an urgent need for trees to provide wood, fruit, shelter from winds, silk (from mulberry trees), and more. According to their view of natural history, the treelessness of the steppe was not a natural state but the result of millennia of fire-clearing and grazing by nomadic pastoralists. The Europeans colonized the land not only with their bodies and their culture but also with their trees.[24]

As its empire grew more powerful, Russia colonized western forests, too. In 1795—within the memory of oaks that still stand—Białowieża was among the lands annexed by Russia in the third partition of Poland, when the country was divided among Russia, Prussia, and the Habsburg Empire. In keeping with her policy of privatizing Russia's forests and entrusting their management to the nobility, Catherine parceled out the primeval forest to her favorites. She gave a whole district of Białowieża to Count Piotr Aleksandrovich Rumiantsev, one of her most important generals. When he died in 1796 in his fortified manor in Ukraine, his heirs clear-cut his whole plot in Białowieża, leaving a sad triangular bald spot on the forest's eastern edge.[25] A swath of forest memory had been destroyed.

Poland's history is a chronicle of division, conquest, and failed rebellions, of hope and paradise lost. Białowieża, once the hunting ground of Polish kings, occupies a special place in Polish consciousness. In his 1834 poem *Pan Tadeusz,* Poland's national epic, Adam Mickiewicz included a portrait of Białowieża that mixed biological exactitude with a fantastical vision of the primeval forest as an animal

Eden. Many of the trees in Białowieża were so old that they had their own names. Now the Russian Empire, having taken Białowieża for itself, was devouring this precious natural heritage, chopping down and selling these natural monuments. By felling the trees in Białowieża, Mickiewicz suggested, Russia was stealing Poland's sacred source of inspiration.

Białowieża was rescued, once again, by its value for the royal hunt, and by its coveted bison. When he took the throne in 1801, Catherine's grandson, Tsar Alexander I, restored the protected status of the forest, prohibiting any hunts except for wolves, bears, and lynx that threatened the bison. The only predators in the forest were to be human ones.[26] The historian Richard Wortman has written about how the hunt was an essential setting for a "scenario of power" for the tsar, an opportunity for him to "display [his] imperial persona." A band provided musical accompaniment as the hunted animal was driven toward the tsar's weapon. The Russian monarchs had learned from the British that hunting was a way to signal the power and daring of a colonizer who asserted mastery over other peoples as well as over animals.[27]

And yet despite Białowieża's renewed status as a protected area, deforestation continued. In 1861, a series of heated dispatches in the liberal dissenter Alexander Herzen's uncensored journal, *The Bell*, decried the felling of trees in the last primeval forest in the western Russian Empire.[28] The forest was still being sacrificed to Peter's old dream of maritime ascendance—even though Russian hopes for a global blue-water presence had been dashed when it lost the Crimean War in 1855. The golden years of Peter and Catherine were long gone, and Russia was being left behind by the Industrial Revolution. Part of the reason for Russia's defeat in the Crimean War was England's steamships and railways. Russia's imperial ambitions were punctuated by the sound of forests falling in vain. Yet the advent of the steamship did eventually halt the use of trees for warship masts, even in Russia. Against all odds, the heart of the forest survived until today.

CHAPTER 4

Subduing the Sublime

The western edge of Russia was wooded and swampy. To the south, where Europe met Asia, Russia pushed against another dense forest—but this one was punctuated by steep, jagged mountains and dizzying green precipices. The Caucasus Mountains were impossibly beautiful. Cold slate water coursed into limpid mountain lakes. Ravines were draped in luminous pines up to the tree line. Then the mountains grew so high that the forest was intimidated by altitude, trees replaced by snow roses, buttercups, purple thyme, and rock bellflower.

In the eighteenth century, the North Caucasus marked the southern boundary of Russian power, as Russia competed with the Ottoman Empire and Persia for regional dominance. Peter the Great and his predecessors had only managed to lay claim to the flatter lands north of the mountain chain. Catherine the Great, encouraged by her success on the Ukrainian steppe, renewed the campaign. In 1785, she expanded Potemkin's responsibilities by making him viceroy of the North Caucasus. Russia desired the North Caucasus in part because they were the only obstacle to a large, fertile Christian land to the south: the kingdom of Georgia, which had long hoped for an alliance against the Muslim Ottomans and Persians. Russia annexed Georgia in 1791, becoming its ruler rather than its ally.

But the peoples of the mountainous North Caucasus, expert horsemen who spoke a baffling array of languages, posed a hostile barrier between Russia and Georgia. Tsarist violence aroused determined resistance, and the Muslim peoples of the North Caucasus launched a series of holy wars against the Russians. Their uprisings were abetted by the landscape. The staggering mountains, the thick forests, and their fierce inhabitants would inspire generations of Russian writers, becoming central to Russia's imperial imagination.

The Caucasian wars coincided with the moment when nature first became an object of sustained aesthetic contemplation for Russians. The early modern Muscovites were famously taciturn in their chronicles, sticking to the bare facts. When they were inspired to flights of rhetoric, they praised God or the tsar, not scenery. Their writings are almost devoid of descriptions of landscape, except as a source of profit, inconvenience, or danger. The era of westernization ushered in by Peter the Great, meanwhile, shunned the unruly natural world, except when it provided the material for mighty warships. Catherine's court poets celebrated gardens rather than forests, palaces rather than mountain ranges.

All this changed at the end of the eighteenth century, when Romantic nationalism swept Europe, beginning in Germany. Soon the Slavs, too, were intoxicated by this new creed, which taught that a nation's essence lay in its land, its vernacular language, and its folk culture. Rather than seeing identity as conferred by empire or religion, Romantic nationalism held that it grew out of the earth—rather like a tree. Intellectuals began to collect, study, and imitate folklore, to visit villages, and to use their vernacular language in their writing.

Poets ventured from manicured gardens into wild spaces, which they now recognized as sublime: not only beautiful but also terrifying. This could mean the central Russian forest, with its bears and witches—or the dense oak groves and stark mountains of the North Caucasus. On the spine of the Caucasus there were no colors left but blue and white; visitors' digits swelled from the altitude. Travelers entered the upper world, staring down at fluttering clouds as wind and sun lashed their faces. What better vantage point for a poet?

Alexander Pushkin was born in 1799, on the cusp of the new century. In the course of his short life, he would transform Russian literature and Russian literary language. He is Russia's national poet, its equivalent to Shakespeare, Goethe, or Cervantes. This is particularly striking since he was the great-grandson of an African abducted from his native land at age seven and brought to Peter the Great's court. The boy, who came to be known as Abram Petrovich Ganibal, was taken from a fortified city called Logone, a center of the Kotoko population near Lake Chad.[1] Ganibal grew up to serve as a military engineer, helping to build fortifications along Russia's expanding borders. Russia's upper classes already included descendants of Tatar and Khanty princes; now an African joined their ranks. Ganibal became a high-ranking army officer and a member of the landed gentry. Peter's daughter, Empress Elizabeth, granted him an estate outside Pskov called Mikhailovskoe: thousands of acres of forest accompanied by hundreds of serfs. This land is now the Pushkin estate museum, where Pushkin's voice is said to whisper from the trees. Pushkin was mocked for his "Moorish" blood and appearance, but this did not stop him from becoming Russia's most celebrated bard.

The young poet was surrounded by an idealistic new generation of liberals who would later become the doomed Decembrists, executed or exiled to Siberia for their 1825 conspiracy against the tsar. By temperament, Pushkin was more interested in women and champagne than in politics, but he partook of the freedom-loving air of the era. In 1820, his odes to liberty nearly caused him to be exiled to Siberia; instead, he was posted to the wilds of the newly conquered Ukrainian steppe. This was far too dull for his taste, and he soon finagled permission to take the curative waters in Pyatigorsk, a Caucasian spa town named for a five-peaked mountain. To his younger brother, Lev, he wrote, "I rode in sight of the hostile lands of the free mountain peoples. . . . You will understand how pleasing this shadow of danger is to a dreamy imagination."[2] For the rebellious young poet, the storied, ferocious mountaineers of the Caucasus were seductive alter egos. The fact that he never made it into the mountains whose "deaf still" hid the "wild genius of inspiration" was no obstacle.[3]

In Pushkin's 1822 poem "Prisoner of the Caucasus," the Circassians, natives of the western part of the mountain chain, have captured a young Russian nobleman. The captive had gone to the Caucasus in search of freedom after being betrayed by his friends in the city. Like many of Pushkin's heroes, he is bitter and cynical. A beautiful young Circassian girl gives the prisoner a drink of cold fermented mare's milk, the nomads' preferred beverage—and that of the Mongols, who had conquered the territory in the thirteenth century. Revived, the young man admires the steppe, the mountain peaks, the thunderstorms, and the fierce, bold simplicity of the mountaineers. He wins their admiration with his own fearlessness. Soon the innocent, passionate young girl is in love with the prisoner. Over the course of the poem, against the sublime mountain backdrop, she gives him life and freedom—and loses her own. The Russian draws power from the Caucasus, destroying it in the process. Pushkin used poetry to make the Caucasus a Russian place, pulling it into the empire by means of his effervescent, violent verse.[4]

"Prisoner of the Caucasus" marked the beginning of a literary trope that has endured to the present. Hostage-taking was an integral part of warfare in the mountains, as it had once been for the Mongols and the Russians; hostages were used as insurance or as a tool of diplomacy. (Indeed, hostage-taking remains a prominent Russian tactic—whether the hostages are American journalists or Ukrainian soldiers.) Samuel Gmelin, a well-known botanist and nephew of the scientist who mapped Siberia's fauna, took part in a scientific expedition conceived by Catherine the Great to map the geography, climate, soil, resources, and ethnographic character of her empire; she had continued Peter the Great's project of classification and inventory. In 1774, Gmelin was kidnapped in mountainous Dagestan. He died while waiting to be ransomed, aged thirty. A 1799 book on the Russian Empire calls him "a martyr to natural history" and explains that "the greater part of the writings he left behind him were forced, not without great difficulty, from the hands of the barbarians."[5]

From the 1820s, tens of thousands of captives were taken in the

Caucasian wars. But the most influential prisoners were those depicted in Russian literature. Mikhail Lermontov, born in 1814, was a hot-blooded Romantic rebel who considered the Caucasus his spiritual home and identified with the persecuted local peoples—even as he helped drive them from their homelands. After an 1837 poem attacking the tsar, Lermontov was sent to the Caucasus for military duty. His 1840 novel *A Hero of Our Time* immortalized the bitter, aimless, womanizing antihero Pechorin, who holds captive an innocent Circassian girl with eyes like a mountain gazelle. She falls in love with him. Like Pushkin's Circassian maiden, she is doomed.

The landscape of Lermontov's novel is all purple abysses, clouds whirling over imposing cliffs, rivers that undulate like silver threads. Real life is insufferable compared to the elation of standing above the world. "On getting away from social conventions and coming closer to nature," Lermontov writes, "we cannot help becoming children: all the things that have been acquired are shed by the soul, and it becomes again as it was once, and as it is surely to be again some day."[6] Romantic nationalism rooted a monoethnic identity in the soil. The literature of the Caucasus put a new twist on the relationship between state and landscape. The "imperial sublime," as the literary critic Harsha Ram has called it, sings of foreign lands that are gloriously free—and yokes these stony mountains and vertiginous forests to distant Russian power.

Though Lermontov adored the Caucasus and admired its mountaineers, his novel, like Pushkin's poem, would become integral to a genocidal imperial imagination. Pushkin ended his poem with a bloodthirsty epilogue that celebrated the generals who had conquered the Caucasus for Russia and "destroyed, annihilated tribes." Without a trace of self-consciousness, the young poet exclaimed, "Resign yourself, Caucasus: Yermolov is coming!" It took decades of fighting, but General Alexei Yermolov, a hero of the Napoleonic Wars who took charge of the Caucasian campaigns in 1816, would ravage the mountain societies that Pushkin and Lermontov romanticized. The process of colonization and ethnic cleansing would also lead to the clearing of the majestic Caucasian forests. For Peter and Catherine, trees had been essential material for maritime conquest. As Russia struggled to conquer the North Caucasus in the nineteenth century, trees became one of its chief enemies, shielding the warriors who fought so hard against Russian domination.

Even before the North Caucasian forests became a military target, Russia's incursions into the region had grievous consequences for the local trees. In the mid-eighteenth century, trees were still seen primarily as an essential building material and fuel—and they were in short supply on the flatter lands north of the mountains. The Cossack forces assigned to conquer the region sought lumber and firewood from farther afield. Commanders were concerned about forest shortages. Mozdok, a city whose name means "dense forest" in Circassian, had forest to its south, but desert to its north. This troubled the Cossacks, who were accustomed to wooden buildings and bountiful firewood. Earlier settlers in the area had often built their homes in the local style, with adobe bricks, wattle, clay, and reeds. But in keeping with their colonial project, the new, more numerous settlers tried hard to maintain their habit of wooden houses, even when it meant building an oak house in summer and another more practical adobe *saklia* for winter. By the early nineteenth century, only narrow strips of forest remained along the river valleys of the area.[7] There was such a shortage of wood that it had to be shipped in from inner Russia—an expensive proposition—or purchased from the mountain peoples who lived in areas that were still forested.

As Russia's campaign against the mountain dwellers escalated, so did the destruction of the remaining forests. In 1830–1831, the Russians destroyed about thirty villages in Chechnya and what is now Dagestan. The resulting resistance movement coalesced in 1834 around the Avar leader Imam Shamil and posed a true threat to Russia's presence in the region. Shamil, who was from the mountains of eastern Dagestan, rallied the support of the Chechens who lived in the lower-lying, heavily forested region bounded by Georgia to the south and the Terek River—the boundary of Russian control—to the north. He also won the support of the Lezghians at the edges of the mountains.

Imam Shamil's twenty-five-year-long leadership of Muslim fighters relied on asymmetrical guerrilla tactics against a conventional army. The Russians found that they could march into the mountains and seize any position they chose—but they were unable to force a decisive confrontation with the local fighters, who vanished into the mountains and forests. Lumbering Russian columns could not survive long in the mountains, making them easy targets for insurgent attacks as they returned to the lowlands. An English history recounted how in 1841, Chechen fighters climbed up beech trees so huge that they could bear thirty or forty men, who fired on the Russians from the branches. "As long as the forest stood the Chechens were unconquerable," the English chronicler wrote.[8]

It was clear that the landscape was on the side of the peoples of the North Caucasus. In the summer of 1845, Yermolov's successor General Mikhail Vorontsov led an expedition to capture Imam Shamil at his mountain headquarters of Dargo. Forced to march through narrow valleys with heavy forest cover on all sides, the Russians found their progress thwarted by barriers made from trees while they were assailed by Caucasian fighters. As the battle intensified, the Chechens reinforced their log forts with Russian corpses. Vorontsov had to retreat, with over five thousand casualties. But he soon changed his tactics against Shamil's forces.

Mountains were immutable, but forests could be cut down. The Russians had emerged from a forest home that had offered protection against foreign conquerors. Now they would expand their own empire by cutting down the forest of their enemies. Vorontsov's troops spent much of the winter felling trees, making space for fortifications and roads. The Chechens fought hard against this campaign. According to the historian Thomas Barrett, "the woodcutters' progress was followed in the newspaper *Kavkaz* as if it was battle news, with the amount of forest destroyed duly noted."[9] Every tree felled was another casualty of the war, the cost of imperial "pacification."

By 1849, Chechnya had been transformed. The Chechens were pushed deeper into the forest, which meant further deforestation as they made space for their pastures and fields. Chechen and Ingush toponyms testify to vanished forests: Grassy, treeless places have names derived from the words "oak," "yew," "chestnut," and "plane tree."[10] Cossack and Russian military commanders eventually began to worry about the complete destruction of the forest, which was caused by practical needs as well as military exigencies. Illegal cutting was rampant, as Cossacks and military colonists broke laws to procure timber and firewood. In 1860, a Cossack ataman wrote, "It is well-known that the banks of the Kuban, Laba, Urup, Terek, Malka, and others were once covered with thick forests of which now remains only a scrawny forest suitable for brushwood and stakes and in some places for wooden plows and poles; in many places not even a trace of such forest remains."[11] As often happens, the destroyers of the forest lamented the results in real time. Elegies described tree stumps four and a half feet wide, a water trough made of a thirty-five-foot-long oak, houses made from planks of a single oak, and "old mutilated trunks, the remnants of giants of the past, with withered branches and tall stumps sending out young shoots"—the last memory of a bygone forest.[12]

Deforestation and flooding created a vicious cycle: The Cossacks cut down trees along the river to make fences to prevent the Terek from flooding into their fields and villages, but every felled tree made flooding and erosion more likely. The trees helped hold water in the soil, their roots held the earth still, and their leaves cushioned the impact of rain. There are some signs that unlike the Russians and Cossacks, the peoples of the North Caucasus understood that forests helped prevent erosion. The Chechens, Kabardians, Ossetians, and other peoples maintained sacred groves, a form of forest preservation. There were rules set against chopping down trees that were close to riverheads, streams, and lakes—a means of preventing erosion.[13] Imam Shamil fortified such protections by issuing laws that limited both wood felling and sale of wood to Russians.[14]

In February 1852, twenty-three-year-old Lev Tolstoy was accepted into service as a fireworksman of the fourth class in the Twentieth Artillery Brigade. His detachment was assigned two kinds of destruction: the felling of the forest and the annihilation of the auls, the villages, as part of the push to destroy Imam Shamil and his coalition for good.[15] A Russian account celebrating the campaign called it "A Pogrom in Chechnya."[16] The Russians always undertook their campaigns in Chechnya in winter, because in summer the dense foliage colluded with the guerrillas. Russian attacks were accompanied by the cracking sounds of fallen trees.

Though Tolstoy shared the aristocratic origins of his predecessors Pushkin and Lermontov, he would bring a graver, more ecologically minded and anticolonial slant to the Caucasian literary trope. Pushkin and Lermontov had their heads in the sublime, imperial clouds. Tolstoy remained rooted in the ground, employing a harsh realism: coagulated blood mixed with dust. He mourned the destruction of the Caucasian forests, in which he saw a parallel with Russia's destruction of the local peoples and ways of life. His grief at what he witnessed in the North Caucasus would reverberate through the rest of his life and work.

In his 1863 novel *The Cossacks: A Caucasus Tale of 1852*, the hero is a young man very much like the youthful Tolstoy. The book's hero, Olenin, is sensitive but without a proper outlet for his passions, prone to gambling and ennui. At twenty-four, he has already frittered away half his fortune. (Tolstoy used the earnings from the novel to pay his own gambling debts.) Olenin has not found a profession and has never even fallen in love. Well-versed in the myth of the Caucasus, he enlists as a cadet in a regiment there in the hope of finding a greater meaning to his life.

It is not necessarily freedom that Olenin seeks; in one early scene, he laments the fact that he is still "free" the night after dancing the mazurka with a beautiful woman. "Why doesn't love come, why doesn't it bind me hand and foot?" he asks himself. He is "intensely conscious of the presence within him of that omnipotent god of youth, that ability to transform oneself into a single desire, a single thought, the ability to will and do, the ability to throw oneself headlong over a fathomless precipice."[17] He hopes that the Caucasus will offer him an appropriate cliff from which to gaze into the distance, purple mountains to serve as a backdrop for heroic exploits.

Though he is joining the Russian army, on his journey south Olenin imagines himself as one of the local horsemen fighting for independence from the Russians. Like any young Russian man of the nineteenth century, he dreams of a Circassian slave girl with a "shapely figure, a long plait of hair and deep, submissive eyes." He will educate her after they fall in love, and soon enough she will be reading Victor Hugo in French. It is a nonsensical dream, he recognizes—but a seductive one, imprinted in the Russian psyche by Pushkin, Lermontov, and others. As Olenin approaches the Caucasus, he feels the freedom of being away from his Moscow friends and acquaintances, from his debts, from the memory of his failures. Liberty is to be found among "coarse beings"—mountaineers, Circassians, Chechens—whom he does not really consider to be people; he is far from "civilization." Every continued reminder of this society—signboards in French, ladies in carriages—is painful. With a sharp, light touch, Tolstoy satirizes the naïve Orientalism of the young person abroad. Olenin has no interest in the supposed "civilizing mission" of colonialism; rather, he seeks freedom in supposed wildness.

Tolstoy was a passionate nature lover even as a young man. *The Cossacks* is full of gorgeous observations of the landscape that he encountered during his real-life military service; he is far more precise than Pushkin or Lermontov. The Caucasus is above all a region of vivid contrasts, the antithesis of the flat, green world of central Russia. Mountains float up from the steppe and rich, dense forests collide with sand drifts. Green is abruptly interrupted by snow. On the Cossack side of the Terek River, the settlements are placed some distance from the eroding riverbank. Century-old oaks stand near rotting plane trees and the remnants of abandoned orchards. The landscape is marked by war; the road between settlements reminds Olenin of a cannon shot through the forest.

Tolstoy displaces the stereotypes of Muslim mountain dwellers fundamental to Pushkin's and Lermontov's stories of prisoners. Instead, Tolstoy's story focuses on the Cossacks who live along the Terek. These are not only Cossacks but also religious schismatics: Old Believers who broke with the Russian Orthodox Church after reforms in the seventeenth century. Many Old Believers escaped into the forest, as we will see later—often to Siberia. Tolstoy's Cossacks sought freedom on the forested slopes of greater Chechnya. Old Believers are known in Russian culture for their capacity to preserve ancient traditions as if in a time capsule, but this particular sect is a strange hybrid. They intermarried with Chechens and adopted many of their customs while continuing to practice their faith and to speak Russian. This, too, is an accurate depiction: Many of the real-life Terek Cossacks were Old Believers.

Like Yermak and his Cossack band, who led the colonization of Siberia, the Cossacks who settled north of the Caucasus were agents of Ivan the Terrible's imperial expansion in the late sixteenth century. But their origins are hazy. According to folklore recounted by Tolstoy, Ivan visited the Terek, granted the Cossacks there a fertile wooded strip of land along the river, and asked them to be friends of Russia, promising not to try to convert them or force them to be Russian subjects. Some historians say they are the descendants of Novgorod River pirates of the fourteenth century, or of a group that splintered from Yermak's band. One unverifiable story even claims that Yermak himself settled in the North Caucasus before moving on to Siberia. All that is known for certain is that free Cossacks were living along the Terek in the mid-sixteenth century, and sometimes worked for the recently established Russian forts there.

According to Tolstoy, after two centuries in the region, the Old Believer Cossacks had a greater affinity to the Circassians and Chechens than to Russians. Russian historians have tended to downplay the Cossacks' ethnic intermixing. But Tolstoy was right to emphasize the extent to which the Terek Cossacks had come to resemble their North Caucasus neighbors. It is likely that the Terek Cossacks were a mix of fugitive Russians, Circassians, Chechens, and Georgians, defined not by race, ethnicity, or religion, but by the fact that they were not bound to any state.[18] As in Siberia, the colonizers mingled with the locals, and soon came to resemble them.

Cossack myth claims that brigand-wanderers were attracted to the North Caucasus for its rich soil and bountiful water, trees, and game.[19] Tolstoy's Cossacks inhabit a fertile land that would sound like Eden if not for the constant warfare. At the edge of the dense forest they have orchards and vineyards, and they grow melons and gourds. Their charming, tidy houses are surrounded by dark green poplars and "gentle bright-leaved acacias with white scented flowers." But the forest is also a gift to the mountain warriors. Chechen raids across the Terek are particularly frequent in May, when the river is shallow and the forest is so thick and lush that it is hard to cross even by foot. Elm and plane trees grow so closely that they form an almost impenetrable screen, and the clearings are overgrown by blackberry bushes and "reeds with grey, swaying heads." For Olenin, the "resilience of the vegetation" is something utterly unfamiliar, as dreamlike as the mountains that he knows lie somewhere in the distance. Perhaps it is a cipher for the resistance of the locals, who will not give up until they are nearly exterminated.

This forest is paradise for a hunter. Uncle Yeroshka is an old Cossack who takes Olenin under his wing. The character is based on an elderly Cossack named Epifan with whom Tolstoy lived and became close during his first days in the Caucasus. But here Yeroshka assumes fairytale proportions. He is so tall and broad shouldered that only when he is alone in the forest can his great scale be forgotten. In ragged deerskin sandals, he hunts wildcats, pheasants, boar, and deer. He reminds Olenin of James Fenimore Cooper's *Pathfinder*, a touchstone of frontier literature for Russians as well as Americans—as we will see later, whole subsections of Russian culture were inspired by Fenimore Cooper. Yeroshka knows how to listen to the rustling forest, to the boar wallowing, the screeching of young eagles, the crowing cockerels, the geese crying out before midnight.

In the end, Olenin finds transcendence in nature rather than military adventure. When Olenin goes hunting with Yeroshka, he finds the forest's flora and fauna "outrageously lavish," the air "hot and pungent." Even the summer gnats begin to charm him, evidence of the forest's surfeit of life. Suddenly he finds that his mind is empty of desire. "Assailed by such a strange feeling of causeless happiness and love for everything," he crosses himself, understanding that he is "not a Russian nobleman at all, a member of Moscow society," "but just a gnat, or a pheasant, or a stag." Olenin came to the Caucasus to search for meaning among noble savages, submissive slave-girls, and the heroic warfare of Orientalist poems, but he has his epiphany in the summer forest.

Tolstoy was unusual in his rejection of conquest and his embrace of the forest. In 1856, after the Crimean War had ended, the Russians reached new extremes in their assault on the people of the Caucasus. They razed villages and resettled whole tribes to the Ottoman Empire; about half the refugees would die during the journey. Russian troops captured Imam Shamil in 1859, putting an end to the greatest threat to Moscow's supremacy in the eastern Caucasus. To the west, the Russians finally succeeded in crushing the Circassians, who had declared a republic in 1861.

A Russian journalist named I. Drozdov described the final struggle of 1862 and 1863. As the campaign began in June 1862, the "highlanders" were visible along the edges of a forest fenced with a barrier of felled trees. Drozdov made clear that the Russians treated the forest as an enemy combatant. They shelled it and assaulted it, cutting it down as they advanced, constructing their own abatis from the rapidly falling trees. The stench of dead bodies permeated the mountain air.

Many of the surviving highlanders had fled, but those who remained were given a deadline for "resettlement." As Drozdov marched east to the Black Sea with the Russian troops, they passed "the scattered corpses of children, women, old people, torn to pieces, half-eaten by dogs."[20]

On May 21, 1864, the Russians declared victory over the Caucasus. "In the mountains of the Kuban district one can now find bears, wolves, but no highlanders," Drozdov jubilated. "Thus ended the long, stubborn, bloody struggle in the Caucasus. It was hard, but it was pleasant to test one's strength in such labors. . . . And life did not pass in vain: there was much charm in dashing battles, and the dry, short ring of a bullet in the mountains gripped the soul more firmly than the sounds of an Italian tenor's song."[21] Tolstoy was haunted for the rest of his life by the violence he witnessed in the Caucasus. In old age, when he had nearly abandoned fiction, he would return to these memories to write his short, late masterpiece: *Hadji Murat*, the tale of Imam Shamil's capture and the end of Chechen independence.

CHAPTER 5

Clear Glade and Murmuring Forest

One of the most extraordinary tales of a Russian prisoner in the Caucasus is memoir, not fiction. Nikolai Shipov—whose name evokes Peter the Great's beloved oak grove, though it is unclear whether there is a connection—was a well-traveled, linguistically gifted serf. Born in 1802 in a village south of Nizhny Novgorod, he was the son of a prosperous peasant trader who, unusually for a serf, was literate and erudite. Serfdom had been established in Russia at the beginning of the seventeenth century to maintain a settled agricultural labor force. Though bound to the land and to the whims of their masters and mistresses, serfs had some latitude to work for themselves, provided they paid the rent or contributed the labor required of them. (Some serfs even owned their own serfs, though this was technically illegal.) Nikolai Shipov and his father traded livestock with the peoples of the southeastern steppe, where the gregarious young Nikolai picked up the Kazakh and Kyrgyz languages. When he was denied manumission despite his father's offer of 50,000 rubles for his freedom, he fled south.

After Nikolai was caught in Pyatigorsk, the spa town in the Caucasus where Pushkin took the waters, he discovered a law saying that any serf taken captive by "mountain predators" and released would win freedom for himself and his family. His brilliant scheme started with a job selling provisions to Russian soldiers in Chechnya, where he quickly learned the area's lingua franca, Kumyk. In February 1845, he ventured out of the Russian fort at nightfall and was promptly seized by a group of Chechen bandits. After eleven days spent playing cards and chatting with his captors, he escaped with the help of a bribe. His legal gambit succeeded, and he and his family were emancipated at last.[1] Before leaving Chechnya, he crossed paths with the famous General Vorontsov, who had felled the forests in his search for Imam Shamil. The illustrious general said with a smile, "Well done! You escaped from them quickly—I suppose you didn't much like it there." The irony was obvious. For Shipov, imprisonment in the Caucasus was the only way to escape a life of bondage in Russia.

When Tolstoy served in the Caucasus, about 40 percent of the Russian population—twenty-three million people—lived as the property of landowners; another 40 percent were "state peasants," bound to state land and required to pay rent. Serf men made up most of the Russian army; in *Hadji Murat*, Tolstoy used the serf soldier Avdeev to make explicit the link between serfdom and imperial conquest. Military service lasted twenty-five years, meaning that few serf soldiers ever returned to their villages alive.

Serf women, meanwhile, often became the lovers of noblemen, the victims of sexual violence, or something in between. As a young man, Tolstoy fell passionately in love with one of his own serfs, Aksinya Bazykina, a married woman from a village about six miles from his family estate. In his diary he described one of their trysts, among fading bird-cherry blossoms in an old-growth forest at his family estate, Yasnaya Polyana. His son with Aksinya, Timofei, bore a marked resemblance to his father. He was raised in the Tolstoy house and ended up working as the family's coachman. Racked with shame over his youthful sexual adventures, disgusted by desire, Tolstoy would go on to renounce sex entirely—though only after having thirteen children with his long-suffering wife, Sophia.

When he returned home from his time in the military in 1855, Tolstoy began to make amends for his sins and those of his country.

Good deeds, he knew, began at home, as did bad ones. He set about educating the local peasants, and he began to replant the forests at his beloved Yasnaya Polyana. As the years passed, he would grow obsessed with the fantasy of returning to the simple, communal ways of the Russian peasant and living in harmony with the land, surrounded by a resurrected forest.

When Tolstoy inherited the estate at age nineteen, Yasnaya Polyana was a self-sufficient idyll of abundance. There were orchards, a creamery, an aviary, a distillery, and hundreds of serfs. Tolstoy's maternal great-grandfather had bought the estate for his wife in 1763. In keeping with the Westernizing trends that started with Peter the Great, Tolstoy's grandfather developed Yasnaya Polyana into a western European–style aristocratic estate, with orangeries, a French garden with pollarded lime trees, and a wilder English-style park. Only the bewigged serf orchestra, which played outdoors as Tolstoy's grandfather strolled among the elms, apple trees, and lilacs, reminded visitors that they were in Russia rather than France or England.[2] Tolstoy's family ranked among the 5 percent of Russian nobles who had more than five hundred serfs.[3] His family's dependence on human bondage would come to torment him, as would the aping of western European ways. But as a child he experienced Yasnaya Polyana as a paradise. It is the basis of his first literary success, the autobiographical novel *Childhood*, which was published while he was serving in the Caucasus.

Tolstoy was possessed of a near-mythical pedigree—and despite his hatred of luxury, he was proud of it. His mother was descended from Riurik, the Scandinavian prince who founded Rus. One of her ancestors had fought the Mongols in the thirteenth century.[4] The history of her estate, too, was entwined with Russian struggles against invasion, and with the importance of trees in Russia's self-defense. The name "Yasnaya Polyana" translates to "Clear Glade," and is derived from "ash tree glade." (In Russian, an ash tree is a *yasen*.) In the sixteenth and seventeenth centuries, the area was a clearing—a kind of gateway—in the Kozlova Zaseka, a stretch of forests and felled-tree barricades that ran for hundreds of miles, protecting Russians from nomadic invasion.[5]

These *zaseki* had once stood as a green cordon across the southern border of Russia. Deciduous trees were cut to leave stumps taller than a grown man. Hazel, berries, and saplings sprouted through them, creating a "green tangle stitched with brushwood," as literary critic Viktor Shklovsky imagined it in his biography of Tolstoy. It was forbidden to break paths through the *zaseki*, cut wood, or collect brush there.[6]

As a young man, Tolstoy was an enthusiastic outdoorsman in the conventional manner: He loved hunting. Like many men of his class, he was also an avid gambler and carouser. While he was in the Caucasus in 1852, he corresponded with his brother Sergei about which of Yasnaya Polyana's forests to sell to pay his debts. Sergei proposed cutting the Chepyzh oak forest, as well as a grove behind the post office and a birch stand. A grove of young aspens could be preserved or sold—as Tolstoy wished. Tolstoy replied that he would prefer to sell one of the estate's houses before the forests. But to pay his debts, he conceded, there was nothing that he would not sacrifice.[7] In a subsequent letter he confessed that if it were necessary to sell off half of Yasnaya Polyana to free himself from the torment of debt, he would be happy.[8]

In the end, he sold not just his estate's forest but also the wing of the house where he had been born. The brick structure was dismantled, carried away, and reconfigured on someone else's land. He had sold off his birthplace, along with the Russian forest he had inherited from his forebears. Russian nobles of Tolstoy's day were often heavily indebted, and selling forests and other assets from rarely visited country estates was an expedient way to fund glittering lives in Moscow or Petersburg. Tolstoy, however, was exceptional in his contrition.

From the later 1850s on, Tolstoy devoted himself to the reforestation of the estate, involving himself personally in forest management. Using the money he had earned with his now famous and celebrated writings, he bought up neighboring land. He was influenced by Franz Meyer, a German estate manager who succeeded in cultivating a German-style forest on the black earth steppe, planting steep, uneven land ill-suited to agriculture with coniferous and broad-leafed trees.

The results were not only pleasing to the forest-loving eye; they also helped prevent erosion and protected nearby fields from wind. Tolstoy visited land Meyer managed at a nearby Tula estate, returning with spruce, linden, and pine seedlings for Yasnaya Polyana.[9]

In 1857, Tolstoy made a proposal to local authorities for the restoration of the *zaseka,* which had been badly thinned by deforestation in the years since the threat of Tatar invasion had receded and the protective forests had been sold off and made private estates.[10] Having returned from the fields of conquest in the Caucasus, he sought to reforest Russia's medieval boundary—a contraction of imperial ambition that mirrored his longing for a simpler past. His proposal, which involved a shift to private ownership and management of the forests, was rejected.[11] But with his wife Sophia, whom he married in 1862, he would more than double Yasnaya Polyana's tree cover.[12] As often happened in the Tolstoy marriage, Sophia was the one to manage the technical details of Lev's guilt-ridden, ecstatic visions. She planted thousands of trees, from exotic North American imports like western red cedar and eastern white pine to Russian staples: alder, fir, larch, birch, linden, and oak. Her diary recorded her distress when cows trampled her planting.[13]

The forests around Yasnaya Polyana were the guardians of old Russia, reminders of a bygone epoch. The local trees also had a highly personal resonance for Tolstoy, who used tree planting as an intervention into his own biography. He later took pleasure in telling visitors, "You see that larch? Right over there where those branches are was the room where I was born."[14] By growing trees, he could help vindicate the errors of his youth and the sins committed by the Russian Empire—and he could invent a new image of his birth, in which he was born outdoors, under a tree, in a world before man's fall from divine grace. He was moving toward the almost pantheistic philosophy of his later life, one that would lead him to reject the Orthodox Church and be excommunicated.

Despite his reforestation efforts, Tolstoy was still chopping down trees—a necessity in a world dependent on wood for building material

A self-portrait by Sophia Tolstoy in the hoar-frosted oak wood of Chepyzh, which Tolstoy refused to sell in 1852. Yasnaya Polyana, 1902. *From the collection of the L. N. Tolstoy State Museum*

and fuel. The great writer was always better at enunciating extreme positions than at carrying them out in his own life, though he did manage to give up hunting and become the world's first celebrity vegetarian. In an 1858 letter to his grandmother, the thirty-year-old Tolstoy recounted a visit to a forest that he had bought and was now cutting down. He described the birches and nightingales that, he imagined, did not want to know that they had been sold, who had no idea that the forest's days were numbered. Ashamed of "the tyranny of drawing imaginary lines," he lamented the persistence of ownership. The forest was bought and sold, and Tolstoy was disgusted by his inability to change himself.[15] Trees, like hunted animals, longed for life. Here was a seed of Tolstoy's later rejection of the very concept of private property.

As the literary critic Thomas Newlin has observed, "Tolstoy famously preached that 'the kingdom of God is within you.' But to find God in his works we almost always need to go outdoors."[16] One of Tolstoy's most famous literary epiphanies is experienced by Prince Andrei Bolkonski in *War and Peace* (published serially between 1865 and 1867). Over the course of the novel, Bolkonski struggles to find meaning and love, tormented by bouts of nihilism inspired by Tolstoy's own darkest moments. Andrei's dilemma over whether to give up desire or embrace it is one of the most profound questions explored in Tolstoy's oeuvre.

During a journey through the countryside on a spring day, Andrei passes through a birch forest that shields him and his servants from the wind. The birches, alders, and cherry trees are budding, and lilac-colored flowers and blades of early grass are dislodging the detritus of the year before. The green fir-trees look "coarse," like a winter hang-over. He notices a very old oak tree, twice as wide as a man's embrace, that shows the scars of a long life. The contemptuous oak seems to denounce spring, love, and happiness as lies, confirming Andrei's own submission to despair. His life is finished, he believes, and he would be a fool to expect any further happiness. The gnarled oak tells him to stand, do no harm, and desire nothing.

Later that spring, on a beautiful, hot day, Andrei visits the Rostov family. That night, he opens his bedroom window and the moonlight bursts in. He leans out to see the pollarded lime trees washed in luminous silver. Andrei hears the daughter of the house, the lovely young Natasha Rostova, above him. She is fantasizing about flying out the open window and into the night. (As a child, Tolstoy had jumped out a window hoping to fly.) Andrei longs for Natasha to know that he exists. In the presence of the moonlit trees, his desire has reawakened.

On his way home, he drives through the forest where he spotted the gnarled oak. Now the forest is denser and greener, full of shade; the pale new shoots on the firs bring them into harmony with their surroundings. When Andrei sees the monster oak, he hardly recognizes it. The old tree has been transfigured by its canopy of dark green leaves. Seeing the oak's spring transformation, he understands the inexhaustibility of nature's power. He realizes that he should live more like a forest—in interconnection with all the beings around him, giving and receiving.

In 1872 Tolstoy used the royalties he had earned from *War and Peace* to buy more than fifty thousand birch and fir seedlings.[17] Most writers merely turn trees into books; he closed the loop, turning his novel into a forest. His oldest daughter, Tatiana, later recalled planting these birch trees with her father and siblings. By the time she wrote her memoir, the birches had grown into a forest, named Abramovsky after the gardener who had helped create it. Every time she passed, she remembered the shining, sticky leaves of the fragrant saplings she planted, as her father told her that someday she would pick mushrooms in the forest she was making.[18] During a visit in 1900, the revolutionary writer Maksim Gorky described watching the elderly Tolstoy walk through the birches in autumn, leaping over ditches and lovingly stroking the "damp satin trunks" with his hands.[19] It has been suggested that visitors to Yasnaya Polyana can feel Tolstoy's "biofield" if they hug a birch tree in Abramovsky forest.

Trees were part of Tolstoy's legacy. In *Anna Karenina* (published serially from 1875 to 1877), Anna's brother sells off forest to pay his debts, to the great disapproval of Levin, the novel's moral compass and Tolstoy stand-in. Levin, like Tolstoy, views the human obligation to the forest as part of the moral duty to family, to society, and to future generations. An 1891 portrait of the elderly Tolstoy by Ilya Repin shows the writer reclining at the foot of a tree at Yasnaya Polyana with a book in hand. The great man's posture makes him look like he is part of the tree's root system. Repin found a visual expression of Tolstoy's belief that humans and trees were constituent parts of a single organism, and that their fates were inextricably linked.[20]

Tolstoy's family was buried in the Church of St. Nicholas, which is reached by a walk through the forest from Yasnaya Polyana. But Tolstoy was excommunicated by the Orthodox Church in 1901, and he was therefore not eligible for church burial. In childhood his oldest brother had claimed he knew the secret to universal love and happiness: It was written on a green stick hidden in the woods at Yasnaya

Polyana. According to his wishes, Tolstoy found his final resting place in the spot where the green stick—which they had never found—had supposedly been buried.[21] A grass-and-earth sarcophagus rises in a forest clearing near the path he used to take to go swimming in the river, in an old, protected forest.[22] The ground is unconsecrated by the Church but made sacred by Tolstoy's love for the natural world.

Though Tolstoy's literary gifts and moral transformation were exceptional, his concern with Russia's forests was not. In the 1850s, many progressive-minded landowners—including politicians, intellectuals, and writers—were growing concerned with the health and survival of Russia's wooded lands. European Russia was rapidly losing its green cover. It was becoming clear that deforestation was causing drought and flooding, both of which could cause famine by destroying crops. Enamored of new scientific advances, many landowners took up the emerging discipline of forestry. One such innovator, a Poltava estate owner who planted forests on his land, was a target of satire in *Dead Souls*—Gogol being a less pious and less ecologically minded writer than Tolstoy. But despite the limitations of their elite outlook, a faction of the Russian aristocracy began organizing their estates to preserve the forest. Some of these landowners were also, like Tolstoy, critics of serfdom and Russia's rampant social injustice.

In some cases, landowners worked together with their serfs to manage and replant their forests. While most of Russia's serfs suffered brief lives of poverty and ignorance, there were striking exceptions—such as Nikolai Shipov, the happiest prisoner of the Caucasus. There were serf orchestras, serf theaters, serf poets, emancipated serfs who became university professors, and serf scientists. Now some green-minded landowners sent their serfs to study forestry. Alexander Teploukhov, for instance, was born in 1811 as a serf of the Stroganov family—the dynasty responsible for colonizing Siberia. The Stroganovs sent him to a forestry institute in Saxony to be trained in the latest German methods. Invited to remain in Germany as a professor, he had to decline: He was still a serf, and was obliged to return to Russia. He went on to teach forestry there and to manage the forests of the twenty-four-thousand-acre Stroganov estate.[23] He published more than fifty scientific works, including Russia's first forest manual and extensive writings on the importance of forests in protecting the water supply by limiting evaporation and erosion. He is remembered as a father of homegrown Russian forestry.

This was an era that saw a strong affinity between serfs and forests. From a legal perspective, serfs were understood as being attached to the land on which they lived—like forests, rivers, and minerals. In the nineteenth century, this connection between serfs and forests came to the center of public attention, as Russia followed Europe in emphasizing the caretaking role of the state. Both serfs and forests were forms of property, but they came to be seen as occupying an exceptional category worthy of special care.[24] Both were at the mercy of landowners, yet both would help decide Russia's fate. As Russian society grew more turbulent and movements for both reform and revolution gathered momentum, serfs and forests gained ever more prominence in the minds of Russia's greatest writers—the consciences of the nation.

One of Tolstoy's early literary models was a novelist who specialized in both nature and human nature: Ivan Turgenev. Born in 1818 to a landowning family in the central Russian region of Oryol, he was raised by governesses to speak French, German, and English. His tales of first love are some of the most poignant in world literature, and he described Russia's social turmoil with unrivaled sympathy and subtlety. He was the first Russian writer to become famous in western Europe, where he introduced Tolstoy and Gogol, among others, to an international audience. And Turgenev was Russia's most eloquent nature writer.

Turgenev was alarmed at the rapid deforestation that he saw taking place before his eyes. In an 1847 short story, he observed that the last forests of Oryol, his home region, would be gone in five years.

The bogs had already been drained.[25] In this and other stories of the period, he immortalized the beauty of a vanishing landscape as he made the case for the idea that Russia's peasants were people, not property. Turgenev advocated for the emancipation of Russia's forests as well as its serfs. Unlike Tolstoy, he was never didactic, nor did he consider becoming a forester himself. Indeed, he was appalled that Tolstoy would waste his literary gifts by spending time "reforesting the whole of Russia."[26]

While Tolstoy donned peasant garb, learned boot-making, and devised his own idiosyncratic philosophy-religion, the genteel Turgenev believed in science and progress, embracing western Europe's technical as well as cultural advances. He spent much of his life in Germany and France, where he became close friends with Flaubert and other writers and had a long-running relationship with the opera singer Pauline Viardot. (His daughter with a serf woman was called Paulinette; Turgenev moved her to France, where she went on to marry a businessman.) He studied philosophy in Berlin, focusing on Hegel. His writing, which shies away from all extremes, shows not only his interest in science and political liberalism but also a fascination with German philosophy, including *Naturphilosophie*, the idea that the world should be seen as a dynamic, organic whole rather than as something mechanical and fundamentally divided from the human mind.

Turgenev's 1852 collection of stories about his travels in the woods and meadows, *A Hunter's Sketches*, united lyrical, lapidary, scientifically accurate descriptions of Russia's natural landscape with compassionate descriptions of the plight of the serfs and peasants. While Tolstoy was still serving in the Caucasus, Turgenev had already succeeded in uniting the two major issues of the mid-century: social reform, including the emancipation of the serfs, and the human relationship to nature. Tolstoy later dedicated to Turgenev his Caucasian tale "Cutting Down the Forest," whose form showed a debt to the older master of nature writing.[27] This was Tolstoy's only dedication to a fellow writer.

A Hunter's Sketches was a sensation in Russia. By illuminating the humanity of the serfs, pointing to the arbitrary and unjust nature of the divide between serfs and landowners, and convincing many readers of the unsustainability of unfree labor, *A Hunter's Sketches* is credited with helping to bring about the emancipation of the serfs in 1861. This emancipation was a great victory: a world-historic act of expropriation on the side of justice. But the ensuing land reforms were poorly conceived compromises with the nobility. The government could not afford to compensate landowners for the full value of the emancipated serfs, even though the indebted upper classes had already mortgaged a large proportion of their land and their serfs to the state. The serfs were therefore burdened with the debt incurred by their emancipation. They were allotted small and often undesirable plots of land, while the commons—including forests and rivers, vital sources of sustenance for peasants—were no longer available. Household serfs, meanwhile, received no land at all.

The shortcomings of the emancipation and land reform caused political, financial, social, and ecological upheaval that would contribute to the 1905 and 1917 revolutions. One of the most visible problems was high-speed deforestation. Suddenly the serfs who had once been a resource comparable to forests were free, and they were demanding their own share of Russian nature. Millions of new peasant landowners came into conflict with old landed classes. The peasants stole timber to sell for cash; the nobles cut down trees to sell before they could be stolen. Arable land was more profitable than forest. Anyone with a plot of woods chopped it down to make farmland. As forest cover vanished, the evaporation cycle in the Russian countryside slowed down. Soon the rivers began to dry up.

The state's attempts to rein in deforestation met with intense resistance from the nobility, which rejected the idea that the state had the right to control their land use. The state now asked that nobles become stewards of the land, but most aristocrats did not even want to live on their country estates—they only wanted to use the land to fund their lives in the city. If the state cared so much, the nobles argued, it ought to expropriate the land and compensate them for it, as it had with the serfs.

In other words, to be saved the forests would have to be "emancipated," too. But in the 1860s, 60 percent of Russia's forests were already state property, and the government could not afford to buy any more. The tumbling price of timber, a result of the helter-skelter deforestation after emancipation, had been a blow to state finances. As the government dithered, the forest fell. Thanks to rumors of forest-related reforms, everyone rushed to cut trees while they could. The price of forests continued to sink, and banks no longer gave credit against forested lands.[28] Gone were the days when a young Tolstoy could sell his forests to repay his gambling debts. In less than two decades, from 1868 to 1887, European Russia lost 5 percent of its forest; in the next two decades it lost another 9 percent—a territory the size of the state of New York or Iowa.[29]

But some areas were too swampy and impenetrable to log. This was the case in Polesia—in Ukrainian "Polissia," in Belarusian "Paliessie"—a densely forested region that spanned the border of Belarus and Ukraine. Polesia was a nearly ungovernable space, a zone of anti-modernity that blurred the boundaries of Russia's imperial authority and defied the encroachment of industry and capitalism. Swaths of marshy forest survived not by royal edict, as in Białowieża, but because the region was so damp and unsteady underfoot that it required a local's knowledge of paths and bogs, rivers and fields, to make the region livable or even traversable. Such a landscape was hardly ripe for urbanization or industrialization. As a result, even at the start of the First World War, much of Polesia was almost devoid of modern infrastructure. Its inhabitants rarely ventured far from their villages, working the land with the simple goal of surviving from one season to the next. Though it was one of the westernmost regions of the Russian Empire, it was one of the least developed.[30]

In the late nineteenth century, the tsarist government embarked on a project to drain the Polesian wetlands, which were fit for neither agriculture nor commercial forestry. For the government, these wetlands were not an ecological treasure but an impediment to the development of a backward region. The government was badly in need of revenue, the empire craved control, and Russia wanted to prove that it was just as modern as the rest of Europe. Germany had once been composed largely of marsh and fen, in an era when the Rhine meandered without any thought of efficiency. But the German rivers had since been straightened to be more profitable, and ungovernable, unproductive German marshes and fens had been drained.[31] Since the days of Peter the Great, Russia had studied Germany's management of the landscape. Now the cash-strapped Russian Empire was determined to dry out Polesia's recalcitrant swamps.

Many of the local peasants who would supposedly benefit from the drainage resisted the transformation of the land. They knew how to navigate this terrain, and they relished the liberty that it preserved. The drainage threatened to replace informal fishing, berry picking, or livestock management with commercialized farming or agriculture. The government's land expropriation and new systems of water management broke up old networks of communication and patterns of habitation. Some scientists, meanwhile, spoke out against the plan, arguing that draining the wetlands might affect river levels or flooding. They were right, but the government, hungry for timber profits and higher tax revenue, ignored their warnings.[32] This plan to drain Polesia's swamps was part of a much larger movement by the Russian government to rationalize and legislate land and resources that had previously been governed by tradition.

In the second half of the nineteenth century, more and more Russian citizens were becoming convinced that forests, like people, could not be private property. The high-speed destruction of European Russia's woodlands showed not only the failures of tsarist reforms but also the dangerous perversity of market incentives where collective goods were concerned. Russian foresters of the era leaned left—sometimes so far left that they ended up in prison. The famous forester Nikolai Shelgunov, author of the most important nineteenth-century history of Russia's forests, was a friend of the influential socialist writer Nikolai Chernyshevsky, author of Lenin's favorite novel. After resigning from the imperial Forestry Department in 1862, Shelgunov ended up in the Peter and Paul Fortress, a prison full of revolutionaries like himself.[33]

Another radical forester, Vladimir Korolenko, was born in 1853 in Zhytomyr, in north-central Ukraine, to a Russian-speaking father of Cossack origins and a mother from the minor Polish nobility.[34] Such blended identities were common on the fringes of the empire; Korolenko's contributed to his principled repudiation of nationalist movements and all forms of ethnic chauvinism. Later in life, he would defend the rights of Indigenous people and Jews who were being persecuted. He embraced socialism during his days as an impoverished student at a liberal forestry school in the woods outside Moscow. He was arrested for the first time after protesting the detention of a radical classmate.[35]

Turgenev was a liberal nobleman who opposed serfdom and sympathized with radicals, but he was not inclined to join the revolutionaries. Younger and poorer than Turgenev, Korolenko had no such hesitations. He was a devoted socialist activist all his life. But his most enduring fame comes from his writing. Like Tolstoy and later Chekhov, he used literature not only to probe human nature but also to argue for justice in an autocratic society. A turn-of-the-century cartoon showed him and Chekhov as the mythical warriors accompanying Tolstoy, the biggest and strongest of them all.[36]

Korolenko saw the forest's promise of freedom from the nobility, from hierarchy and property, from domination by class, nationality, or sex. His 1885 story "The Murmuring Forest: A Polesian Legend," one of his most enduring works, is a socialist fable about the swampy Polesian forest's capacity to support rebellion against the ruling class. Roman, a forester, lives beyond the normal rules of human conduct. People whisper that the bears are Roman's brothers and the wolves his nephews. He fears no animal, but he cannot stand the sight of people.

When the local landowner comes to Roman's forest dwelling and orders him to marry a woman named Oksana, Roman refuses. The lord has him flogged until he submits. This is what was sometimes called the droit du seigneur: the lord's right to marry off the peasants who dwelled on his land. We soon learn that the lord has impregnated Oksana, probably by rape. He forces Roman to marry her, presumably so that the child will not be born out of wedlock.

There is a third man in the equation: Opanas, a charming Cossack with a bandura, the traditional stringed instrument of the Ukrainian bards, wandering singers and bearers of folklore and folk memory. Opanas falls in love with Oksana and asks the lord for her hand, but the lord refuses. If she married Opanas, who is not tied to any patch of land, the lord would no longer have access to her. This is the logic of serfdom: People who are property—even, as here, illicit property—must be held in place. At the climax of the story, Opanas plays an ominous song on his bandura, warning the lord that he will be punished. The lord does not listen. On a stormy night, Roman kills the lord in the forest, out of the reader's view.

Opanas's cautionary song is only a brief interlude. The more pervasive music is the eponymous murmur of the forest:

> There was always sound in this forest—even, long-drawn, like the undertones of a distant bell, peaceable and indistinct, like a quiet song without words, like dim memories of the past. There was always sound in the forest because it was a dense, ancient pine forest, still untouched by the saw and the ax of the timber merchant. The tall, century-old pines with their mighty red trunks stood in frowning ranks, their thick green tops pressed against one another as they thrust toward the sky. Beneath them the air was still and fragrant with resin; bright ferns broke through the carpet of needles covering the ground, displaying their sumptuous fringe and standing motionless, not a leaf moving. Tall green blades of grass grew in dark, damp corners; white clover bent its heavy head, as if in a quiet trance. And above, endless and uninterrupted, droned the forest sounds, the indistinct sigh of the ancient pines.[37]

The story's narrator is an orphan boy adopted by Roman. Raised to understand the language of trees, he can hear when the pines are singing or groaning in fear. When the storm is coming, so is the "Forest Master"—in other words, the *leshii*. Storms appear when he runs "laughing and crying, dancing and spinning" through the forest, diving down to the oaks and trying to rip them from the roots. The *leshii* is quick-tempered. But as a master, it is obvious that the wood goblin is preferable to the lord. Better to be ruled by the laws of the forest than by a nobleman.

Opanas the Cossack is an earthly embodiment of this freedom from human laws. The music he plays on the bandura is the music of nature. When Opanas runs his hand across the strings it tells him everything: "How the dark pine forest murmurs in bad weather, and how the wind rings through the thistles on the empty steppe; how the dry grass whispers on a high Cossack grave." Opanas is himself a force of nature, rising "like a dark cloud" when he realizes the lord's intentions toward Oksana. The lord is no match for the forest or for Opanas, who has united the power of forest and steppe, the two shaping forces of northern Eurasian history. In Siberia and the Caucasus, the Cossacks served as mercenaries for the Russian Empire. But here they symbolize freedom from the injustices of tsardom.

Throughout the nineteenth century, folklore inspired national movements around Europe, including in Ukraine. The songs of the Cossack bards and the work of Ukrainian poets like Taras Shevchenko, who was himself born a serf and whose poetry Korolenko cherished, were touchstones in the movement for Ukrainian independence. An early draft of "The Murmuring Forest" was so full of Ukrainian words and expressions that Korolenko had to rewrite it before publication.[38] But Korolenko, a socialist rather than a nationalist, used a supposed folk legend as his coded plea for another kind of freedom. For him, the sound of the forest represented the promise of liberty and justice for the common person. A new generation of socialists and anarchists would share Korolenko's hope.

CHAPTER 6

Prince, Peasant, Tungus, Yakut

All of great Rus' will hear of me,
All her tongues will call my name,
The Slavs' proud grandson, and the Finn, and now the savage
Tungus, and the Kalmyk, the steppe's friend.
And I will be long beloved of the people,
For rousing goodness with my lyre,
For celebrating Freedom in my cruel age
And calling for mercy for the fallen.

—Alexander Pushkin, "I have built myself a monument . . ."

If revolution had not summoned Prince Peter Kropotkin, future father of the anarchist movement, he would have been a geographer. From childhood, he had an avid interest in the natural world. In his 1899 *Memoirs of a Revolutionist,* he includes a loving description of his father's country estate in the central Russian province of Kaluga, where the family spent every summer. To reach Kaluga from their mansion in Moscow, the family crossed miles of beautiful pine forest. The soil was deep and sandy, nothing like the springy dark earth farther south. The family and their servants had to descend from their carriages and carts and cross the pine barren on foot as their horses struggled to drag the vehicles. These journeys were among Kropotkin's happiest childhood memories.

As a teenager, Kropotkin took pleasure in leaving his family entourage and crossing the forest alone, listening to the voices of the enormous, centuries-old red pines. He drank cool, refreshing water at a spring in a ravine. Someone had left a birch bark ladle nearby, as if for communal use. It was this forest that first instilled in Kropotkin his love of nature and his "first dim perception of its incessant life."[1] He learned alertness to the contours of the land and the reaches of history. From the balcony of his family estate, he could see the Serena River and the ruins of an old earthen fortress where the Russians had once defended themselves against the Mongols. Fields of yellow grain were enclosed by wooded expanses where a lucky boy might spot a wolf. Kropotkin and his siblings liked to pick mushrooms there. Sometimes the family had tea in the woods with an elderly beekeeper, tasting the pleasures of forest life.

These rustic journeys were a dramatic contrast to the lavish celebrations of the Russian aristocracy. When Kropotkin was eight years old, in 1850, he took part in a fancy-dress ball in honor of the reactionary Emperor Nicholas I. The theme was the display of all the "nationalities"—what we would call ethnicities—of the Russian Empire. The emperor was to be honored with a pageant of his conquests. Kropotkin's relatives dressed in Russian, "Caucasian," and Mongolian costumes. His uncle was dressed as a Tungus (Evenk), the most romanticized of Siberia's Indigenous peoples. In his memoirs, Kropotkin recalled feeling "dizzy with admiration of his fine leather coat, his bow, and his quiver of arrows." The young Kropotkin carried the coat of arms of Astrakhan, on the Caspian Sea, and wore the region's distinctive fur headgear. His appearance charmed Emperor Nicholas, who poured biscuits into his funny hat.[2]

Under Nicholas, Russia's empire reached its apex, covering 7.7 million square miles—twice the size of Europe, larger than South America. Nicholas died of pneumonia in 1855, an unhappy man: His expansionist spree had met a humiliating end in the Crimean War. His son and successor, Alexander II, ushered in an era of reform—and Kropotkin served as Alexander's head page boy. In 1862, the year after the emancipation of the serfs, Kropotkin made an unusual decision. His true wish was to study mathematics or physics at the university, but his

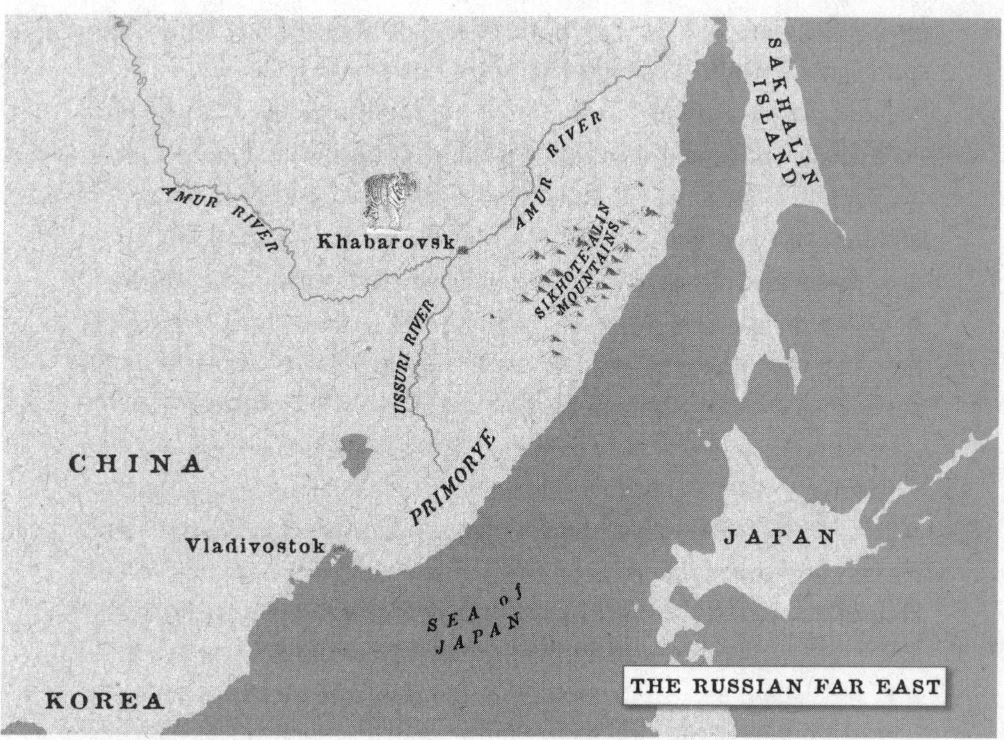

father would not allow it, and the young Kropotkin could not finance his studies alone. He would have to be a military man, as his father intended. Rather than choosing an assignment that would allow him a life of ballrooms and parades, Kropotkin petitioned to join the newly formed regiment of mounted Cossacks of the Amur, in the newly Russian Far East. Count Nikolai Muravyov, the governor-general of East Siberia, had annexed the Amur and Ussuri territories between 1858 and 1860 through a sequence of treaties with the Qing Empire.

The mighty Amur River was the "Mississippi of the East," realm of Russian frontier dreams. Its tributary the Ussuri River was surrounded by subtropical forest. With little resemblance to either European Russia or to Siberia, the region was tantalizingly exotic to Russian visitors. A lush gateway to the Pacific, it had long attracted Russians, but for centuries they had been unable to wrest it from Chinese control.[3] Now the region was theirs, and Siberia's riches could be unlocked at last.

Kropotkin went east in search of scientific discovery, adventure, and independence in Russia's New World.

His political curiosity was piqued by Russia's easternmost territories, where serfdom had never taken hold. Kaluga, where he had spent his summers amid the fragrant forest, was the realm of old Muscovy, with one of the highest rates of serfdom in Russia. Kropotkin's father was descended from the medieval Russian princes, like Tolstoy's mother's family, and possessed some 1,200 male serfs. The Kropotkins, like the Tolstoys, had a serf orchestra; they also had serf tailors, shoemakers, and even a serf pastry chef.[4] One of Kropotkin's relatives scandalized society by marrying a brilliant serf actress, who continued her career after her marriage—an even more shocking transgression.[5] Like much of the Russian nobility, Kropotkin was raised by serfs who treated him with tenderness; he was appalled to see them beaten and abused. At twelve, he wrote his first novel. Inspired by tales of republican noblemen of the French Revolution, he abandoned his aristocratic title and signed his work simply "P. Kropotkin," the signature he would use for the rest of his long life.[6]

Siberia functioned in the Russian imagination as a paradoxical place of liberty and exile, possibility and punishment: a land of bandits, rebels, recluses, and adventurers. When Kropotkin arrived, eastern Siberia was sparsely populated by Indigenous pastoralists and hunter-gatherers, Cossacks and political exiles, escaped prisoners and serfs, and hardy, long-suffering settlers. Its climate was harsh, and its north-flowing rivers impeded trade and travel. But it had plenty of fertile soil, fish and game, and precious minerals in its rocky depths. The Far East, meanwhile, was imagined as a land of untold natural riches. Kropotkin was seduced by the thrill of discovery and by the promise of a new, freer society in the eastern mountains and forests.

The young man set out to join the Amur Cossack regiment in 1862, traveling by train past the swamps and forests of the Vladimir region and through the immense coniferous forests near Nizhny Novgorod. Precious oaks were always cause for special comment in his diary. Peter the Great's dream of naval supremacy had been dashed, but oakwood was still valuable, and oaks had an almost sacred aura. Kropotkin traveled along the Kama River, where huge forests shone blue in the west. Gray-blue fog, he observed, was the perpetual companion of the conifer. The scent of resin wafted from the shore, and the sky seemed to frown in the silence. European Russia may have been hacking down its forests, but here on the edge of the Urals the trees still seemed infinite. Profligate use of firewood was a testament to the limitless supply.

After leaving Perm, Kropotkin was pleased to observe that the forest was growing more diverse, with spruce, aspen, birch, and willow among the pines. When the railway ended, he entered Tobolsk province on a road made of logs piled over swamp. "The forest, at first small, becomes taller and denser," Kropotkin wrote in his diary. "There is open space and freedom for wolves and hares, of which there are many; there is no other animal." Near Tyumen the black earth was so "exciting" and rich that he imagined mixing it in his porridge.[7] This was land that could clearly be used for agriculture.

Moving east, he approached Lake Baikal, the world's largest freshwater lake and a sacred space for the local Buryat people. Kropotkin observed that Russian settlers viewed the crooked coniferous forest on the rocky slopes as a rival. Humans believed that they were competing with trees for scarce arable land, though the conifers were occupying territory that was probably no good for farming. There was a reason that so many of Siberia's Indigenous inhabitants were hunters, fishers, foragers, and pastoralists rather than farmers.

In early October, the trees on the steep mountains around the magnificent Baikal were bare and unbeautiful. As Kropotkin approached the Stanovoy mountain range, which had until recently marked the border between Russia and China, he wrote, "The ridge is overgrown with forest, now completely bare and so lamentable. Sand, crooked pine trees . . . the forests are burning, no one puts them out because it is not worth it."[8] Even if the few inhabitants of the area had tried, they probably could not have stopped the fire with the primitive means available to them. In the eastern Siberian town of Chita, Kropotkin observed a forest fire that made a mountain look like a volcano, with a red glow and a halo of smoke, the trees reduced to black silhouettes. There had been no rain for a long time. When the peasants plowed the earth, it was like ash.[9] Kropotkin saw so many fires that he began to feel that there was a conspiracy against Siberia's larch-giants: Like martyrs killed several ways, they were burned, flooded, uprooted by wind. The forests had a sorry look—but, he wrote optimistically, "the young tree will grow again and come back into the struggle."[10] Kropotkin was only twenty years old, but he was already developing a political philosophy that encompassed plants and animals as well as people.

If Russia's annexation of the Amur and Ussuri territories was to hold, Russian settlers would have to remain on the land. Kropotkin was tasked with helping to maintain these settlements through the delivery of regular barge loads of grain. Like previous generations of Siberian governors, Count Muravyov was so desperate for settlers that he had to rely on ex-convicts. In order to help the unsavory settlers to multiply, Muravyov married off the single men to freed female convicts.[11] Women were so scarce in Siberia that men jumped at an opportunity to marry a woman convicted of murdering her previous husband.

Homicide was one of the region's more minor dangers. Monsoons, hordes of hungry migrating birds, and the intimidating nearly virgin forest caused the settlers many brushes with famine. Food shipments could only reach them at certain times of year. If barges loaded with food ran aground or sank, as happened on one of Kropotkin's delivery missions, the settlers were in danger of starving to death. More than two centuries after the first Russian colonization of Siberia, Russia still struggled to keep its easternmost settlers alive. In Ussuri Krai, close to the Pacific Ocean, rare oak forests—a sign of arable land—were cleared to make way for farming. In the Far East, as in the North Caucasus, imperial expansion was a process of deforestation. Kropotkin's diary from his journey shows how his loss of faith in state reform progressed in tandem with the deforestation he witnessed in the region.

The early days of the reign of Alexander II were a time of emancipation, optimism, and ambitious plans. Count Muravyov was an intelligent, capable man intent on improving life in the Far East for Russians, if not for Indigenous people or the Chinese and Korean populations that had lived there long before the Russian settlers arrived. Though he was hardly radical, he was open to novel political ideas: Muravyov hosted a conversation of young officers in which they discussed the possibility of forming a United States of Siberia that would be part of a federation with the United States of America. Muravyov's cohost at the event was his cousin Mikhail Bakunin, another father of anarchism. An ardent, hotheaded revolutionary, Bakunin had been exiled to Siberia in 1857 for his involvement in failed uprisings in Prague in 1848 and in Dresden in 1849.[12] The cousins partook of a new Russian enthusiasm for the ideas of federalism and regionalism. In one line of reasoning, Siberia was analogous to the United States: an abused and exploited colony that could be transformed into a realm of egalitarian pioneers who would live in freedom on the great land.

But in Siberia Kropotkin observed how all attempts at reform—for example, of the violent, corrupt police—came to nothing or produced new, unforeseen harms. He would later write an influential book arguing that mutual aid—what biologists now term altruism—rather than competition was the dominant factor in the evolution of both humans and animals. He came to believe that the state was the root of all evil; once the people overthrew it, they could revert to older, more egalitarian forms of self-organization, like clans, guilds, and the Russian village commune. For him, as for Tolstoy (a de facto Christian anarchist) and for many anarchists of later generations, the development of strong, centralized states was not a mark of human progress but a fall from grace. A state only enabled ever-worsening property accumulation, hierarchy, inequality, and social control—the qualities traditionally associated with "social complexity," as we saw in chapter 1—as well as learned helplessness among people who forgot how to provide for their own needs and those of their friends and neighbors. For Kropotkin, hunter-forager-gatherers knew more about justice than city dwellers did. He had set out on his eastern journey with high hopes for the future of the Russian state and for the role he might play in advancing these reforms. The five years he spent in Siberia during the 1860s instead crystallized his anarchist theories and prepared him for a life of principled asceticism, teaching him "how little man really needs as soon as he comes out of the enchanted circle of conventional civilization."[13] The young prince slept on a blanket placed on a bed of spruce twigs—and liked it.

Kropotkin would spend years trying to understand the mountain formations of northern Asia, the "primitive backbone" of the continent. A few years after his sojourn in Siberia and the Far East, he was imprisoned for his political activities. He struggled with scurvy as he wrote up the results of his research, an important contribution to Russia's middling understanding of its own eastern territories. He later delayed his flight from the country so that he could present his findings at the Geographical Society. Thanks to his devotion to science, he was arrested and imprisoned in the infamous Peter and Paul Fortress. After two years of incarceration and a daring escape, he did not return to Russia until 1917.

Another revolutionary who found himself enthralled by Siberia was Vladimir Korolenko, whose "Murmuring Forest" we encountered in the previous chapter. Having been expelled from Moscow's College of Agriculture and Forestry in 1876, he enrolled at the Saint Petersburg Mineral Resources Institute. But in 1878 he was exiled from the imperial capital to Perm, on the banks of the Kama River. Korolenko had been reported by a police spy for his work with a Narodnik group. This movement of agrarian socialists believed that the salvation of Russia lay in "going to the people," educating peasants in rural areas. The Narodniki had some affinities to Tolstoy's idealization of the Russian peasant, and to Kropotkin's; the traditional peasant commune and village council appeared to them to be forms of proto-socialism. The mostly urban, intellectual idealists were convinced that the rural peasantry was the repository of the peaceful and virtuous essence of the Russian soul, a purity that had been corrupted by tsarist autocracy and aristocratic pretensions. But where Tolstoy taught nonviolence, some successors to the Narodniki embraced political assassination. In 1881, the radical group the People's Will succeeded in killing Alexander II, "the Emancipator," by blowing up his carriage with a bomb.

All prisoners and exiles were now required to swear allegiance to the new emperor, Alexander III. When Korolenko refused, he was punished by being exiled even farther away: to Yakutia, in eastern Siberia. His time there would inspire one of his most beautiful short stories, "Makar's Dream." The protagonist, Makar, is an example of the assimilation of Russian settlers into local cultures. "While Makar's fathers and grandfathers fought with the taiga, burned it with fire, hacked it down with iron, they themselves grew wild without noticing it," Korolenko writes. "After marrying Yakut women, they adopted the Yakut language and Yakut customs." Makar tries to remember his Russianness, but this is difficult. He speaks Russian poorly, dresses in Yakut garb, and eats Yakut food. When he is sick, he summons a shaman. Like many Indigenous people and Russian peasants alike, he suffers from alcoholism, though it is hard to find real vodka among the taiga traders. His cosmology is a blend of Christianity and Yakut tradition.

Some Russians portrayed Siberia as analogous to North America, celebrating the potential for its development and exploitation by Russian settlers. But as Korolenko's portrait of racial and cultural blending suggests, there were crucial differences. Siberia was far less inviting than the Americas had been for colonists. Russian fur trappers reached the Pacific in 1639. By 1700 some 100,000 Russians and other Europeans had crossed the Urals into Siberia, but there were twice that number of Indigenous people in the region.[14] Nearly two centuries later, the population of Yakuts living in northeastern Siberia recorded by the 1897 census was about 227,000—nearly as large as the entire Indigenous population recorded by the US government in 1900.[15] Nine-tenths of Siberia was still designated by the Russian resettlement department as "completely uninhabited and badly explored."[16] This is radically different from the situation in the United States, where by 1900 the Indigenous population accounted for 0.3 percent of the population and historians had declared the frontier "closed." By 1911, the Russian population of Yakutsk province had actually fallen from the 1897 total, to just 7 percent.[17]

These numbers make it easy to see why Korolenko's Makar looked more Yakut than Russian. Another distinctive feature of Russian colonialism in Siberia was a remarkable degree of ethnic blending and cultural syncretism, with some descendants of Russian settlers forgetting how to speak Russian entirely. The 1897 census was complicated by the fact that some people surveyed did not recognize traditional ethnic categories at all, identifying "peasant" as their nationality.[18] Some old Russian settlers viewed Yermak, conqueror of Siberia, as an enemy invader.[19]

Unlike the nineteenth-century frontiersmen who took their entire families with them to settle the American West, the plains of Canada or the savannas and deserts of South Africa and Australia, Russian explorers in Siberia were almost exclusively men. The only region where Russian settlers included large numbers of men and women was the Ukrainian steppe, where agricultural labor required larger family units. Having traveled for years to reach Siberian hunting grounds, Russians relied on the local peoples. They traded, bartered, and caroused with them; they married and had children with them. In the mid-seventeenth century, the town of Yakutsk, the northeastern-most outpost of Russian settlement in Siberia, consisted of forty-six yurts of Yakut design and twenty-four Russian-style wooden huts, inhabited by 280 men. Of these, 68 were Cossack soldiers, 86 were hunters or trappers, 3 were traders, and the remaining 123 were Yakuts. There were only two women in the settlement, both natives.[20] In the nineteenth century, regiments of Cossacks were transplanted to Siberia to push back the frontier with Qing China. As Kropotkin noticed during his trip in the 1860s, these men had so few marriage options that they were grateful to wed a convicted murderer. A native woman was often a more appealing choice, or simply the only one available, and these relationships produced mixed offspring.[21]

Although both the conquest of Siberia and the conquest of North America involved displacement and subjugation, the population trajectories of Native Americans and Indigenous Siberians, Tatars, and descendants of the Mongols were very different. Native Americans in North America numbered perhaps two million in the seventeenth century, but by the 1890s just one-tenth of that number survived. In sharp contrast, the non-Russian population of Siberia grew from about two hundred thousand in the early 1700s to about six hundred thousand in the early 1900s, though it also decreased as an overall share of the population, from 40 percent to 22 percent.[22] The westward expansion of the United States and Canada to the Pacific involved a catastrophic population collapse and vicious exterminatory warfare. The non-Russian Siberians were often immiserated and cut off from their traditional ways of life, but they were not exterminated. The Chukchi, whale and seal hunters and reindeer herders who lived on the forbidding, frozen edges of the Bering Strait, were the most remarkable example: They avoided Russian rule until the twentieth century. The first state with which they had to compromise was the Soviet Union.

Due to the vastness of Siberia's forests and tundra and the inhospitable nature of its terrain, geography, and climate, Russian settlers were forced to rely on Indigenous peoples and their knowledge of the land to a much greater degree than Anglophone settlers in North America did. When Kropotkin was searching for a route from the gold mines of Yakutsk to the mountainous region east of Baikal, for instance, a Tungus man showed him a map etched on a piece of birch bark. Kropotkin set off with a Yakut guide who had followed that same route twenty years ago. The birch bark map was perfectly accurate, leading the travelers through the disorienting expanses of mountains and forested valleys. This long-term reliance on Indigenous people helps explain why, although some Indigenous Siberian groups and their languages went extinct, several larger ones persisted and preserved their religion and customs throughout the era of high imperialism.

In Yakutia, Korolenko discovered that the line between Russian Siberians and Indigenous people was often thin. He saw what aristocrats like Pushkin, Lermontov, and even Turgenev missed, but what the escaped serf Nikolai Shipov had grasped: that peasants and non-Russians had a natural affinity. The end of serfdom had done little to end economic hardship in Russia, and nothing at all to help the Indigenous population. With Alexander III's reactionary regime, the tsarist era came closer to its fiery end.

CHAPTER 7

Tigers Listen to Water Talk

But the Earth stood empty and naked. Only high above birds were flying past. One day a duck flew across the earth and dropped a larch branch from its beak. After some time it became a tree, and a larch forest began to rustle on the banks of the river. A black grouse flew by and dropped from its beak a pine sprig on the ground, and pines began to grow in the larch forest. A tit flew by and dropped from its beak a willow catkin that landed on the very shore of the river, and willows began to grow on the shores and islands. A crow flew by and dropped from its beak a sprig of birch, and from it the trunks of birches whitened the land. The swamps blushed with cranberries.

The Earth became the Earth, and the taiga became the taiga.

—From a Nanai creation myth[1]

At the end of the nineteenth century, Russia set out to build a trans-Siberian railroad. The project was intended to further strengthen the empire's grip on northern Asia, increase the profits from the vast territory, and, perhaps above all, project state power both inside and outside Russia.[2] The railroad ties, sleepers, and bridges came from the bountiful—if not always durable—timber of the surrounding lands. The railroad was a machine for devouring forests. Like the American railroad, Russia's train system consumed more wood than coal; in 1913 alone, Russian locomotives consumed 7.7 million cubic meters of wood—enough to fill more than three thousand Olympic-sized swimming pools.[3] It facilitated the felling and burning of forests for other purposes—for example, coal mining, which requires large amounts of timber to hold mineshafts open—as it made it possible to transport wood across long distances.[4] Completed in 1916 in a last gasp of imperial achievement, the Trans-Siberian was the longest railway line in the world, running from Moscow to Vladivostok, on the Sea of Japan.

Construction required a detailed study of the land's contours—a continuation of Kropotkin's geographical work. In the first years of the twentieth century, the Russian government sent out surveyors to map the railroad's future route. The most accomplished and illustrious of these was Vladimir Arsenyev, who became one of Russia's greatest naturalists. Like Kropotkin and so many other Russian travelers, Arsenyev would depend on Indigenous guides. Arsenyev's account of his own pathfinder and protector, Dersu Uzala, would bring both men enduring fame. Nineteenth-century populists like Korolenko saw Indigenous peoples as analogous to Russian peasants—innocent, downtrodden, and in need of enlightenment.[5] Arsenyev's story merges the stereotype of Indigenous people as nature's children with a more heroic, tragic narrative. In his account, Dersu is the savior, rescuing the explorer again and again. But like the eastern taiga he calls home, Dersu is doomed.

Arsenyev's biography testified to the social transformations enabled by the emancipation of the serfs, imperfect though it had been. Born in St. Petersburg in 1872, Arsenyev was the son of a former serf who ascended the ranks of the Moscow District Railway. Continuing the family's trajectory up the social ladder, Arsenyev became an officer in the Russian Imperial Army. A man of even more diverse talents than Kropotkin, Arsenyev was a self-taught naturalist, geologist, cartographer, ethnographer, archaeologist, and demographer.[6] He took part in numerous expeditions to explore and map the forests of the Russian Far East, where a sickle of land borders Manchuria in northeastern China, the base of the Korean Peninsula, and the Pacific Ocean. This place, Primorskyi Krai, whose name means "area along the sea," is home to an extraordinary biome not found anywhere else in Russia, and unique in the world. It escaped the ice cover that once blanketed

Siberia, allowing a far greater diversity of flora and fauna to survive and flourish. Subject to wild shifts in temperature, it is very humid. The local climate's volatility is a constant reminder that humans live at the mercy of the elements.

On his expeditions through the forests of Russia's southeastern coastline, Arsenyev encountered vast stretches of old-growth forest. The names of the tree species he catalogued were a list of the many peoples who inhabited the border region—including those who had disappeared. The Daurian larch was named for Dauria, the region of Siberia and the Far East that was inhabited by the Mongolic Daurian people until they were driven out by Cossacks in the seventeenth century. Arsenyev described Korean pine, Manchurian linden and ash, Japanese angelica tree, and Mongolian oak. There was Amur cork, with its velvety bark, and Manchurian walnut, whose large leaves at the ends of its branches made it look almost like a palm. As the names of these species suggest, this was a region where the Siberian taiga met a coastal climate inhabited by species that also lived in Japan and Korea.

The Far Eastern forest was lush, diverse, almost fantastical to a Russian accustomed to a more austere climate. Pointy-leaved red currant and white-flowered Manchurian viburnum covered the forest floor. Persian nightshade inched up trees, and fresh-faced yellow honeysuckle flowers made a youthful contrast with the plant's wizened bark. Vines grew as thick as a human arm, and pines, spruces, firs, birches, and poplars grew to sizes Arsenyev had never encountered.[7] In one area, the branches overhead were interwoven so closely that the explorers could not see the sky. Even the lilacs grew to be 30 to 40 feet tall.

What, Arsenyev wondered, could these giants say about what they had seen in their centuries on earth? He felt that the virgin taiga was full of secrets, seductive and awe-inspiring: a "quiet display of nature's strength."[8] Raccoon dogs snapped at trout teeming in a river, and Arsenyev and his men caught a flying squirrel that was more than a foot and a half long.[9] He named his dog Leshii, for the wood goblin of Russian folklore. This forest was magical.

But like any magical creature, the forest could vanish in a moment. As Arsenyev climbed closer to the Sikhote-Alin mountains, the altitude increased and the soil grew rocky and shallow. With little purchase for their roots, the trees became slender and precarious. Scrawny spruce and larch crouched on the surface of the ground, cushioned only by moss, so that it was possible to push over a twenty-year-old tree. Some of the trees had already died but were still held upright by their roots, so that they crumbled like dust at the slightest pressure. Primorye's abrupt, extreme weather posed a constant threat to the region's trees.

Dersu Uzala

Wind could blow away the poorly anchored mountain forests, and in a valley Arsenyev saw a whole forest submerged by a flood.

Dersu Uzala introduced himself to Arsenyev as a member of the Gold people. Also called the Nanai, this was one of the most numerous of the Indigenous groups of the Russian Far East, a Tungusic people living along the Amur River basin. Their language is related to that of several other native peoples of eastern Siberia: the Evenki (Tungus), Even, and Udege. According to Arsenyev himself, Dersu's name was more accurately spelled "Derchu Odzhal"—Derchu from the Odzhal clan—but Arsenyev felt his version would be more palatable to the Russian audience. It has been argued that Dersu was in fact Udege, based on his location, clothing, and seminomadic taiga lifestyle.[10] Today, Udege people understand Dersu as a Nanai who lived among the Udege in the taiga—a frequent occurrence.[11] As Korolenko's Yakutized Russian peasant Makar showed, Siberian identities were often hybrid, and the Nanai and Udege are close relatives.

Dersu captured the hearts of the Russian public. Arsenyev's greatest literary success came not with his full-length scientific travelogues but with an abridged, condensed, and simplified version titled *Dersu Uzala*, first published in 1926. The book was acclaimed by high-ranking Soviet writers, and it became a classic wild adventure story of Russian literature, what might be called an "Eastern."[12] It was directly inspired by the novels of James Fenimore Cooper, author of *The Last of the Mohicans: A Narrative of 1757* (1826) and its sequel *The Pathfinder* (1840).* *The Last of the Mohicans* is an adventure-romance set in upstate New York during the French and Indian War. In it, friendly Mohicans—the last of their tribe—cross cultural and ethnic lines to help a daring frontiersman and the ladies entrusted to him during a conflict with other, less friendly Indians. The peaceable, vanishing Mohicans seem to endorse the European conquest of the land; those Indians who resist colonization are caricatured as bloodthirsty vil-

* In Andrei Sinyavsky's story "Tenants," the house spirit wants to read *The Last of the Mohicans.*

lains. The novel has little literary merit, but it was extremely popular in Europe as well as in America, where it perpetuated the false idea that the Indians were dying out and the ownership of the land was passing to the European settlers as if by an almost inevitable, quasi-evolutionary process.

In Arsenyev's eastern adventure tale, Russia's assertion, through the railway, of full control over the Far East is a kind of mirror image of the American conquest of the West. In these narratives, the frontier was bountiful and largely empty, and the explorer was a glamorous hero. The Indigenous people encountered along the way were sometimes a threat, sometimes local color, but always endangered. Like Fenimore Cooper's Mohicans, Dersu is the last living member of his clan, having watched his wife and children die of smallpox. This had been the real-life fate of many Far Eastern natives after the Russian annexation and ensuing high-speed settlement, which caused smallpox epidemics and widespread displacement of non-Russian residents. As in Siberia and North America, colonization brought pathogens, war, and other pressures that caused the decline in population of many (though not all) Indigenous groups.

Arsenyev's story differs from Fenimore Cooper's in that there are no hostile Indigenous people. Dersu's continuation of his traditional way of life as a taiga hunter makes him an exception. Other Indigenous peoples Arsenyev encountered were settled in villages, under miserable conditions. Centuries of domination by Russia and China had separated them from old ways of life, and communities were ravaged by alcoholism. The enemies of Arsenyev's narrative are mostly Chinese, reflecting the political mood of his day. Arsenyev's book also stands out from other colonizing narratives in its insistence on the superiority of Dersu and his way of living. In its loving, expert focus on the natural world, *Dersu Uzala* is very far from the torrid clichés of Fenimore Cooper's novel. And yet even as he celebrates Dersu, Arsenyev sees clearly that his exploration and the construction of the railway will mean the destruction of both the region's unique, pristine forests, which are already disappearing, and its native inhabitants.

From the beginning of Arsenyev's narrative, Dersu is associated with wild nature—and like wild nature, he is in constant peril. When Dersu first appears at the camp, Arsenyev describes how the Cossack soldiers mistake him for a bear and nearly shoot him. Arsenyev's description of the newcomer starts from what might charitably be called a biological perspective. He feels the urge to enumerate Dersu's physiological features in order to identify his genus, as he has done with so many plants and animals. Dersu looks about forty-five, stocky, barrel-chested, and muscular, though not tall; his legs are slightly bowed; he has a small nose, high cheekbones, and "eyelids with epicanthic folds." But Arsenyev also notes that Dersu's eyes glisten with a special integrity.

The forested landscape is Arsenyev's great love, and his fascination with Dersu is correspondingly intense. In his guide, he sees something he has never encountered. "Before me was a primitive hunter," he writes, "someone who had spent his entire life in the forest; the ways of the city and of civilization were foreign to him. . . . He told me that he was fifty-three years old and had never had a home. He always lived under the open sky, and only in winter would he build a temporary birch-bark yurt."[13] From his first moments in the camp, Dersu distinguishes himself with his capability and his uncomplaining assumption of responsibility for everyone around him. He insists on leaving supplies in a lean-to for the next person who comes along—after all, they might be on the brink of starvation. Here is taiga mutual aid that would thrill Kropotkin.

The morning after Dersu's arrival, the forest comes alive to Arsenyev in a new way, while his civilization looks pitiful. As sunlight rushes over the mountainous horizon and the green forest brightens, the campfire is revealed as a gray heap. The ground surrounding it looks not cozy but squalid, scattered with empty tins, the grass trampled where the tent once stood. Dersu's arrival shows Arsenyev that "progress" is only ashes.

Dersu's skills, meanwhile, seem almost supernatural to his astonished new friend. A master tracker, Dersu is a Sherlock Holmes of the taiga. (Like the last Mohican, Sherlock Holmes was a popular import to Russia.) Dersu can discern virtually every detail of a person's identity—nationality, profession, age, health, what he is carrying, direction of travel, purpose of trip, moral failings—from the slightest traces. From tracks and other signs, he can tell exactly what animals have passed and what they have eaten. It all seems obvious to him. By comparison, Arsenyev and his Cossack companions are insensate beings, illiterate in the language of the forest. Here is an early version of a more recent stereotype, of Indigenous people as inherently superior in their pure relation to nature.

Fluency in natural signs is accompanied, in Dersu, by an animistic belief system. In his broken Russian—which seems an invention of Arsenyev's more than a convincing rendering of how someone speaks a second language—Dersu calls everything "people," addressing objects and natural forces directly and ascribing them will and agency.[14] When the fire crackles too loudly, he admonishes it to be quieter. For him, water can yell, cry, or play.

He sees the links between life forms of all kinds, in an even more intense, taiga version of Tolstoy's vision of interconnection in *War and Peace*. When Arsenyev complains about the wet, depressing weather as they tramp through a particularly thick area of forest, Dersu replies, "This ground, hill, forest—all same people. Now his sweating. Listen! . . . His breathing."[15] At night Dersu finds a spot under a tree, between two large roots that serve as wind breaks, and he sleeps on a strip of bark. When they come face-to-face with an Amur tiger—a rare species that stalks the forests of Primorye to this day—Dersu defuses danger by kneeling and bowing to the tiger before walking off. The tiger accepts his tribute.

"Nature is pitiless to man," Arsenyev observes. "After a brief caress she will attack, as if intentionally underlining his helplessness. . . . The forest itself is an element. More than the rest of us, Dersu was in harmony with his surroundings."[16] This description celebrates Dersu by suggesting that he is something other than human, better adapted to the forest and more capable of surviving in it because he is himself an integral part of it. Arsenyev does not need to make explicit the assumption beneath his romantic complacency: Man is merciless to nature, too. As in *The Last of the Mohicans*, the narrative will end, inevitably, with extinction.

Over the course of their travels, Arsenyev absorbs some of Dersu's animism. When Arsenyev arrives in an area devastated by repeated forest fires, likely ignited by campfires and the railroad, he sees the charred tree stumps as "gigantic fingers" pointing to the sky, calling for rain and floods in revenge for the fires that have destroyed the once-glorious taiga.[17] He hunts for food, to obtain scientific specimens, and even for pleasure, but on many occasions he cannot bring himself to shoot at an animal, to deprive it of its life, in scenes reminiscent of Tolstoy. He learns from Dersu, who takes only what he needs and does not kill for the pleasure of conquest. "To shoot for nothing is a sin!" Arsenyev thinks. "What a true, simple thought! Why do Europeans so often abuse our weapons, and take the life of animals left and right, just for the sake of shooting, for the sake of amusement?"[18] In an observation that would reverberate through later Russian forest writings, Arsenyev writes that wild animals are perhaps the most minor of all forest dangers—they usually respond to encounters with humans by fleeing. It is human encounters that are the most perilous.

When Arsenyev visited, half a century after Kropotkin's journey, the Far East was still a land of plenty. He and Dersu arrive at a stream overflowing with keta salmon, so many that thousands are stranded in creeks and shallows. But the days of bounty are numbered. Arsenyev sets Dersu's frugal approach to the forest, rivers, and sea that sustain him in marked opposition with the profligate exploitation of the Russians and Chinese. He describes how Russian concession holders fell huge tracts of forest, cutting the oldest trees and thereby killing many smaller ones that are knocked over in the process, collateral damage. Russian peasants cut down fertile areas of forest and turn them into farmland. The Chinese market's hunger for deer tendons, sea-lion hides, and the glands of musk deer, Arsenyev laments, leads hunters to massacre hundreds of animals, the carcasses left to rot in heaps, or to harvest freshwater pearls until the mussels that produce them are extinct. Dersu remarks, "Another ten years, no more deer, sable, squirrel."[19] This is the Far Eastern version of Turgenev's warning, in *A Hunter's Sketches,* that in a few years the forests of Oryol would be gone.

Pushkin and Lermontov wrote tales of beautiful Circassian maidens who sacrificed themselves to rescue Russian prisoners of the Caucasus. In the 1830s, there was an efflorescence of Russian stories about beautiful Tungus maidens; Fenimore Cooper inspired the first wave of Siberian tales of romantic-imperial conquest.[20] Perhaps this romantic trope underlies Arsenyev's intense attachment to Dersu. In one of the most memorable scenes in both the book and in the legendary Japanese director Akira Kurosawa's 1975 film adaptation, Dersu and Arsenyev get caught in a blizzard on a small grass-covered island in a marsh. They are on a daytime expedition without warm clothes, a tent, or other supplies. There are not even any trees to use to start a fire—none of the safety or resources of the forest.

Dersu works frantically to braid grasses into a makeshift tent that will insulate them from the cold as they sleep. Arsenyev is almost useless, uncomprehending, and Dersu has to shout at him to follow instructions before it is too late. As they cut grass, their wet clothing freezes solid on their bodies. The wind is so strong that it almost knocks them over. When Arsenyev collapses, Dersu covers him with a tarpaulin and a mountain of cut grass. After he has finished constructing the makeshift nest, he puts his deerskin coat over Arsenyev and his fur boots on the explorer's feet. The rapidly growing snowdrift on their grass nest acts as insulation.

Kurosawa's film shows the two men lying side by side in the grass house; one is tempted to say that they are spooning. When Arsenyev opens his eyes, Dersu is already awake, and jokes that it is time for the "bear" (that is, Arsenyev) to wake up and go to his own den. But this blizzard was no joke: "Last night many people die," Dersu says. The "people" were birds.[21]

Dersu saves Arsenyev, who finds it hard to live without him. When the expedition is finished, he asks Dersu to return to Vladivostok with him. Dersu refuses, of course: The forest is his home, and he does not know how to sleep indoors. Arsenyev is "overcome with sadness." In a highly cinematic scene—the kind, no doubt, that made Kurosawa so eager to make the book into a film—Arsenyev watches Dersu depart across a low hill, where he is silhouetted by the sun as he reaches the crest and then disappears on the other side. "It was as if something had broken in my chest; I felt that I had lost someone close to me," Arsenyev writes.[22] On his next expedition, Arsenyev hopes for an encounter with Dersu as fervently as a man in love, secure in the faith that with his tracking skills, Dersu will always be able to find him. When they meet again, they are as joyful as long-separated lovers.

But as in the Caucasian prisoner romances, the native savior will not live to see the next chapter of the story. Tellingly, Arsenyev is constantly on the brink of killing Dersu. During their second expedition together, in 1910, there is a terrible moment when Arsenyev goes boar hunting and accidentally shoots Dersu. He is terrified at the thought that he may have killed his friend, but it is only a glancing wound. The magnanimous Dersu, whose generosity often borders on servility, blames himself for standing in the wrong place and not alerting Arsenyev to his presence. He goes out of his way to absolve Arsenyev of any guilt.

Later, Dersu realizes that he can smell a pig in the woods but cannot see it. He is losing his sight. For a man who relies on hunting to survive, blindness means death. This gives Arsenyev his own chance to become a savior—but Dersu's demise is now overdetermined. The loving and solicitous scientist brings his friend back to Khabarovsk, a large city by local standards. Dersu fails to adjust to city life, though Arsenyev is willing to provide any comfort he can. Dersu simply does not understand how to live there, how to abide by urban rules. He tries to cut down a tree in the park, indignant at the idea of paying for firewood. Before Arsenyev can equip him with something more than an old rifle, Dersu departs.

Soon Arsenyev gets word that Dersu has been murdered, killed in his sleep by thieves who wanted his rifle. When Arsenyev goes to see his friend's body, the police are burying him in the forest. In the final scene of the book, a sunbeam pushes its way through the canopy of firs and illuminates Dersu's face. This is the forest's final caress of its native son. Dersu seems to look up at the sky like "a man who had forgotten something and was struggling to remember it." Arsenyev commits to memory the two huge Korean pines that extend their arms over Dersu's grave. But when he returns a few years later, the trees have been cut down along with the rest of the forest. Instead of trees there are roads, a town, and a granite quarry, a wound in the earth.

Dersu Uzala is a late frontier fantasy that lodged itself in the Soviet and Russian unconscious. It is also a memorial to the forests of the Russian Far East, and to the people who call them home. A few decades earlier, the serfs and forests of European Russia had been linked in debates about protection and emancipation. In Arsenyev's writing, an Indigenous guide was synonymous with the eastern forest. Both were at risk of disappearing thanks to Russian settlement and the Russian railroad.

Many readers have understood *Dersu Uzala* to be a work of nonfiction, a document of Arsenyev's explorations and of his friendship with Dersu Uzala. And Dersu was a real person; there are photographs of him. But Arsenyev took many liberties with his story. In reality, he knew Dersu Uzala for a much shorter time than he does in the book, and he had a number of different Indigenous guides—Nanai, Udege, Yakut, and Evenk—who helped him during his travels.[23] Dersu is a composite character, inspired by a real person but elaborated to stand for the central ideas of Arsenyev's narrative. He is an archetypal child of the earth uncorrupted by modern ways, naïve and pure. In other words, he is fictional. His total isolation, his position as the last of his "species," reflect a trope borrowed from North America, not the reality of the Tungusic peoples of the Amur and Ussuri territories.

It was Arsenyev, not Dersu Uzala, who was the last of his kind: the last celebrated explorer of imperial Russia. The eastern frontier had closed. It was not until the Soviet period that the Indigenous peoples of Siberia and the Far East would start to write their own novels. Their self-expression would be sharply curtailed by the Soviet censors, guided by the strictures of Soviet ideology.

During the Russian Civil War that began in 1918, eastern Siberia and the Far East were the last regions to fall to the Red Army. The White Army, Yakuts, Evenks, Tatars, Buryats, Russian peasants, and bandit gangs alike offered fierce resistance. After the last uprising was finally suppressed in 1925, the Soviets set about trying to remold the peoples of Siberia and the Far East into modern Communist citizens. Since the days of Peter the Great there had been campaigns to baptize and educate Siberia's Indigenous peoples, but this was something new. The Soviets required not only the collectivization of hunting, fishing, and herding, but also the production of literature that would testify to the ascent of the supposedly innocent natives to a Marxist-Leninist utopia.[24]

Every member of the family of Soviet peoples was to be represented by its own official writers. In the Far East, one of the first of these was the Udege writer Dzhansi Kimonko, son of a nomadic hunter much like Dersu Uzala. Born in 1905, Kimonko spent his childhood hunting and fishing around the Khor River basin, south of Khabarovsk. During the civil war, he worked as a guide for the Red Army; even then, Russians relied on Indigenous knowledge to find their ways through the unfamiliar territory. The first Udege person to receive a formal education, he did not learn to read and write until he was twenty-two, during the Soviet literacy campaign—a common story for Siberian and Far Eastern "small peoples." Now the last Mohicans were to be replaced by historic novelties. Articles called Kimonko "The first of the Udege."[25] The Soviets saw themselves as ushering in a new world; in it, they imagined that Indigenous peoples, too, could be reborn, though many of them were simply repressed. Even Kimonko was arrested in 1936 on false charges of espionage, kept in prison for two years.[26]

Like other writers of the period, Kimonko wrote condemnations of tsarist oppression and paeans to Soviet power. But his poetry and lyrical prose also celebrated the natural beauty of life in the eastern taiga, where "birds listen to the water talk, and rivers listen to the birds as they call out to one another," where Kimonko's childhood "flowed, crying and laughing, along the forest's impassible roads and noisy creeks."[27] A poem in his unfinished autobiographical novel *Where the Sukpai Flows* sings of his native landscape:

> Sukpai meets the Bikin River,
> Sukpai meets the Izdi,
> Sukpai meets the ocean.
> Graylings spawn there,
> Taimen and lenkas rush.
> Elks graze at quiet streams,
> Bears swim to and fro,
> Otters dig under the steep banks
> And sables make their way along the shore . . .
> This is Sukpai, my land![28]

Early in the novel, which is the story of his own transformation into a Soviet man, he wrote,

> I began to remember myself when we still lived near the mouth of the Bolshaya Bolinka River. It was a hot summer. I can see, as if it were now, the burnt mountains along the banks of the river. The remains of granite rocks stick out on the slopes. They resemble human figures. After a fire, enormous tree stumps turn black as bears. From the top of the mountain you have a good

> view. You look up the river: the water sparkles and shimmers in the sun. When you look down, it darkens and foams. How many times did I climb to the top of the hill? How many stones did I cast in the water? I still love these hills, although they have long kept my people's life away from the world.[29]

This glorious natural world, Kimonko's homeland, is only an obstacle to the one-way journey into the Soviet future. We sense a hint of regret in his celebration.

CHAPTER 8

Cutting Orchards and Moving Mountains

After electricity, I abandoned my interest in nature. Too backward.

—Vladimir Mayakovsky, "I Myself"

In 1890, Anton Chekhov embarked on a three-month trip from Moscow to Sakhalin Island. At thirty, he was already suffering from the tuberculosis that would kill him. Friends thought he was insane to make the journey. There was not yet a trans-Siberian railroad, and the journey across Siberia involved boat trips down turbulent rivers and bone-shaking rides in rickety carts. Most Russian writers who went to Sakhalin made their journey in chains. The long, narrow island off the coast of the Amur region was the traditional home of the Ainu, Nanai, Oroch, and Nivkh peoples, but it was best known in Russia for its penal colony. Indeed, Chekhov's goal was to study the living conditions of the prisoners there. Stung by accusations from radical writers like Vladimir Korolenko that he was indifferent to the plight of Russia's downtrodden, he had decided to devote himself to a cause. The recent, humiliating failure of his first play, *The Wood Demon* (*Leshii*), had also pushed him east.[1] The journey would yield a series of investigative articles that united luminous literary precision with meticulous collection of data.

Like Vladimir Arsenyev, Chekhov was part of an upwardly mobile generation that had risen from serfdom. His paternal grandfather Egor was born a serf of a certain Count Chertkov in Voronezh, at the edge of old Russia's heartland. By an odd coincidence, the count was the grandfather of Tolstoy's acolyte and literary executor, Vladimir Chertkov. Two of Russia's most influential writers stood on either side of the historical master-serf relationship. In 1841, Egor Chekhov used his life savings to buy his family's freedom. The Chekhovs moved south to the steppe town of Taganrog, the cosmopolitan southern port first conquered by Peter the Great. Anton's father and his brothers joined the lowest ranks of the merchant class.[2] Anton's childhood was marked by deprivation and hard work, bouts of poverty relieved by idyllic summer holidays spent fishing and exploring the countryside. His father sent him to school to become a tailor. Anton became a doctor instead—and a progenitor of both the modern short story and modern stagecraft. His writing would help change the course of Western literature.[3]

Given his family background, it is not surprising that Chekhov was deeply attuned to social injustice. In a famous 1889 letter, Chekhov wrote to a friend about the struggle to squeeze "the slave out of himself, drop by drop."[4] His vocation as a writer, his life as a habitué of Russia's most elite artistic circles, required a constant effort to transcend the dismal circumstances of his childhood. But he was melancholy and contemplative by nature, with none of the single-minded fervor of a revolutionary. Until his journey to Sakhalin, Chekhov had stood at some remove from the ideological ferment of his day. While admiring his literary gifts, his progressive peers were disappointed by his lack of full-throated political commitment. Now he won Korolenko's approval by embarking on a mission of study and self-sacrifice.[5]

The Yenisei was the most magnificent river Chekhov had ever seen. The landscape from the Urals through western Siberia had bored him, but the Yenisei's thundering waters inspired him with the kind of rhetoric that had characterized Russian descriptions of Siberia for decades. The European Volga, Chekhov wrote, was a "beautifully dressed, melancholy beauty" on which "a man starts out with spirit, but ends with a groan which is called a song." The Yenisei, on the other hand, was "a mighty, raging Hercules, who does not know what to do with his power and youth." The river functioned as a kind of noble savage: The colonized periphery could rejuvenate the tired heartland. On the Yenisei, Chekhov wrote, "Life commences with a groan and finishes with the kind of high spirits which we cannot even dream about." The nearby mountains reminded him of the Caucasus, that other imperial borderland, "with the same smoky color and dreaminess."[6] For Chekhov, European Russia was drained and pessimistic, poetic but dissolute. Siberia, like the Caucasus, was strapping, artless, and full of brute energy. The depressed, chronically ill writer's affinities lay with weary, refined Europe, but he had great admiration for Siberia's life force.

At first the famous taiga disappointed him. The trees were not particularly large, the species were familiar. Instead of the terrifying silence and absence of scent he had read about in books, he encountered birdsong, insects buzzing, and the fragrance of resin, pine needles, and flowers. He concluded that the power of the taiga lay in its vastness: Only migratory birds could know its true size. When asked where the taiga stopped, locals would reply that it had no end. It swallowed exiles and convicts without remark. This was frightening but also somehow reassuring, especially for a writer with a notoriously gloomy view of humanity. Here was a place, Chekhov wrote, where man could never master nature. Even if all the inhabitants of Siberia set out to fell and burn the forest, their efforts would leave no lasting trace.

In European Russia, as Tolstoy and Turgenev had warned, the situation was quite the opposite. Chekhov was acutely aware of the "forest question." It had been a central theme in *The Wood Demon*, whose failure had helped drive him to Sakhalin. When he returned from his journey east, he told a friend, "God's world is good. One thing is not good: us."[7] His biographer Donald Rayfield has observed that Chekhov's "confirmed distrust of ideology, and his preference for unspoilt nature over spoiled humanity are Sakhalin's legacy."[8] The journey transformed Chekhov, who in turn transfigured the failed *Wood Demon* into *Uncle Vanya*. The 1897 play won Chekhov the unofficial title of

Russia's best playwright.[9] The incurably ill writer was the greatest dramaturge of a dying society.

Set on the country estate of a cash-strapped elderly professor, *Uncle Vanya* is a play about disillusionment and disappointment, about a vanishing society and a vanishing forest. Chekhov recognized that more than just the century was ending. Unlike the Yenisei River, the tsarist status quo had run its course. Russia was in need of rejuvenation—but Chekhov was not optimistic about its prospects for revival. The overwhelming sense in the play is of impending collapse. The Russian intelligentsia seemed to Chekhov to resemble the Volga, groaning out its exhausted song.

Tree plantations and the protection of the countryside offer the play's core of hope. Of all its characters, only Astrov, the family doctor, possesses a positive vision for the future along with the will to act. He has a model orchard and nursery, as well as a government plantation that he supervises. Like Tolstoy, Astrov does not eat meat. But he does have a weakness for vodka and beautiful, lazy women such as Elena, the much younger second wife of the estate's owner.

Elena wonders why the doctor bothers with trees, which she finds monotonous. But Sonia, the grown daughter of the family, understands. Astrov's love for trees has inspired her own secret passion for him. In his defense, she attributes astonishing powers to forests, reflecting the enormous faith placed in trees in an age when many foresters were also revolutionaries:

> He works hard to stop the old forests from being destroyed. . . . He says that forests make the earth beautiful, that they teach humankind to appreciate beauty. . . . Forests make a harsh climate milder. In countries with a mild climate people spend less energy on the struggle with nature, and so they are gentler and more tender; people in such places are beautiful, flexible, responsive, their speech is elegant, their movements graceful. Science and art blossom, their philosophy is not gloomy, and their attitude to women is full of elegant generosity.[10]

In Sonia's naïve, idealistic account, forests even teach men to treat women better—for instance, teaching men to love plain but virtuous women like Sonia. They impart culture, happiness, and refinement, which are in short supply in the Russian provinces. They even impart beauty to people, who become as supple as saplings. Nature is culture. We should not mistake this for Chekhov's opinion. In his writings on Siberia, he makes clear that the taiga is a place devoid of artistry. And though he had faith in nature, he was less hopeful about the possibility of human improvement.

In his response to Sonia, Astrov echoes the anxieties about the destruction of the forest that were expressed by Turgenev, Tolstoy, and others. "The Russian forests are groaning under the axe," he tells her, "billions of trees are dying, the dwelling places of animals and birds are being laid waste, the rivers are getting shallow and drying up, marvelous landscapes are disappearing forever," all because Russians continue to insist on using wood as their primary fuel. He shows Elena a series of historical maps documenting how the forests have been cut, telling her about the disappearance of swans, geese, ducks, goats, elk, woodgrouse, and also small farms, monasteries, and mills—the "decay" of the landscape in every respect. The earth is being destroyed by the laziness and stupidity of humankind.

Astrov goes on to describe the hope that lies in protecting and cultivating the forest:

> When I walk by the peasant forests that I have saved from felling, or when I hear the murmur of the young forest I planted with my own hands, I realize that the climate is in my power too, at least a little, and that if in a thousand years humankind is happy, I'll be at least slightly to blame. When I plant a young birch and then see how it grows green and sways in the wind, my soul is filled with pride.[11]

For all his irony, skepticism, and melancholy, Chekhov placed great value on the green world. An early outline for *The Wood Demon* presents the cultivation of plants as a kind of art. The play's protagonist, Chekhov wrote, "realizes his ideas not on canvas or paper, but on earth, not in dead paints but with organic materials."[12] The playwright is explicit: The cultivation of living organisms is a form of poetry. Perhaps Tolstoy was not so wrong, then, to devote his later years to planting trees instead of writing fiction. By 1899, Chekhov had trouble tearing himself away from his own garden, which he often preferred to his writing desk.[13]

Chekhov had been preoccupied with cherry blossoms since before he went to Sakhalin. He first wrote down the title *The Cherry Orchard* in 1902, after hearing that the beautiful cherry trees at his former country house outside Moscow had been cut down by the new owner.[14] This would become the title of his final play, the story of an indecisive, ineffectual landowner who can no longer afford to keep her country estate and its cherry orchard.

Chekhov wrote it with great difficulty in 1903, while suffering the terminal stages of tuberculosis. (He would die the next year, aged forty-four, in a spa hotel in Germany's Black Forest.) His anger at the unjust status quo, fortified by his time in Sakhalin and by his work providing medical care to peasants in the Russian countryside, was not enough for him to believe the promises of the revolutionaries who were soon to overthrow the government. In *The Cherry Orchard*, the radical student Trofimov persuades Anya, the young daughter of the family, not to be sad about the destruction of the family's orchard: "The whole of Russia is our orchard. The earth is great and beautiful and there are many, many wonderful places on it." But Chekhov makes Trofimov's optimism sound hollow. These cherry trees will not be replaced. There is a whole world, but only one home.

Trofimov points out that Anya's forefathers owned "living souls"—"Don't you see human beings looking at you from every cherry tree in the orchard, from every leaf, from every tree trunk, don't you hear their voices? . . . to begin to live in the present, we must first atone for our past and be finished with it, and we can only atone for it by suffering, by extraordinary, unceasing exertion."[15] Here, the idea of the parallel emancipation of serfs and forests, which had become prominent in Russian public discourse in the preceding decades, takes a literal form. At the end of the play, Lopakhin, the entrepreneurial son of serfs on the estate, buys the orchard and cuts it down. The liberated serf has liberated the land from its trees. Chekhov, the son of an entrepreneurial serf himself, reminds us that emancipation is not a simple matter.

The play's cherry orchard is a symbol of the old order. Trofimov rejects it along with the very idea of property, for himself as for Anya. This vision of emancipation, like that of the Bolsheviks, is iconoclastic: creation through destruction. To move into the radiant future of Communist revolution, the cherry orchard must be cut. Trofimov's speech presages the new phase of the destruction of Russia's trees that would accompany the revolutions of the coming years. The old world was dying; a new one would be born from the ashes of Russian forests.

By the revolutionary year of 1917, Chekhov and Tolstoy were dead. Two-thirds of Russia's forests were controlled by the state, thanks in part to the rapid clearing of private forests over the previous decades. When the Bolsheviks took power after the October Revolution, it became evident that they intended to nationalize all of Russia's forests, along with everything else in the country, and manage them along German lines. Some prominent foresters had already recommended the nationalization and state management of the forests, which they saw as the best hope of protection for Russia's trees. Others worried that if the state controlled all the forests, no one would be able to protect the forest from the state. Peasants were skeptical that the state would manage the forests in their collective interest. They continued to believe in their right to use the forests as they always had. As a Russian folk saying said, "The forest is God's, so the forest is no one's."[16]

The Bolsheviks sought to maximize efficiency in forest exploitation and to repress what they considered the backward, unscientific ways of the peasants, enemies of the urban, industrial, proletarian revolution.

But the Bolsheviks' desire for high-intervention German-style forestry was stymied by a lack of funding and qualified workers to enact such a program.[17] In the immediate aftermath of the revolution, civil war, poverty, and hunger led to yet another spate of acute deforestation. Forest fires raged unchecked. War is almost always bad for forests.

As Chekhov had foreseen in *The Cherry Orchard*, the revolutionaries wasted no time mourning lost trees. Some Bolsheviks believed that deforestation was a good thing. Radicals saw forests as "rotten places," blots on the map of Russia whose loss was nothing to regret. Fire, after all, was the traditional means of turning forest to farmland. The conquest of nature was a fundamental tenet of Soviet ideology. In his 1923 essay "Literature and Revolution," Leon Trotsky wrote,

> The current arrangement of mountains and rivers, fields and meadows, steppes, forests and seashores can in no way be called final. Man has already made some changes, and not small ones, to the picture of nature; but these are only student experiments in comparison with what will be. . . . Man will re-register mountains and rivers and . . . correct nature. In the end he will rebuild the earth, if not in his own image, then in his own taste. We have no reason to fear that his taste will be bad.[18]

Trotsky's grandiose words exemplified the Soviet belief that anything in nature could be bent to human will, made to serve human purposes. His sanguine tone was characteristic; blustering Soviet self-confidence left little room for second thoughts about the possible consequences of rerouting rivers, draining seas, and rearranging forests.

Soviet rhetoric often expressed horror at the disorderly, irresponsible laziness of "untouched" nature. In *Uncle Vanya*, Dr. Astrov is troubled by the beautiful Elena's indolence. The Soviets were angry at the rivers and forests. One avant-garde Soviet writer, Sergei Tretyakov, wrote in 1928 that "delight in nature 'untouched by the blasphemous hand of man,' in 'virgin' forest, in 'chaos,' in the great masses of tree trunks rotting irresponsibly and unmethodically, is just a belch of reactionary Romanticism. Would it not be more correct to express interest in nature organized to human advantage? In fields plowed and sown, in forests cleared and cultivated, in rivers locked in the casemates of dams turning hydroelectric turbines?"[19] Soviet beauty was to be found in orderly, geometric landscapes cleared by human labor and human reason. The whole world would be a city.[20] In a particularly memorable phrase, Tretyakov described swamps as "weeping eczema." Ironically, Tretyakov was a great admirer of Arsenyev's book *Dersu Uzala*. He admired Arsenyev's closely observed, scientifically accurate prose, which he saw as a prototype for the new "literature of fact," while ignoring Arsenyev's celebration of Dersu Uzala, whom Tretyakov dismissed as amusing, exotic, and as primitive as the irresponsible taiga.[21]

For the avant-garde Soviet photographer Alexander Rodchenko, pine trees were of aesthetic interest only thanks to their resemblance to telegraph poles; otherwise, the rural landscape outside Moscow was just boring. For him, trees became beautiful only when they were transformed by human will into the materials of industry.[22] In the Ukrainian director Oleksandr Dovzhenko's influential 1930 film *Earth*, trees cut into utility poles pulse with the magnificent rhythm of connection and modernity across the countryside. The only good trees were working trees.

But this extreme rhetoric did not necessarily dictate policy. In the early 1920s the Communist Party adopted a measured approach to forests, thanks to advocacy by the union of forest workers. There was still some concern for the forest as a resource, and perhaps even respect for the forest's symbolic potency. In 1921, the extremes of War Communism, a total abolition of private property and commerce, yielded to the more moderate New Economic Policy. As a result, early Soviet forest management continued some conservationist trends from the late tsarist empire, when the imperial government had established a system of *zapovedniki*, or nature preserves, as well as other forest protections.[23]

From 1924 on, the Soviet Ministry of Agriculture and Food

attempted to inculcate the people with a tender attitude toward the forest, part of its effort to enlist the peasantry into forest management. The government, it turned out, needed peasant manpower. Authorities organized a "Forest Day" holiday and tree plantings, lectures, excursions, and traveling museums devoted to the forest. A 1924 book about the holiday mixed socialist rhetoric and ecology, explaining that "the forest is not a simple gathering of trees, but a very complex social organism, constructed according to its own social laws and consisting of tight and permanent bonds between everything living there." In keeping with Russia's longtime cultural fixation on the forest, instructions for Forest Day also included an order that lectures should include "Russia's rich artistic literature about the forest." Sample conversation topics for Forest Days in the 1920s included "The Nature of the Forest and Its Imprint on the Life Patterns of the Russian People," "The Forest as Protector of Water," and "The Forest as a Symbol of the Collective." In Vladimir province, northeast of Moscow, an audience of six hundred peasants attended a lecture on "The Forest and Its Significance in the Life of Man."[24]

The early Soviet period showed a tension between Prometheanism—the idea that humans could harness all of nature's power—and conservationism. The forest was an ambiguous character in Soviet life: It may have been disorderly and unproductive, but it was also comforting and restorative, a place of refuge and pleasure. Though it had sometimes been a rival to farmland or a source of danger to humans and livestock, the forest did not instill the same kind of fear as the Arctic tundra or a surging river that threatened to overleap its boundaries. In fact, as Russians knew well, forests helped keep rivers in check with their root systems and prevented drought by sustaining a healthy evaporation cycle. The forest moved slowly, its murmur a lullaby as well as an existential question. The woods were the site of dachas, the country houses that formed such an important part of Russian life, and the place where Russians ventured on happy mushroom-picking expeditions—a tradition that continues to this day. Chekhov was not alone in his fondness for trees; this affection was a cornerstone of Russian culture.

Many Soviet writers continued to feel a close bond to the natural world. In 1926, at the Congress of Siberian Writers, a novelist named Vladimir Zazubrin described his struggle to accept the new Soviet approach to the taiga:

> For us, people who feel an animal love for Siberia's expanse of taiga, it is hard to think of the city, of urban culture, of the clang of factories. But let it be so, let the human being in us knock down the animal, drag it by the mane. Let Siberia's flabby green breast be clad in the cement armor of cities, be armed with the stone craters of factory chimneys, be bound by iron railroads. Let the taiga be scorched and cut, let the steppes be trampled.[25]

Zazubrin's declaration captures the brutality of Soviet rhetoric about nature. The railroads in the taiga sound like instruments of torture. Despite Siberia's status as a place of exile and prison camps, the taiga was still strongly associated with freedom. Encasing it in concrete, burning and slashing it, would mean the end of a core myth in Russian history and culture. Violence toward the forest was accompanied by violence toward people: Zazubrin was shot in 1937, during Stalin's purges.

Stalin's rise to power and his first Five-Year Plan, which began in 1928, meant an end to the more moderate years of the New Economic Policy, and the beginning of a more radical approach to forest exploitation. A new round of political attacks targeted the principle of limiting cutting to allow sufficient regrowth, the "sustainable yield" technique that still dominated forest policy. By 1929, it became evident that the current approach to forestry was not producing enough timber for Stalin's Five-Year Plan. To achieve the high-speed modernization of the country, enormous quantities of timber were needed for construction and fuel. Though there were voices of caution, the momentum of the plan and the danger of opposing it were irrefutable. Radical industrializers were granted control of the forests. The concept of sustainable yield was denounced as bourgeois, and the idea that the forest could be irretrievably damaged was mocked as a scary fairytale. Forest management was to be replaced by forest exploitation. One hardliner announced, "We need revolution in the forest."[26]

The new hyper-exploitation of the forest took place alongside the forced collectivization of agriculture. No longer partners to be coaxed into assisting with conservation, forest management, and tree planting, peasants were once again the enemy. The days of Turgenev, Tolstoy, Korolenko, and Chekhov's sympathy and respect for the people of the countryside were over. Korolenko had died in 1921, appalled by the suffering unleashed by the revolution and ensuing civil war. Kropotkin died the same year, under house arrest for his rejection of Soviet authoritarianism and violence. Nearly all Soviet anarchists, including Tolstoyan pacifists, ended up in Soviet prisons. Millions of Soviet citizens were to be starved, deported, or executed over the coming decade, as the forest fell. On Forest Day, participating foresters were instructed to use slogans like "The development of socialist construction demands the strengthening of the exploitation of the forests of the Soviet Union!" In 1930, a forest journal instructed that Forest Day was to "proceed under the slogan of the strengthening of the struggle with the kulak," the rich peasant who was the great enemy of collectivization. To mark the holiday, peasants cut trees down rather than planting them.[27]

This was the beginning of a war on the forests. In 1931, the union of timber workers announced, "Logging under the Five-Year Plan is logging of a military order."[28] It was too complicated and time-consuming to log only portions of mature forest, as more sustainable plans had required; instead, industrialists bulldozed huge territories. Replanting was desultory, if it happened at all. Soon forests in accessible areas of central Russia were being cleared faster than they could possibly regenerate. Some foresters risked their lives to save the forests under their supervision from destruction.[29]

At the first All-Union Congress on the Protection of Nature in the USSR in early 1933, attendees declared that now that the damage of tsarist exploitation had faded, it was essential that Soviet science overcome the "fetish" of the absolute inviolability of nature preserves, or *zapovedniki*.[30] Now any natural space could become an outdoor factory. Nature would be fully instrumentalized. In the early 1930s, Mikhail Prishvin, one of the Soviet Union's most beloved nature writers, had a dream about visiting a dark, dense primeval forest and seeing that every tree bore the mark of an axe. As he ventured deeper into the forest, looking for an area where the trees were not doomed, he could not find a single untouched trunk.[31]

When the concept of sustainable yield in forestry was denounced as bourgeois, however, those committed to conservation responded by referring to theories linking hydrological stability to forest cover. The link between rivers, drought, and deforestation had been at the heart of the "forest question" in Tolstoy and Turgenev's day. Now conservationists connected it to the viability of hydroelectric dams, a linchpin in the Soviet project to "electrify" the country as quickly as possible, and in Stalin's scheme of high-speed industrialization.[32] The best strategy to save the forests, they saw, was to treat their preservation as instrumental to Soviet modernization. This was a precursor to more recent ideas that ecological protections must be justified with economic rationales. Decades before the concept of carbon credits had entered global discourse, the Soviets decided that to earn its existence, the forest would have to work.

CHAPTER 9

Electricity and Resurrection

Art, I think, does nothing but convert matter into spirit and vice versa—just like the plants which, in breathing and feeding themselves, create our soil and atmosphere by a continual process of transference up and down their stalks, making this labor into a mode of existence.

—Andrei Sinyavsky, "A Voice from the Chorus"[1]

Andrei Klimentov arrived in the world in 1899, on the cusp of the new century, at the outskirts of Voronezh, the boundary between the central Russian forest and the southern steppe. Coming of age with the revolution and passionately devoted to the Communist cause, he studied electrical technology before becoming a writer. He chose the pen name Andrei Platonov. Lenin had written in 1920 that "Communism is Soviet power plus the electrification of the whole country"—electricity being seen as the power source of revolution and equality. It was the task of artists to document this process, and to thereby electrify the new Soviet literature and art. But Platonov soon proved himself to be a sui generis writer who slipped free of the dogma of his age.

Like Arsenyev, author of *Dersu Uzala*, Platonov was a railway worker's son. But Platonov's father had also painted church cupolas with gold: Remarkable professional leaps ran in the family. Platonov is the rare writer who wrote three novels but also helped build three power stations. The author of poems, short stories, plays, and novellas as well as several major novels, he is the most idiosyncratically brilliant Russian writer of the twentieth century. His work offers a case study in the ambivalent treatment of nature and industry in the early Soviet Union.

By his early twenties, Platonov had already published a poetry anthology. But in 1921, disturbed at a famine triggered by the disruptions of revolution and civil war, Platonov gave up writing to become an engineer. "Being someone technically qualified," he wrote, "I was unable to continue to engage in contemplative work such as literature."[2] Like Chekhov ministering to sick peasants, Platonov put literary work aside for humanitarian reasons. He helped reclaim land, supervising the draining of 2,400 acres of swamp and the digging of 763 ponds and 331 wells.[3] This deeply unliterary activity would inspire Platonov's writing for the rest of his life. Chekhov had found the key to transforming *The Wood Demon* into *Uncle Vanya* after his journey to Sakhalin Island; Platonov had his artistic awakening after half a decade of engineering work.

Though Platonov supported the revolution, his works were not the wholehearted paeans to the future utopia that had come to be expected of writers. Under Soviet censorship, any ambiguity or hesitation was anathema—and Platonov was too sophisticated and original a thinker to write single-minded propaganda. In 1931, he was sent by the People's Commissariat of Agriculture to report on the collectivization of agriculture in the central Volga region and North Caucasus. There he witnessed firsthand the violence, irrationality, and misery of collectivization, which led to so many unnecessary deaths. Unlike most of his peers, he wrote about it honestly.[4] His story "For Future Use," on collectivization and peasant life, made Stalin so angry that he is said to have scrawled "bastard" in the margins.[5] Platonov was unable to publish any new work for years—though this was a mild punishment by the standards of the times.

In 1934, Maksim Gorky, the most politically influential Soviet writer, arranged for Platonov to take part in a "writers' brigade" trip to Turkmenistan, to document the achievements of a decade of Soviet power in the region. Gorky famously wrote that "changing nature, man changes himself"—the epigraph for the infamous book he edited celebrating the construction of the White Sea Canal, a huge infrastructural project ordered by Stalin. An army of Gulag prisoners dug through the Karelian forests, in northeastern Russia near the border of Finland, between 1931 and 1933. Tens of thousands of these laborers died in the process. In keeping with early Soviet rhetoric, nature was not only to be changed; it had to be defeated. In a speech to the "shock workers" of the White Sea Canal, Gorky called nature "the principal, ancient enemy" of the Soviet people, a "blind tyrant" tormenting humankind with earthquakes, hurricanes, and droughts.[6]

After the trip to Turkmenistan, Platonov was invited to contribute to a collective volume called *People of the Railway Kingdom*, a tribute to the heroes of the Soviet rail system. Platonov first wrote a successful story based on a meeting with a Donbas railway station director who had won the Order of Lenin. Next he visited a railway station in the forests of Karelia, where he interviewed Ivan Alekseyevich Fyodorov, a switchman who was a recent winner of the Order of the Red Star. This trip yielded the remarkable story "Among Animals and Plants," which, for its failure to conform to Soviet ideological standards, met with such brutal denunciation and censorship that it was little known until recently.[7]

The story begins with a man in "the gloom of nature," carrying a hunting rifle as he crosses a sparse forest.[8] This opening echoes the familiar trope of the literary hunter, a staple of Russian literature that reached its apotheosis in Turgenev. But the familiar song is being played in a new and dissonant way, beginning with the sparseness of the trees. Readers of Turgenev are accustomed to forests that are lush and beautiful. Here the woods are almost pitiful. This is not the kind of forest that could be mistaken for an ocean. Boulders make an unflattering contrast with skinny, diminutive birches—the secondary trees that grow after the primary forest has been cut. The soil is poor, though by now the trees and grass are used to it, and simply do their best to survive. The parallel with Soviet citizens, accustomed by 1936 to a great deal of hunger, deprivation, and fear, is obvious.

Rather than being populated by sylvan giants, the forest is a city crowded with insects, worms, and birds. It screeches, squeaks, and mutters—emitting not a divine song without words, as in Korolenko's murmuring forest, but an inarticulate slur. With Platonov's characteristic ambiguity, it is unclear whether this sound indicates joy, satisfaction, or a recent death. The boundary between hope and annihilation blurs. This is one of many moments in the story that can be read as an almost outright criticism of life under Stalin. A small animal whimpers with the terror of existence, "not daring to surrender to its own heart's joy in the loveliness of the world."[9] It is terrified of being eaten, but its whimper will probably give it away.

The Soviets envisioned progress as linear, often representing it as a train speeding into the glorious, electrified future. This ideal was utterly at odds with the natural cycles of growth and decay, life and death. In Platonov's story, these endless cycles are the domain of the forest, and a human being must struggle to escape them. In this sense, the story conforms to the Bolshevik hostility toward the natural world. But "Among Animals and Plants" has none of the triumphalism of most "official" literature of the Stalin era. For one thing, it is hardly an advertisement for the lifestyle of the Soviet worker. Fyodorov lives with his parents, wife, and baby daughter in a hut whose wooden roof is rotting and covered with moss, its lowest logs buried in the ground and, mysteriously, beginning to sprout new branches. Fyodorov's father is allowing his home to return to the earth and nourish a new tree, in the manner of an untouched forest. What falls is left to decay and live again in a new form. The family is subject to the metabolism of the woods. The song of the rails is a response to the murmuring of distant leaves and branches—the murmuring of the forest immortalized by Korolenko. It seems possible that the murmur of the forest will remain when the song of the railroad has died out. This recalls the enduring Russian fear of being engulfed by primordial forest, dragged into the past.

Yet Platonov also offers the possibility, in the story, that the Soviet project will replace the stunted taiga with mighty oaks, the heroes of central Russia's deciduous forests. Fyodorov's father is in the business of cutting down trees and making them useful—he works at a sawmill—and he plans to move somewhere better soon. He has decided to say goodbye to the past, to forget what has come before. In this, he resembles a good Soviet man, but he lacks the self-confidence of a Soviet hero. As often happened in Platonov's writing, many aspects of the story seem to conform to Stalinist prescriptions on a superficial level, but the mood and the details are utterly out of keeping with the high Stalinist mood.

Even worse, from the perspective of a Stalinist censor, was the fact that "Among Animals and Plants" is full of subtle allusions to the White Sea Canal.[10] In reality, most of the people traveling on trains through the northern forest would have been prisoners, not bright-eyed builders of Communism. Fyodorov becomes a hero by stopping a runaway train from hitting a crowd of people—perhaps an indication of the lethal role played by the railroads in the age of the Gulag. This is not to say that the story is simply a between-the-lines indictment of Stalin's repressions. In Fyodorov's world, it is not the woods but the railway that sings an "eternal song," one more intelligible and more beautiful than the forest's screeches and muttering. The railroad carried prisoners to hard labor and death, but as Platonov knew well from his experience in 1921, it could also help prevent famine. He shared the Bolshevik reverence for technology.

"Among Animals and Plants" offers a surprising argument for tenderness toward machines, which in Platonov's description need more care than living things do. When Fyodorov first started work on the railway, he

> treated metal and machines as he had treated animals and plants, with caution and foresight, trying not only to get to know them but also to outwit them. Then he had realized that such a relationship was insufficient and just wasn't enough. Being with metal and machines required a great deal more sensitivity than being with wild animals or with plants and trees. You can outwit something living and it will yield to you; you can wound it

> and, being alive, it will heal; but machines and rails don't yield to cunning—they can be won over only by pure goodness; and you can't afford to wound them, because they don't heal. A break is mortal.[11]

This is an almost shocking reversal of the usual idea (at least to modern readers) that what is organic is irreplaceable, whereas machines are lifeless, soulless things. It is possible to read it as a satirical comment on the Stalinist glorification of industry at the expense of human life, and that aspect is surely present. But there is also the engineer's affection for his mechanical charges and their tenuous magic, and a scientist's faith in the regenerative powers of nature, including the forest. In our age of ecological crisis, we tend to emphasize the risk of extinction. But Russia, with its extremes of both climate and history, is a testament to the resilience of living organisms, whether trees or human beings. At the end of the story, Fyodorov goes out into the forest "to look for his father among animals and plants." He is looking backward rather than forward; for all his celebration of machines, he is returning to the inhuman music of nature.

As Stalin's purges escalated in the 1930s, more and more Soviet citizens found themselves forcibly returned to the inhuman music of the taiga, conscripted into the project of transforming nature to serve Soviet needs. Chekhov's voluntary trip to Sakhalin remained an anomaly. A steady stream of Soviet writers was sent to be "reeducated" in the Gulag, many of them never to return. For some, the taiga was a torment. But for others, nature's music had come to seem more human than the manmade kind.

In 1933, Osip Mandelstam composed a poem that called Stalin a "peasant slayer" and compared him to a cockroach. Mandelstam recited his so-called "Stalin Epigram" at several gatherings. It was an attempted suicide by poem; he must have been surprised that it took six months for the secret police to arrest him. He expected the death penalty, but his wife, Nadezhda, and the poets Anna Akhmatova and Boris Pasternak helped save him. His sentence was remarkably light: three years of exile in Cherdyn, in the northern Urals. This was an unusual act of clemency, attributable to the Soviet desire to avoid bad press just before a major international Writers' Congress in Moscow. The poet was even allowed to bring his wife into exile with him. The Mandelstams followed Chekhov's route up the Kama River in a steamboat.

In a poem about his journey into exile, Mandelstam described how darkness filled his eyes and lines of trees on the banks looked like wooden cities brought to their knees. He imagined that a burning fir tree was running into the river's cold Siberian water to be saved, like a person trying to extinguish flaming clothing. The vast forests of the Urals became a poetic metaphor for the thoughts of a condemned man. In reality, Mandelstam did not see the trees. He hallucinated throughout the trip. The curtains on the windows of his boat were closed: The convict did not have the right to look out into the distance.[12] The loyal Nadezhda stayed awake for five days, watching over him. Mandelstam had suffered psychotic episodes in jail, where he had been interrogated and tortured. Now the psychosis returned. When he was calm enough to listen, Nadezhda read him Pushkin.[13]

Unlike Platonov, Mandelstam was entranced by the past. His imagination had been nourished on ancient classics like Ovid; he longed for Italy, and his greatest love was the Mediterranean. He experienced the taiga as a hell—and not the calm, well-ordered underworld of the Greeks. For him, the coniferous forest was a distinctly Russian place of banishment, suffering, and madness, devoid of the comforts of civilization. Like Chekhov, Mandelstam experienced Siberia as a place without art. It was Russia's New World, but as the memoirs of many Gulag survivors would attest, it was also a place of misery, starvation, and huge, even lethal, swarms of mosquitoes.

Not every Gulag survivor had such a harsh view of the taiga. Many later remembered how the forest saved their lives. Yevgenia Ginzburg was a devoted Communist, a professor of Leninist history, when she was falsely accused of counterrevolutionary activities. After being expelled from the party, she was arrested in 1937 and sent to a camp in the Kolyma River basin, on the easternmost edge of northern Siberia, an area even harsher than the terrifying forest on the Kama River. The Kolyma region straddles the edge of the Arctic Circle, and much of it is covered in permafrost and tundra. This is the northernmost edge of the world's forest, a place where even the hardy larch struggles to survive. The Gulag was situated there because of the gold and other minerals buried underground. Prisoners labored in mines or at forestry, since lumber was needed for buildings and fuel to support mining efforts.

Journey into the Whirlwind, Ginzburg's memoir, was smuggled abroad and published in the West in 1967. At the end of its first volume, she describes trudging with other prisoners through the virgin forest and its deep snow cover, their feet soaking and frostbitten. The guards order her to cut down a tall tree with the help of only one other woman. "Poor trees—how they must have suffered at being mangled by our inexpert hands!" she wrote. She was an intellectual, and her fellow inmate was a nurse. They did not have the slightest idea how to cut down a tree. Ginzburg and other prisoners who failed to meet the impossible quotas were denied their food ration, then punished as "saboteurs." They were locked overnight in an unheated shack, taking turns sitting on three logs fastened together—the only furniture.

Ginzburg's life was saved by a woman named Polina, who miraculously fulfilled the quotas alone with a handsaw. Polina explained that the forest was full of piles of wood cut by other gangs of prisoners and never counted. She took the old wood, cut the very end to make it look fresh, and passed it off as her own felling. Ginzburg and her friends survived on this trick until the cut timber was taken away by truck, after which their output plummeted.

Soon Ginzburg was once again on the brink of death. This time salvation came from "sour, bitter, northern berries" left from the last season and revealed by the spring melt. As she was cutting branches from a felled larch, she saw a sprig of five or six crimson berries, perilously close to bursting. They were too fragile to pick, but she found that she could lie on the ground and suck their precious, coral-red juice directly from the branch with her chapped lips. "Their taste was indescribable," she wrote, "a fine wine of excellent vintage. It could hardly be compared with the sourness of ordinary cranberries: here was the sweetness and aroma of victory over pain and winter." She told her companions about what she had found, and they all ate their share of berries. "From then on," she writes, "we went into the forest every morning not in despair, but in hope."[14]

Ginzburg was among the lucky ones who survived the Gulag. Mandelstam did not. After being arrested again in 1938 on spurious charges, he was deported to Kolyma. He died of a heart attack in a Vladivostok transit camp. A piece of wood with his inmate number was attached to his toe before he was cast into a mass grave.[15] That same year, Platonov's fifteen-year-old son was arrested on similarly risible charges and sent to the Gulag—likely as a hostage to ensure his father's compliance.

For many of those who survived to make art or write memoirs about their time in the Gulag, the forest offered the promise of salvation through hope as well as precious vitamins. Varlam Shalamov was born in 1907 to a priest father: a dangerous family history once the Bolsheviks took power. After becoming involved with the political opposition against Stalin, he ended up in camps in Kolyma from 1937 until 1951—the year Platonov died of tuberculosis he contracted while nursing his dying son. After his return from the camps, Shalamov wrote the autobiographical story cycle *Kolyma Tales*, the greatest literary chronicle of life in the Gulag. One story, "Cherry Brandy," imagines Mandelstam's death in the transit camp.

As for Ginzburg, in *Kolyma Tales* the forest is a source of nutrients for the starving, malnourished prisoners. It is also a source of dangerous temptation, as if in a fairytale. In the story "Berries," the narrator and a fellow prisoner are sent out on a winter day to tear up tree stumps and saw and stack them up. Whenever possible, the men pick bluish gray lingonberries; bright, crinkled blueberries; and purple mountain briar hip berries frozen on the bushes after the long winter. The frosted berries have an alluring scent and a subtle but intoxicating taste—the flavor of life that has been preserved. The narrator's companion collects them in a jar, intending to trade them to the camp cook for bread. At dusk, seeing a tussock with an especially lavish spread of berries, the companion crosses the boundary line set by the prison guard—who shoots him without warning.[16] Inured to death, the narrator picks up the jar of berries and slips it into his pocket. The warm corpse lies between the tussocks of the taiga berry patch. Against the backdrop of the sky, river, and mountains, the body looks "surprisingly small." In the Gulag, humans are dwarfed by nature—but this can be a source of reassurance as well as horror.

In Shalamov's story "Lend-Lease," the prisoners harvest timber from streambeds. This is the best source of timber in Kolyma because in a deep gully, trees grow especially tall and straight as they reach for the sun, protected from the harsh wind. At first, most of the work is done without the help of any technology. The inmates drag felled Daurian larches by hand up narrow, twisting hillside paths and over hummocks. This is exhausting work even for a healthy person.[17] The "Lend-Lease" convicts receive the unexpected aid of American bulldozers that can hoist the trees for them, lifting two-meter-wide trunks too heavy for any prisoner. But soon the prisoners and the bulldozer come to a slope stripped of every tree that once anchored it, the biggest stumps blown out with explosives. A mass grave has burst out of the stony ground, and undecomposed corpses lie like felled trees across the denuded hill.

This is a horrific vision, but here, again, Shalamov finds a counterintuitive comfort. "Permafrost preserves and reveals secrets," he writes. The frozen corpses force the guards and the prisoners to bear witness to their murders. The bodies seem to crawl down the hill, "perhaps about to be resurrected." At first the narrator mistakes them for tree trunks that have not yet been stacked into piles. As in Mandelstam's poem, where trees fled into the water, Shalamov's people and trees become almost interchangeable.

But most of all, the trees in *Kolyma Tales* are gnarled yet resilient symbols of suffering and survival. Among six-hundred-year-old larches, the human life span seems trivial even without being curtailed by forced labor. One of Shalamov's most memorable meditations on trees is in the story "The Dwarf Pine." The seam of taiga and tundra has denied the tree the chance to grow to maturity; it remains a bush, its trunk only a little thicker than a man's arm and a few meters in length. The diminutive tree grows where it can, its roots snaking into fissures in the rocky slopes. It is "courageous and stubborn, like all northern trees," and gifted with an almost supernatural sensitivity. When it senses that bruised storm clouds are coming, bearing snow, it lies down in preparation, "as if under an immense, ever-growing weight . . . it presses itself to the ground, stretching its emerald paws. It prepares for bed."[18] When snow buries the landscape, the shapes of the supine dwarves are blisters on the white expanse.

The first harbinger of snow, the dwarf pine is also the first sign of spring. Before human senses can detect any change in the weather, the dwarf pine "shakes off the snow, straightens up to its full height, and lifts its green, icy, red-tinted needles to the sky." For Shalamov, the dwarf pine, the only evergreen in the landscape, is "a tree of hope," "the most poetic Russian tree." In summer it seems to disappear among the hasty clouds of blossoms and berries. But in autumn, the larch, a deciduous conifer, loses its yellowed needles. The grass fades and dries, and only the dwarf pines remain, like "huge green torches." The year-round permafrost is matched by the endurance of the pine, the evergreen that may grow a little faded—as in *War and Peace*, when the conifers Prince Andrei passes look dismal, almost dirty. But for a laborer condemned to a slow death, the pine's stubborn green vibrance in the desolate sea of white is an inspiring reminder of eternity.

In Shalamov's late story "The Resurrection of the Larch," a man in the Far North sends a woman in Moscow a package by airmail. The woman's husband, a poet, died in Kolyma. Shalamov was likely writing about Mandelstam's widow, Nadezhda, who was a close friend. The package contains a gift to commemorate the woman's husband: a branch of Daurian larch, "dried-out and wind-blown by the airplane air, crumpled, broken in the post wagon, bright brown, tough, bony." The woman puts it in an empty jar filled with tap water.

Three days and three nights pass—the magical triad of fairytales—and the woman is awoken by a strange scent. Dazzling, bright green needles have emerged from the hard skin of the plant. The larch has been resurrected; the larch is immortal. Its turpentine odor, the overwhelming smell of Kolyma in spring, is "the smell of life . . . the smell of victory."[19] Despite the best Soviet efforts, the taiga was still unconquered.

CHAPTER 10

Young Oaks

As the taiga offered its meager fruits to desperate Gulag prisoners, war was fracturing Europe. In September 1939, Nazi Germany invaded Poland. Three weeks later, Soviet troops advanced into the Polish Republic from the east. For twenty months, the border between Germany and the Soviet Union lay just west of Białowieża Forest. But the truce between the two dictatorships was brief. In June 1941, Hitler invaded the Soviet Union. For the next four years, the forests of eastern Europe and the western USSR would be battlegrounds.

Among the first Soviet units to be encircled in the invasion were three armies bottled up in the Białowieża region. Hundreds of thousands of Red Army soldiers surrendered, but many were able to sneak through the forests and rejoin their comrades farther east. The Nazis were now in possession of Białowieża Forest, the old prize of Lithuanian grand dukes, Polish kings, and Russian tsars. Hermann Göring, Germany's "chief huntsman," was particularly fascinated by the legendary hunting garden. He dreamed of making Białowieża his own forest-fiefdom.

In 1934, Germany had officially mandated that all its forests should follow the so-called *Dauerwald* model. This "continuous" or "eternal" forest, composed of vigorously growing trees of different ages and species, was intended as a more natural corrective to the homogenous, clear-cut outdoor wood factories that had become common thanks to the older approach to forestry. According to the *Dauerwald* concept, a beautiful, harmonious forest would have better soil and produce more timber. Göring enshrined *Dauerwald* as the Third Reich's official approach to silviculture, linking sustainable forestry to the Nazi nature cult. As he put it, "Eternal forest and eternal nation are ideas that are indissolubly linked."[1]

The *Dauerwald* concept was quickly discarded from forest policy, but Göring's fascination with the perfect forest endured. Now he had the opportunity to run Białowieża, the most celebrated primeval forest left in Europe, according to his nationalist fantasy. Białowieża's trees and animals would be protected from anyone except German hunters while the forest was cleansed of Jews, partisans, and poachers.[2] Göring's dream was a sadistic revision of the Polish poet Adam Mickiewicz's fantasy, in *Pan Tadeusz*, of an area of Białowieża that was free of humans and free of predators.

The Nazi authorities set out to purge the forest of everyone who had sought refuge there. When Poland had fallen to Germany, Polish soldiers and partisans had taken to the woods, where it was easier to wage guerrilla warfare. Jews went to the forest to hide, sometimes becoming partisans as well. An estimated twenty-five thousand Jewish men, women, and children escaped to the forests of Poland, Belarus, Lithuania, and Latvia; some lived there for up to four years. Like other partisans, they survived on food requisitioned at gunpoint from nearby villages and slept in dugouts disguised by conifer branches, sometimes waking beneath several feet of snow that had fallen during the night. From the forest they made sorties to blow up bridges, derail trains, cut down telephone poles, attack German soldiers, and bring other Jews into the woods, sometimes liberating entire ghettos. Danger came not only from German soldiers but also from local inhabitants, many of whom collaborated with the Nazis.*

* This is the subject of a large body of scholarship, documentary film, and popular writing—most recently, the film *Four Winters*.

Germany classified partisans as "bandits," which deprived guerrillas of their status as combatants under international law and obliged even ordinary citizens to denounce or simply kill them. After deporting many of the local Slavs, the Nazis repopulated the region with Germans. Resettled German foresters became sharpshooters, their experience as trackers and hunters now focused on human beings. Special anti-partisan troops called "hunting commandos" were deployed. In 1942, the chief of the Wehrmacht General Staff called for the use of hunting techniques originally intended for wild game. The German soldiers murdered Jews, partisans, and recalcitrant villagers in swamps and fields, forests and farmhouses. As the historian Philip Blood puts it, "patrols and Jagdkommandos [hunting commandos] recorded the kills as if they were competing for trophies."[3] Białowieża had become a Nazi hunting garden in which "bandits" were the prey.

It was not only the Germans who used hunting tactics for warfare. Such strategies were also used by those resisting the Nazis. Peasants in the region had long been forbidden the use of guns and had thus developed other techniques. For instance, they could kill a large animal with primitive instruments if they used their collective force to push it onto a small island in the wetlands. In at least one incident, this method was used against German troops. The soldiers' bodies were found scattered across an island in the swamp, stabbed, hacked, slashed, and beaten.[4]

The Nazis viewed the Slavs, like the Jews, as inferior beings: *Untermenschen.* This racialized disgust extended to the environment. The Germans had long been suspicious of Polesia, with its isolated, independent Slavic and Jewish villages. The marshier the forest, the more they abhorred it. In the 1930s, German visitors had proposed that the Pripet marshes in Ukraine and Belarus, the swampiest part of the Polesian forest belt and today the largest wetlands in Europe, be drained and reclaimed as farmland, the rich peat dug up and burned for fuel. The Germans were appalled by the unruly, ungoverned, unproductive nature of this marshland, by its useless wolves, boars, and birds, and by its Slavs, who were portrayed as disgustingly fecund. Above all, Germans were repulsed by Polesia's Jewish inhabitants, whose very body fat was compared to viscous swamp mud. In his history *The Conquest of Nature: Water, Landscape, and the Making of Modern Germany*, David Blackbourn shows how the draining of Polesia's wetlands was associated with the damming up of the "Slavic flood" that had long served as a manufactured race panic in Germany. Later, the Nazis planned to resettle Jews in Pripet and force them to drain the swamp, so that they would forfeit their lives in the process of reclaiming the land.

The plan to drain the swamp was abandoned—but not the plan to exterminate its inhabitants. In July 1941, Himmler ordered that all the Jews at the northern edge of the Pripet marsh were to be shot, Jewish women driven into the marshes to drown. Within the span of just two weeks, the SS killed fifteen thousand people in Belarusian Polesia, supposedly as part of an anti-partisan operation. "Driving people into the marshes" became a euphemism for mass murder.[5]

For the Nazis, the swampy forests of Polesia were a blight, a metaphor for the people they hated, and an instrument of genocide. But for those escaping and fighting the Nazis, forests and swamps were spaces and tools of resistance. Much of the fighting on the Eastern Front occurred around areas that still had plentiful forest, despite the deforestation of the preceding centuries. Once again, the forest became a central character in Soviet war stories—in modern legends of partisans and soldiers stranded behind enemy lines.

Russians had learned the value of well-coordinated guerrilla fighting in 1812, when partisans nearly caught Napoleon himself. The decades-long success of local guerrillas in fending off Russian conquest in the Caucasus was another, less pleasant reminder to Russians of the potency of nimble fighters in the forest. During the Russian Civil War, there had been partisans fighting for every faction, but the victorious Red partisans of Ukraine, Belarus, the North Caucasus,

Siberia, and the Far East were the most numerous and the best organized, and they played a significant role in subduing the many sources of resistance to the revolution.[6]

But the partisans of the Second World War outdid all their historical predecessors, distinguishing themselves with their bravery, self-sacrifice, and military effectiveness. Like the guerrillas of Imam Shamil's day, they found their greatest ally in the forests. But unlike Shamil's forests, the hiding places of Soviet partisans were often swampy, crisscrossed with rivers, marshes, and lakes that posed a formidable obstacle to German troops. The poor quality of Soviet roads made railroads the only reliable means of transport through the region, and the partisans focused their efforts on sabotage. When they were short on explosives, they took the rails apart and hid them in the forest or dropped them into marshes, lakes, and rivers. By doing so, they deprived the Germans of access to the forest's timber, which was cut at local sawmills and transported on these railways. By August 1943, partisans had destroyed half the sawmills in Belarus. The Germans were distressed at the loss of 80 percent of crude logs and processed timber produced in Ukraine. Because wood was necessary for frequently replaced pit props in the mines of eastern Ukraine, by cutting off access to wood, the partisans also stopped the Germans from extracting coal there.[7] Partisan forest sabotage compromised German access to building materials, energy, and all manner of other supplies.

The guerrillas moved only at night, choosing the most forbidding terrain to minimize the likelihood of any encounters with the enemy. They marked their paths for comrades by leaving subtle signs: cracked twigs, broken blades of grass, discreet arrangements of stones, even artificial animal scents. To be a good partisan meant possessing the skills of an expert forest tracker.[8] The Germans attempted to encircle areas of partisan activity and then comb them for combatants. Anyone caught was executed. But the wet, wooded terrain and its sheer size made this a hard task, especially for foreigners. In 1942, a German report detailed the difficulties of this approach, as soldiers followed trails of bloodstains in the snow along twisting forest paths, struggling to distinguish false trails from real ones and getting lost in the woods themselves, disoriented and facing enemy fire from the trees. Sometimes the clever partisans even put dummies in the forest, guns in hand. Germans approaching from a distance opened fire, revealing their whereabouts to the real partisans lurking nearby.[9]

The partisans managed to take control of whole regions in Ukraine, Belarus, central Russia, and Crimea. By spring 1942, partisan-held territories were as big as Belgium, Denmark, and the Netherlands combined.[10] Partisans from Pskov and Novgorod, in central Russia, managed to smuggle forty-eight tons of food across enemy lines to the starving citizens of besieged Leningrad, where the streets were littered with the corpses of people who had collapsed from starvation.[11] "As far as agriculture is concerned," a German detachment in Belarus reported in spring 1943, "the security situation has deteriorated again. By night the entire region becomes the partisans' area of operations. From every forest, fires burn and rockets climb into the air to light the way for the Red Air Force."[12]

One major Soviet World War II legend concerned a Soviet fighter who fell from the sky—and was saved by the forest. In April 1942, the successful fighter pilot Aleksei Maresyev was shot down over the Demyansk Pocket, an area south of Leningrad where the Soviets had encircled a large number of German troops. Maresyev made an emergency descent into the forest but badly injured his feet in the crash landing. For eighteen days, the twenty-six-year-old pilot first limped, then crawled, then rolled east through forest and swampland, avoiding German patrols, until he was discovered by Russian villagers. When they were finally able to get medical help for him, his gangrened legs had to be amputated at the shin. Less than a year later, equipped with primitive prostheses, Maresyev returned to flight, shooting down more German planes and becoming one of the rare double-amputee fighter aces in history.

Maresyev's story was recorded by the war correspondent Boris Polevoi, who went on to write a documentary novella about the episode, *The Story of a Real Man*. The book became a fable about the indomitable Russian will to defend the homeland. It celebrated Maresyev's ability to miraculously overcome the limits of the human body, first through perseverance and later through the use of prosthetic limbs. The book was immensely popular in the Soviet Union and abroad. It was added to the Soviet school curriculum and made into a 1948 film. By 1954, there were 2.34 million copies in circulation worldwide.[13]

The Story of a Real Man was even made into a 1948 opera by Sergei Prokofiev. As in the novella, tree imagery is central. Prokofiev's opera starts and ends with a song called "A young oak grew in a grove." Maresyev was a Soviet superman, but he was also a young Russian oak: powerful, righteous, and almost immortal, the strong wood on which Russian society was built.* The forest was the place where he undertook the saintly, superhuman feat of heroism and endurance that would make him immortal, at least for Soviet purposes.

In Polevoi's book, we meet the woods before we meet the hero. The story opens with a description of a forest that is just awakening to the cold dawn, soughing as it is ruffled by fresh wind. Century-old pines whisper to one another, and the sounds of a woodpecker are like notes being played on a violin. A tree has saved Maresyev's life. When his plane fell, he landed in the arms of a hundred-year-old spruce and slid down its branches into a snowdrift. While the wounded man drags himself through the woods, the forest does its best to sustain him. When he falls into the embrace of a pine sapling, he is inspired to cut it and use it as a crutch. He eats moss, lingonberry leaves, young spruce bark, bitter birch and linden buds, and the "tender, sticky gruel of young linden bark."

These do little to sate his hunger, but on the sixth night, when he lies

* The post-Soviet writer Victor Pelevin later wrote a satire of the Soviet space program that was a cynical retelling of *The Story of a Real Man*, a testament to the story's importance as a Soviet myth.

down to sleep under a spruce tree, a squirrel above him starts to throw down cones. In one of them, the starving Maresyev discovers a tiny seed with a pleasant aroma of pine oil. He finds more spruce cones on the ground, heats them, and shakes out the seeds. The squirrel and the tree have conspired to save him.

This is the turning point. The next day, he sees the signs of spring. The melting snow looks like honeycomb and the forest has the "powerful scent, like home-brewed beer, that makes all living things dizzy." No longer able to walk, he crawls across the hummocks of a swamp where he finds bog cranberries to sustain him. In a dense young pine forest, he hears Russian voices at last: two young boys. When he asks them who is here, the Soviets or the Germans, one of the boys answers, "How do I know? No one tells me. The forest is here."

Maresyev learns that rather than working for the occupying Germans, as they had been ordered to do, the inhabitants of a nearby village fled to the depths of the forest, where they joined the partisans and continued to live according to collectivist Soviet ideals. The story ends as it began, with Maresyev back in combat and the forest murmuring a song that cannot be drowned out by the sound of warfare. *The Story of a Real Man* is also the story of the forest, which shelters the Soviet people in its depths during their moment of peril.

In the later 1940s and in the 1950s, one-note patriotic World War II stories like *The Story of a Real Man* were a staple of Soviet culture, proliferating in fiction, film, journalism, and even opera. Yet for Soviet citizens, the memory of the war was hardly simple. The losses incurred were incalculable, and the trauma of the experience marked several generations. It was almost impossible in those first postwar years to make a great work of art about the war, given the strictures of patriotism and Stalinist censorship. But with the loosening of censorship after Stalin's death and the distance of time, a new honesty became feasible.

By the 1960s, there was room to express the true pain of the war in which the USSR suffered nearly twenty-seven million casualties. Several of the greatest and most harrowing of all Soviet films are about partisans in the forests of the western Soviet Union—soldiers who crossed enemy lines under the cover of trees, and ordinary people in occupied territory who escaped to the forest. In these stories, the swampy forests of the region are both refuge and Golgotha.

Andrei Tarkovsky's first feature film, *Ivan's Childhood* (1962), opens with the sound of a cuckoo. We glimpse a young boy, the eponymous Ivan, behind a tree. The camera pans up a slim pine and the boy becomes visible from a distance—prefiguring the similar shot in Tarkovsky's *Andrei Rublev*. This is a boy's wartime dream of a moment when his mother and the rest of his family were still alive, before his family tree was cut down by the Nazi invasion.

Awake again to the horror of reality, Ivan wades through a flooded

Ivan crosses the flooded forest *Mosfilm*

forest. A village nearby has no roofs left. In the forest and in the village, ordinary life has been disfigured.

Ivan is a partisan scout, seeking revenge for his lost family. He and two older soldiers wade through the marsh of denuded trees and algae-covered water, flares illuminating them at dangerous intervals. After Ivan is sent across enemy lines, an older soldier gazes at the reflection of trees in the water. This is no jingoistic victory film. Ivan is caught and hanged by the Germans. In a devastatingly beautiful conclusion, we see Ivan and his mother at the beach, playing around a tree, chasing a little girl—no doubt his sister—along a spit of sand. The tree is dead.

Tarkovsky's film resonated through Soviet culture for decades. It demonstrated that the stories of the partisans and the villagers who bore the brunt of the Nazi anti-partisan operations were more powerful and persuasive without the addition of patriotic embroidery. *The Story of a Real Man* obscured the pain of the most traumatic episode in Soviet history.

One reason for the success of the Soviet partisans was the unfathomable brutality of the Nazi occupiers toward the Slavs as well as toward the Jews. Hitler told his advisers, "As for the ridiculous hundred million Slavs, we will mold the best of them to the shape that suits us, and we will isolate the rest of them in their own pigsties; and anyone who talks about cherishing the local inhabitant and civilising him goes straight off to a concentration camp!"[14] This was the philosophy that motivated Nazi behavior in occupied territories. In Turgenev's old hometown, Oryol, partisans were strung up in the public square.[15] The Germans massacred whole villages on mere suspicion of support for the partisans. Many of those not murdered by the Nazis were sent to forced labor camps.

Slavs in occupied regions understood that they were being enslaved and exterminated, and that fighting the Germans was a matter of survival for themselves, their communities, and their land. At least a quarter of the population of Belarus died during the war. A scorched-earth policy in areas that could not be controlled led to the creation of "dead zones" that the Germans looted and evacuated so that no one would be able to work the land and produce benefits for the partisans or the Red Army.[16] In total, not including the millions of Soviet Jews killed in the Nazi genocide, the Germans executed or starved 5.8 million Soviet citizens—prisoners of war, partisans and suspected partisans, and civilians who were suspected of aiding the partisans or who were murdered in acts of collective punishment.[17] Among these were large numbers of women and children. Resistance was not only men's work. Women and children fought back, too, as Ivan does in Tarkovsky's film. Nazi policy treated anyone over ten as fully responsible for their actions, which meant that children of eleven were executed for helping the partisans.* About 10 percent of Soviet partisans, meanwhile, were women.[18]

It is fitting, then, that one of the most enduring cultural monuments to the partisans was a woman's work. Ukrainian director Larisa Shepitko's 1977 film *The Ascent* opens with an enigmatic black-and-white shot of a featureless expanse rippled by a tidal movement. We hear gunfire and see that this is a snowy field punctuated only by the occasional barren tree, twisted and dark against the white ground. Then a human figure pops up from behind an embankment, like a fox going hunting. At his gesture, more figures rise up from the snowdrifts. Suddenly the blank field is populated. These are partisans and their charges: women, children, old people. Human warmth emerges from the nothingness of winter.

The gunfire starts again, and the partisans return fire. Some are wounded and some are killed. A little boy hangs onto a tree branch, his legs dangling, after the adult carrying him falls, shot. In wartime trees have different meanings: They are shelter from marauding air-

* The partisans also executed villagers who collaborated with the Germans, sometimes even in very small ways. But this death toll is minuscule compared to the massacres committed by the Nazis.

craft, but also hanging posts. Those who make it back to the protection of the forest share the band's last food, a tiny bag of seeds. Each person tips their portion tenderly into their mouth.

On the bare, snowy slopes, human figures stand out from a perilously long distance, easy marks. But in the forest, the partisans blend into the patterns made by dark branches. Mustaches and beards are rimed with frost, heavily mended sheepskin and wool coats dusted with snowflakes. The more the partisans look like forest, the safer they will be. The black-and-white film makes it mercifully difficult to imagine blood, violence, or compromised flesh. In Shepitko's film, trees offer camouflage and comfort.

The Ascent, which was based on a novel by the Belarusian veteran and war writer Vasil Bykaŭ, concerns two young partisans, the ethereal Sotnikov and the hardy Rybak, who leave the forest to find food. Sotnikov is soon wounded in a firefight with German soldiers. With just one bullet left, he is about to commit suicide when Rybak, a good-hearted peasant type, rescues him and drags him back into the woods, saving his life.

In one of the film's most memorable scenes, Sotnikov lies propped against a big tree, hollow-cheeked and luminous with virtue. Rybak has gone ahead to scout. The camera caresses the tree's rough bark and slender branches stippled with ice. Translucent snow collects in Sotnikov's hair, on his long eyelashes, on his mustache, on his coat, and on his inadequate little military cap, with its hammer and sickle. His face is partly obscured by a trembling lattice of twigs.

When Rybak returns from his scouting mission, Sotnikov is frozen to the tree's trunk. Rybak uses the warmth of his breath to release him, stopping the Christlike Sotnikov from merging with the tree, from dying peacefully in the forest.

"I was only afraid to die out in the open field," Sotnikov tells him, "in the night, alone like a dog. In the woods, it's not frightening. You just have to get used to the idea."

Rybak's desire to live, embodied by the warmth of his breath, proves greater than his sense of honor. When the two partisans are captured, Rybak saves his own skin by giving up information and agreeing to join the collaborators. He is not a bad man; he is simply afraid to die. Shepitko reminds us that pure heroism was a difficult choice to make.

Throughout the film, Shepitko lingers on Sotnikov's drawn face as he gazes out at the sky and the landscape, his selfhood seeping out from his round, eerily transparent eyes. If Rybak is too attached to his body, to his corporeal existence, Sotnikov is hardly attached to it at all. He is liable to dissolve into the landscape, to fuse to a tree, to become a part of the forest. In *Ivan's Childhood*, the tree of life is everything that Ivan, and by extension the Soviet people, have lost. In *The Ascent*, the forest is the afterlife.

The filming of *The Ascent* was a process of self-mortification that paid tribute to the suffering of the partisans. Shepitko shot on location in January's winds and blizzards, when the temperature dropped to –40°C. The actors refused to bundle themselves up in warm clothes, wanting to feel the same cold the partisans had experienced. The film's many extras chose to emulate them, even while filming scenes set in snowdrifts. Their hands had black spots from frostbite. When Shepitko asked a twelve-year-old extra why he had not put on gloves, he said he wanted to know what his father had felt during the war.[19] This was the ethos of the film: No sacrifice in filming could compare to the sacrifices made by the partisans thirty years earlier.

At the end of *Come and See*, a 1985 partisan film shot in vivid color by Shepitko's husband, Elem Klimov, the camera follows a column of partisans into an evergreen forest. Then the camera parts from them, wandering for a while through the woods. Time is passing. When we rejoin the fighters, snow covers the ground. The camera travels up the tree trunks and looks up toward the sky. By the summer of 1944, the front lines had returned to the forests of Belarus. Here the advancing Red Army linked up with the partisans who had survived in the woods for three years. On June 22, the third anniversary of Hitler's invasion, the Soviet high command launched Operation Bagration, named after a Georgian princely general who had fought for the tsar and died in the Battle of Borodino against Napoleon in 1812.

After Red Army armored divisions broke through German lines, more than 100,000 partisans attacked the retreating enemy from their forest hideouts, blowing up railways and ambushing convoys. Entire German units disintegrated and fled for their lives amid the trees, abandoning roads that were clogged with destroyed vehicles. Tens of thousands of soldiers were never found again. In the space of three weeks, the Wehrmacht suffered 450,000 casualties. Twenty-eight of its thirty-five divisions in the central sector of the Eastern Front were annihilated.[20] Months after the war had ended, in the fall of 1945, there were still groups of dazed stragglers emerging from the woods. Operation Bagration remains the largest defeat in German military history—a forest Stalingrad. Göring had dreamed of making Białowieża his hunting garden. Now the swampy border forests became a graveyard for Nazi forces.

CHAPTER 11

Stalin and the Wood Goblin

When a forest is felled, splinters fly.

—Russian proverb

The Second World War reminded the Soviets that the forest provided not only lumber but also protection from invaders. They recalled that enemies were always lurking at the gates—or at the edge of the woods. The Soviet historical imagination linked the Nazi invasion of 1941 to Napoleon's campaign of 1812, to early modern invasions from western Europe, and to the days when nomads galloped in from the dangerously barren eastern steppe. After the war was won, the fantasy of conquering nature merged with older visions of the forest as protector to create a strange, distinctly Soviet brand of what we would now call eco-nationalism.

Flush with victory, in 1948 Stalin revived a dream that had reverberated through Russian culture for many decades: to plant a forest that would protect Russia, its water, its people, and its culture. With typical Soviet pomp, the scheme was called "The Great Stalin Plan for the Transformation of Nature." The Nazis were vanquished and the Mongol Horde was a distant memory. Now it was the arid, supposedly Asian winds and sand that were the menacing invader. Deforestation had caused drought and desertification in a country already ravaged by the long war. Sandstorms tormented farmers and city dwellers. Unchecked winds damaged crops at a time when the war's survivors were going hungry. The Soviet Union needed more food, more water, and more peace—including a respite from sand and wind.

Stalin decided to plant forests on the steppe, creating a new, more deeply rooted version of the *zaseki,* those barriers of stumps and logs that warded off the nomads in earlier centuries. The *zaseki* were to be turned into national parks that were also national defenders. Eight huge forest belts were to be planted that would, in the fervent imaginations of their progenitors, protect agricultural fields, stop sand and dust storms, and transform dry southern Russia into a leafy refuge as cool, moist, and verdant as Muscovy. Russia would be saved, and so would the ancient Russian culture of the forest.

Stalin's Great Plan had recent precursors in more modest, rational efforts. Since the 1930s, Soviet deforestation had alternated with attempts to protect the forests, especially along riverbanks. In 1931, the Council of People's Commissars asked for a report on the potential value of "a screen of forest belts between the Urals and Caspian Sea to defend against winds originating in the eastern deserts."[1] Early attempts yielded poor results. As Russians had learned as early as the eighteenth century, it is exceedingly difficult to plant a forest from scratch. The development of healthy trees depends on a web of other supporting organisms and environmental factors with which the trees have evolved.

After the Second World War, there were renewed efforts at afforestation, this time taking into account climate, soil type, and other local factors that determined the best tree species and planting methods for a given area. Siberian larch, pine, and birch were selected for the strip linking the cities of northern Ukraine; currant and white mulberry for the drier, hotter region stretching from eastern Ukraine down to Moldavia; and oak, ash, and birch for the belt of Volga steppe stretching from Saratov to Astrakhan. According to the initial plan, the approach was to be incremental and patient, in keeping with the

We will conquer drought, too! 1949 Soviet poster celebrating Stalin's Great Plan. Victor Govorkov. *From the collection of the Russian State Library, Moscow/HIP/Art Resource, NY*

rhythm of the forest—though the project was not for the good of the forest so much as for the improvement of agriculture, an urgent Soviet priority. In 1946, drought had caused a disastrous grain harvest, which had led to famine in Ukraine.

Under Stalin's guidance, the afforestation plan became ever more ambitious as the 1940s advanced. The historian Stephen Brain classes the Great Stalin Plan for the Transformation of Nature as "the world's largest ecological engineering project" to date, as well as "the world's first explicit attempt to reverse human-induced climate change."[2] The technocratic caution of the earlier afforestation plan was replaced by Promethean arrogance that recalled 1920s declarations of a war on nature. The new forest belts were to cover an area equivalent to that of France, Italy, Britain, Belgium, and the Netherlands combined. Hungry citizens were promised berry patches and oases in areas that had once been deserts. As often happened with titanic Soviet plans, rhetoric was more extreme than practice. The actual plan for species largely followed the older, specific recommendations. But propaganda for the project envisioned a Russia newly peopled by powerful oaks, the tree most symbolic of old Russia and its strength.

A fatal turning point came when the project was hijacked by Trofim Lysenko, the most sinister charlatan in Soviet biology. Lysenko had risen to prominence by tailoring his scientific theories to Soviet ideology and vigorously denouncing his professional rivals and critics, many of whom ended up in the Gulag. He had nearly been discredited just before the Great Plan was announced, but he managed to win back Stalin's favor and achieve the official denunciation of the entire field of genetics—which was politically suspect because it suggested that living things were not entirely subject to human will. Lysenko's ascendance was a blight on Soviet science that would last for decades.

According to Lysenko's anthropomorphizing theories—which could be seen as a Stalinist distortion of Kropotkin's theory of mutual aid, or as a bizarre precursor to Suzanne Simard's theory of the "wood wide web"—plants could work as a collective, helping each other to grow and acting in the interest of the greater good. Oak acorns, for example, could be planted in nests in a formation that would allow them to defend each other against malevolent outsiders such as weeds. This would allow the forest to win its struggle against the steppe at last. The victory of the new forest would stand for socialism's triumph against capitalism, and the Soviet Union's triumph over its foreign foes. In Lysenkoism, political metaphor always trumped scientific methods.

Inspired by Lysenko, one official involved in the plan wrote,

> I want to say a few words about the struggle of the steppe with the forest and the forest with the steppe. Until now, in the majority of cases the steppe has defeated the forest. This happened because the forest is not always in a position to fight the steppe, and because the interference of man under conditions of anarchic capitalism always enabled the victory of the steppe . . . but

> can't we, workers of science, bring together forest plants and agricultural crops against their common enemy and win?[33]

The Great Stalin Plan was to be the final act in the showdown of forest and steppe that had defined Russian history from its earliest days. At the same time, it would be an unprecedented act of cooperation between woods and farmland, traditional rivals. Farmers would no longer battle against the forest, slashing and burning it to produce arable soil. Instead, they would look outward to join forces against the foreign enemy. Communism would bring the solidarity of forest and agriculture, of scientists and workers, that would allow Russia to conquer the Asian steppe at last.

In 1949, the composer Dmitrii Shostakovich debuted a humiliatingly propagandistic oratorio called *The Song of the Forests*, which won him the Stalin Prize by using folk song themes to celebrate Stalin's rescue of Russia through afforestation. That summer, hundreds of poorly prepared, underequipped young people were dispatched to plant oak forests and agricultural crops on the dry, windy steppe of the south, with its intimidating sandstorms and climatic extremes. Their untended nests of oaks had no real chance of survival, especially in the southernmost regions. The project relied on peasant collective farm workers, though they had long shown themselves unwilling and unable to successfully fulfill afforestation projects. There was no way to plant viable forests at the scale required. Meanwhile, the crops planted alongside the trees sucked away the water from the oaks. Those oaks that did survive did so thanks to foresters who deviated from Lysenko's plan. The dream of solidarity of forests and agriculture against the steppe was not only bad science. It also showed a refusal to acknowledge the failures of solidarity even among Soviet humans.

Many scientists fought hard against Lysenko's scheme. They lobbied successfully for a more rational, realistic revision of the plan, and they won. But then, in March 1953, Stalin died. His Great Plan was abruptly abandoned, along with a large share of forest conservation efforts more generally. Only one stretch of the belt was ever completed.[4] Nikita Khrushchev, the new leader of the USSR, was an expert tractor driver from the forest-steppe region of southern Russia; his passion was not forests but corn to feed the masses. He visited corn farms in the American Midwest to study their technique. Instead of planting trees, he built groves of flimsy apartment buildings to address the Soviet housing crisis. The Soviet Union had entered a new chapter, one defined more by compromise than by Prometheanism.

When Stalin died, a fifty-three-year-old writer named Leonid Leonov was finishing an epic novel called *The Russian Forest.* Begun under draconian Stalinist censorship, the book was promptly reedited to conform to the new requirements of de-Stalinization. Leonov was once ranked among the most talented Soviet writers, admired both at home and abroad. His fortunes have since waned; today, even connoisseurs of Russian literature may not recognize his name. But his willingness to reject the Soviet subjugation of the forest, which he celebrated as a wellspring of Russian identity, marks a hinge point in the treatment of nature in Soviet culture.

In *The Russian Forest,* Leonov juxtaposed Stalin's xenophobic, nationalist reverence for the forest with a defense of sustainable forestry and forest conservation—two concepts that had been under siege since the 1917 Revolution. With this unorthodox blend, Leonov ushered in a new era of Russian eco-nationalism. Influenced by Leonov, the next generation of ecologically conscious writers would combine literature with remarkably effective ecological activism—and, in many cases, with Russian chauvinism.

Leonov's rise to the pinnacle of Soviet literature is surprising, because his early biography should have marked him for political persecution. He was descended from the hated peasant class; his father was a self-taught peasant-poet. Though his family had made their way to the city, from an early age Leonov strongly identified with the woods and their promise of protection and escape. He spent the happiest days of his childhood near a forest populated by towering old-growth trees. As a young man he lived in Arkhangelsk, where he worked with his father as a journalist. Father and son were both socialists, but of the agrarian, Socialist Revolutionary variety. Both men published writings critical of the Bolsheviks during the Russian Civil War. Heirs to the Narodniki, who had "gone to the people," the Socialist Revolutionaries hoped to redistribute the land to the peasants. After the Bolsheviks took control, many SRs were imprisoned or forced to emigrate. One, Fanny Kaplan, tried to assassinate Lenin in 1918. This meant that Leonov's past involvement with the SRs was a dangerous liability.

But Leonov was soon even more severely compromised. When the White Army took Arkhangelsk, Leonov was apparently forced by the anti-Bolshevik Whites to enter a school for young officers.[5] After the Reds conquered the city and consolidated power, Leonov switched sides with alacrity. Still, it is a miracle that he survived. He would have been shot for his service with the Whites if not for a kind woman who deleted his name from a list of former White officers. Instead, he became one of early Soviet literature's brightest stars, rising to the peak of the literary hierarchy. For the rest of his life, he would live under a secret, suspended death sentence. Though he tried to hide his ambivalence, he was never a wholehearted supporter of the Soviet project. He was, after all, a peasant's son who loved the woods.

From the beginning of Leonov's career, the forest appeared in his work as a place of refuge from political conflict. His first published story, "Buryga," was about a *leshii* who is driven out of the forest by unbelievers and axes, and ends up living in exile, in a doghouse. The tale expressed deep ambivalence about the Soviet project to domesticate the forest—to put it in the doghouse. In Leonov's 1923 poem "A Note on Birchbark," young people escape in wartime to the northern boundary of tundra, swamp, and forest. After being conscripted into anti-Bolshevik forces, they escape into the pine forest, building a simple, idyllic house surrounded by flowering rowanberry and white strawberries with translucent flowers. In Leonov's first novel, 1924's

Badgers, characters hide from the Revolution in the forest with a band of deserters and bandits. They are called "badgers" because they live underground. The anti-communist peasants evoke the long history of Russian peasant rebels who found refuge in the forest.

As Stalin consolidated power, Leonov moved toward political orthodoxy. If he wanted to publish and to survive, he had no choice. When a new Union of Soviet Writers was formed in 1929, Leonov was chosen as its first president. Like Andrei Platonov, Leonov made trips to sites of industry such as factories and newly collectivized farms.[6] His 1930 novel *The Sot*, informed by real-life visits, is a "production novel" about a paper mill being built on the banks of the Sot River in Karelia, the setting of Platonov's "Among Animals and Plants." The mill's director dreams of converting the pine forests into "rivers of newsprint."[7] Trees will be transmuted into human ideas.

The Sot celebrates the construction of the mill, because industrial celebration was obligatory in such works. But Leonov's grief at the violence done to nature seeps out from between the lines. The opening paragraphs of *Sot* are not a celebration of muscular young workers or whirring turbines but a description of an elk drinking from a sweet stream, "gorged with happiness." A *leshii*, a gnarled old man with telltale too-long arms, emerges from behind a tree, listening to "the deafening racket of life awakening." He is frightened off by the smell of sulfur, a byproduct of paper production. The forest darkens and the birds fall silent.[8] When Leonov describes the beauty of the forest and the river, his regret at industrialization is obvious, his love for nature unmistakable. He was reluctant to sign on to the avant-garde eagerness to treat the whole nonhuman world as an instrument for human gain. *The Sot* sold well and earned positive reviews, but Leonov's skepticism attracted negative attention. By 1930, even subtle dissent was dangerous. By defending the forest, Leonov was risking his career.

Unlike many of his peers, Leonov survived political attacks on him during the Great Terror of the 1930s. It was a time when anyone could be arrested after a wrong word or a denunciation from a jealous colleague, hostile neighbor, or friend seeking to save themselves.

But despite his doubts about the Soviet project, Leonov was adept at navigating the treacherous waters of Stalinist cultural politics, and his literary success insulated him from criticism. Early in his career, he had been endorsed by Gorky, the "dean" of Russian literature, who told Stalin that Leonov had "the right to speak on behalf of Russian literature."[9] For Stalin, a former aspiring poet, a literary gift was sacred. Gorky's praise for Leonov would act as a kind of protective talisman even after Gorky's death in 1936.[10]

Leonov also had the right temperament for survival under a whimsical despot. Unlike the passionate, impulsive, unstable Osip Mandelstam, Leonov was restrained, discreet, and willing to reproduce the required dogma, at least superficially. By 1946, he was a patriarch of Russian literature—Gorky's heir. But harassment from fellow writers took a toll on his work, and he found himself unable to write fiction. During this unhappy time, he found refuge in the question of the management of Russia's trees. In 1947, he published an article that elicited a flood of correspondence on the profligate treatment of Russian forests. When the article was read aloud at the meeting of the board of a forestry agency, it prompted energetic debate.

The avid response to Leonov's article confirmed the desire for a collective effort to save Russia's trees, just after a war that had killed a large proportion of its men. Leonov helped to establish multiple societies to protect forests and natural resources in Russia and in Georgia, which he had visited several times. He formed close relationships with forestry professors, one of whom would become the model for the hero of his next novel—*The Russian Forest.* The diligent and well-connected Leonov ordered up masses of books and journals and assimilated them with remarkable thoroughness.

Based on years of Leonov's historical and scientific research, *The Russian Forest* tells the story of the woods and the nation from the early days of Slavic civilization. *The Russian Forest* was Leonov's first novel published in two decades. With all mentions of Stalin removed, it won the 1957 Lenin Prize. But it came into the world at a moment when the forest was no longer a priority for the highest levels of the Russian government. "Not all trees are useful," Khrushchev warned Leonov. "From time to time the forest must be thinned."[11] Still, the story of the Russian forest pleased the authorities. Soviet policy matched print runs to official approval, and more than a million copies of the novel were printed in the twelve years after it was first published. It was also adapted for the radio and stage.[12]

The novel's hero is a forestry professor named Ivan Vikhrov, who is at odds with another forestry professor, Gratsiansky, a villain who cares little for trees and is only motivated by the desire for power. Their opposition gives Leonov an opportunity to recount many of the major debates in Soviet forestry and Soviet science. The third major character is Vikhrov's daughter, Polya, who at first believes Gratsiansky's slanderous attacks on her father. She is a classic socialist realist heroine: brave, wholesome, and ardently Communist. The novel's primary plot line takes place during the Second World War, and Polya's foray across German lines provides Leonov with a classic war story that gives cover to the novel's more controversial environmental and political elements. When Polya and her father reconcile, progressive, conservationist approaches to forestry are symbolically fused to triumphant postwar patriotism.

Through flashbacks to Vikhrov's earlier life, Leonov's novel also tells the story of Russia's forests from the end of the nineteenth century through World War II. These passages are the ones that hold the greatest interest for today's readers. Despite their strong ideological slant, they offer a lively historical portrait based on Leonov's comprehensive research as well as his own experience. As a peasant boy in the countryside, the young Vikhrov witnesses the prerevolutionary destruction of Russia's forests. In the process, he finds his vocation as a forest defender, and learns to recognize the central importance of forests to the Russian national idea.

In one of the novel's most vivid scenes, the young Vikhrov watches with horror as an army of drunken peasants descends on the forest where he loves to roam. They are destroying their own historical livelihood, on the orders of a predatory merchant who plans to sell the magnificent old-growth trees for cheap timber. Leonov imagines the forest as an army that stands its ground for two days, seeming to bring up fresh troops every night. But on the third day, the forest begins to fall to the axe. The war imagery is especially striking in a novel written so soon after the worst war in Russia's history. Leonov took deforestation seriously.

When the loggers reach a huge, ancient tree that shelters the source of the local river, a *leshii*-like old man who lives there warns of the consequences of their actions: "You'll have a summer without clouds, and sometimes a winter without snow, and folks will curse the sun. . . . And when you've cut down the last tree in Russia's forests, then, my dears, you'll be going to foreign lands for your bread."[13] Deforestation will imperil agriculture, cause droughts, and compromise national self-sufficiency and the whole Russian way of life. The old man is right about much of the science. He is also channeling the values of the Soviet 1950s, fusing socialist ideals with a celebration of Russia's national spirit and self-sufficiency.

Through Vikhrov and his travels, we see the panicked deforestation that preceded the revolution in northwestern Russia, as landowners and peasants rushed to sell anything that would raise cash. A deforested Russia is hurtling to disaster. Logging leads to drought, which causes fire and famine. "Clad in the glow of forest fires, Russia was entering the twentieth century," Leonov writes. Pillars of blue smoke march across the land like supernatural armies, stepping over the rivers. The coastal forests of Arkhangelsk are "wrapped in crimson gloom," the Vistula River flows under a film of ash, and the Siberian taiga smolders.[14]

The apocalyptic fire—which might also be read, between the lines, as the revolution itself—threatens to engulf commerce, agriculture, and even civilization. Boats risk being set alight by the burning shores. Old ladies stand with icons as young people try to beat out flames with fir branches, and a priest sprinkles holy water in the direction of the flames. And yet Russians are dreadfully slow to understand the disaster going on before their eyes. Both private owners and the state continue to cut down trees. This happens even in Shipov, the grove protected by Peter the Great, and in the "denuded, ravished" Tula *zaseki* that Tolstoy hoped to replant. In Leonov's account, Russia's history and its tradition of self-defense are being annihilated with the forest, the oaks, and the old line of arboreal defense—the same forests that Turgenev and Tolstoy roamed and celebrated.

Other characters in the novel refer to Vikhrov as a *leshii*, with a mixture of admiration and derision. Anticipating recent ideas of granting citizenship to nonhuman entities like rivers, Vikhrov espouses the idea that the "forest should be granted the same rights of citizenship as other sources of public welfare."[15] Indeed, the forest is the most engaging character in this uneven, overstuffed novel. Nodding lungwort, a golden carpet of lesser celandine, pale green clusters of rockfoil, "blue eyes of newly blossoming hepatica whose eyelashes fluttered almost imperceptibly," and coltsfoot blossoming "among the purplish shadows of still bare branches" are more compelling than most of *The Russian Forest*'s people.[16] Vikhrov keeps polished slabs of different tree species on his bookshelves—they can easily be mistaken for books. In Leonov's world, trees are knowledge; trees are art; trees are people, or something better. Retreating from the dilemmas and strictures of Soviet life into the forest, the author sometimes seems tempted to abandon humanity entirely.

Above all, trees are protection. Leonov makes a quick cut from forest fires to a scene in which Vikhrov's daughter Polya extinguishes incendiary German bombs on Moscow rooftops. Deforestation, forest fires, and Nazi invasion are grouped together as existential threats. Later in the novel, like a real-life partisan, Polya finds a measure of safety in the welcoming forest. When she volunteers for a dangerous mission crossing enemy lines to her home village, the trees of her native region shelter her. Their arboreal guidance clearly evokes the invisible presence of the *leshii*, as if that familiar folkloric creature has forgotten his grievances at the advent of Christianity and returned as a Russian patriot. As Polya dodges Nazis in the woods, she catches sight of something big and shaggy "nodding after her from under a snowy, swinging paw."[17]

Despite the forest's interventions, Polya is captured. During her interrogation, she cannot conceal her patriotism and reveals herself in an angry tirade: "It's easy enough to kill me. You'll pluck me, a single pine needle, from the tree, but look how many will remain."[18] Here, Russians are pictured as constituent parts of a single tree, which is in turn part of a forest. Leonov has too accurate a knowledge of science to imagine, like the charlatan Trofim Lysenko, that forests and farmland can find common cause against the enemy steppe. But he does use trees as tropes of collectivity and signs of the power of society, as of nature, to cooperate and regenerate. Leonov succeeds in reimagining the old wood goblin of folklore as a socialist patriot.

This is a vision of the collective in which humans and trees cooperate: Polya's native forest contributes to the war effort by helping with her mission. *The Russian Forest* explicitly rejects the Soviet fantasy that nature can be subjugated and reduced to a machine that serves human ends. It also criticizes the politically motivated attacks on science that ran rampant under Stalin, reaching their apotheosis with Lysenko. In the novel, Vikhrov has been vilified for writing a long, dense book, a "poem on the bitter fate of the forest" that denounces the "vulgar formula which understood the forest and the tree as factory and worker producing timber."[19] Spurious political campaigns have attacked him for associations with class enemies and for corruption, all as a cover for personal enmity or rivalry. The disputes bear a close resemblance to real-life Soviet scandals.

With a delicacy refined by decades of experience negotiating Stalinism, Leonov points to the similarity between capitalism and communism: Both share a commitment to the high-intensity exploitation of nature, with little concern for the cost. In this sense, the ambitious but destructive Western and Soviet visions of modernity stand on the same side, though they are often taken as enemies. Leonov counters them with a more balanced vision of national rootedness and solidarity, one that proceeds at a pace that allows trees as well as people to thrive. Part of the hubris of the modernizers was to believe that they could realize their grand projects in the lifetime of human beings.

Against this, *The Russian Forest* embraces a more-than-human sense of time, making an argument for forestry's inherently socialist qualities. In one scene, Vikhrov reflects on why forestry does not fit into the Soviet timeframe, or into its idealization of boldness and valor. Medicine, mining, hydropower, agriculture, warfare, and technological inventions make great leaps in a matter of years. Forestry, on the other hand, is bound to the lifespan of trees, which is often measured in centuries. Foresters rarely die a hero's death. And the best approaches to the forest are the ones that take the longest view; the logic of the five-year plan can only bring the forest's downfall.

Though he believes that forestry must reject the Soviet ideals of heroic martyrdom and breakneck speed, Vikhrov makes the case that forestry is a quiet but essential manifestation of socialist cooperation. Forestry embodies the spirit of collective achievement and socialist concern for future generations. We might say that sustainable forestry is a form of mutual aid, which Kropotkin characterized at the beginning of the twentieth century as an essential ingredient in evolutionary success—whether for people, animals, or insects. According to Vikhrov, the forest is also the one truly socialist national resource: Unlike minerals hidden and locked underground, the forest is open wide, available to all.

The Russian Forest articulates a distinctly socialist ethos of forest defense. But Leonov's myth of the Russian forest is also deeply national. It is important that this is the *Russian* forest, not the *Soviet* one. This emphasis on Russian identity is an essential part of the novel's appeal to subsequent generations of eco-nationalist writers. The book's centerpiece is a nearly book-length lecture Vikhrov gives to incoming students at his university. In it, he echoes the rhetoric of Stalin's Great Plan, describing the forest as the first obstacle in the path of "molten human lava" from Asia. In his view, only the forest and the will of the Russian people can save Russia from conquest.[20] By this logic, the loss of trees is not a problem confined to the environment; it has broad implications for Russian liberty. Vikhrov argues that when forests fell in the nineteenth century, the country was exposed to invasion by alien species. Green Russia risked becoming hot, dry, and Asian:

> Sandstorms were knocking at the gates of Ryazan like a crowd of yellow ghosts from the past, while the salt marshes, the wormwood, and all kinds of devilish, prickly undergrowth, in addition to what the Mongolian cavalry had brought on its hooves and in its manes, crept forth from beyond the Caspian bent on conquest. Over three and a half million hectares of land were overrun by shifting sands in the Astrakhan River during the last century. The Don and the Dnieper were becoming steppe dwellers, and once-meek brooks burst their dams in the spring, but at the height of the summer they hibernated, timidly burying themselves in the sand like Asiatic lizards.[21]

The racism and xenophobia here are blatant. This passage exemplifies the nationalist environmentalism that was rising in Leonov's day and that finds intense expression in many countries around the world today, when immigrants are compared to invasive species that upend local ecosystems.

"In the ancient struggle between forest and steppe," Vikhrov warns, "man has been taking an active part on the side of the latter." By cutting down its forests, Russia is destroying itself. Though Leonov's book was the subject of acrimonious debates among Soviet writers as well as Soviet foresters, Vikrov's speech was met with unanimous enthusiasm.[22] Leonov's account of the history of the forest and its importance in Russian life was a comprehensive fusion of real history, Russian cultural myths, the nationalist view of forest and soil, and early Cold War xenophobia. The forest was Russia's god, Russia's home, and Russia's hero.

After *The Russian Forest* won the Lenin Prize in 1957, Leonov had even greater latitude for his environmental activities. The once-prolific writer hardly published anything literary for the remainder of his life.

Forests had allowed him to return to art one last time, with his literary monument to Russia's trees. Now environmental activities took the place of literature in his life. A deputy to the Supreme Soviet, he met often with forestry workers, initiated inquiries, and worked to save thousands of trees.[23] A new, post-Stalinist generation was taking the stage, and Leonov's literary oeuvre was fading into irrelevance. But his voice as an environmentalist remained powerful. In the Khrushchev and Brezhnev years, as environmental concerns mounted, *The Russian Forest* provoked thousands of admiring letters.[24]

Once an acclaimed "engineer of the human soul," now Leonov was a forest guardian. His vision of Russia's wooded lands as a repository of Russian memory was taken up by the next generation of ecologically conscious, nationally oriented Russian writers. They would view literature as a means of protecting Russian nature—and the Russian soul along with it.

CHAPTER 12

The Tsar-Larch and the Flood

The taiga is the law, and the bear is its prosecutor. (Old proverb)[1]

—Andrei Sinyavsky

In Siberia, there had never been any "forest question" or need for afforestation. By the mid-twentieth century, the forests of the conquered half-continent still seemed limitless, despite the Siberian smoldering that Leonov described. And the dense forests of northern Asia were still hiding hidden treasure: not fur this time, but gold and diamonds. Foresters, whose work revolved around growth cycles that were often longer than human lives, had little chance of fitting the mold of the Soviet hero. The geological cycles that produce minerals are so slow that they are hard for a human being to comprehend. But the moment of discovery of gold or diamonds was a perfect climax for an adventure story. In the 1950s and 1960s, geologists became a new breed of Soviet hero.

Natural resources are valued by all countries, but the USSR's simultaneous geopolitical isolation and high-speed industrialization demanded especially vigorous use of its vast natural resources. As Stalin put it in 1931, "We are fifty to one hundred years behind the most advanced countries. We must cover this distance in ten years, or we will be crushed."[2] The forest had to be exploited at high speed, and so did the minerals buried under the trees, in the tundra, and under the sea. Oil and gas were power; gold was wealth; diamonds were essen-

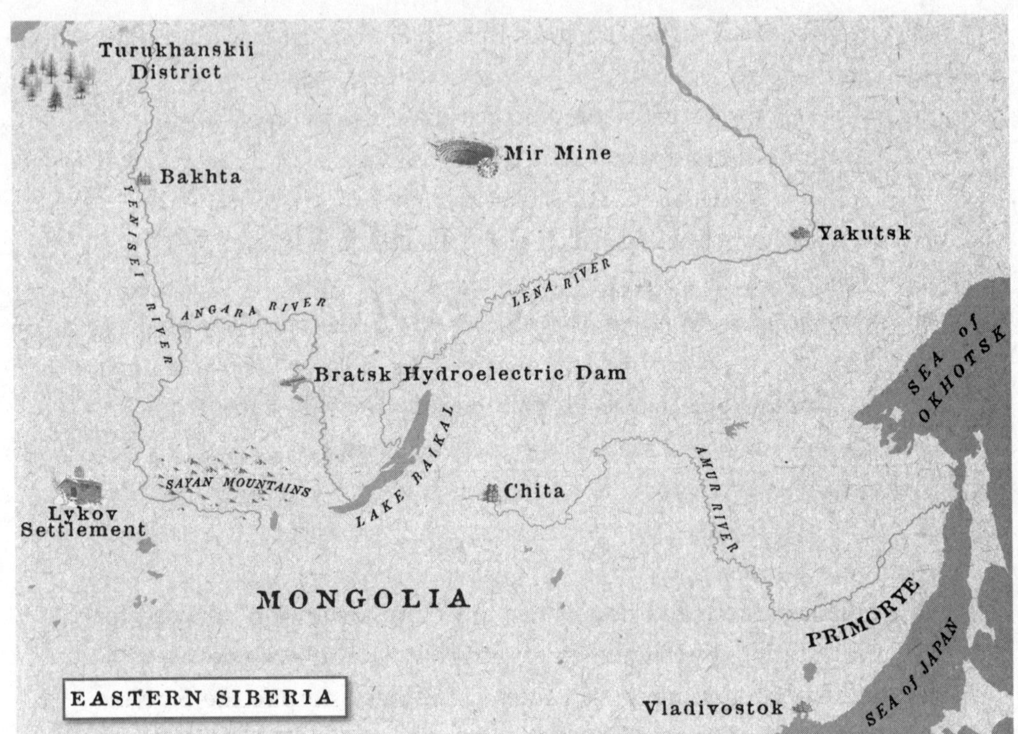

tial for industrial and scientific equipment, including the technology needed to explore outer space. Soviet rhetoric portrayed nature as a "senseless emptiness" filled with riches. Geologists were the fairytale heroes who triumphed over the monstrous wilds to find buried treasure, thereby giving those riches sense and purpose. They kissed the taiga and woke it from its slumber.[3]

Soviet geology was alluring and even sexy because of the adventure involved, the possibility of great fame and (relative) riches, and because of its promise of escape. Geologists risked starvation, malnutrition, illness, and frostbite. They had memorable and sometimes dangerous encounters with locals: Siberian settlers and workers, Indigenous people who served as essential guides, and escaped or recently released Gulag prisoners, not to mention bears. Geology was romantic, a quest in the forest and fog. And becoming a geologist or simply joining an expedition was a way of retreating to the freedom of nature, a reversion to "taiga laws" rather than the repressive surveillance of the Soviet state. In the forest, mutual reliance and hospitality were central values. Snitching was forgotten, at least most of the time. As the historian Alla Bolotova puts it, "nature was not simply the 'house of treasures' that official rhetoric cherished but also an archipelago of freedom."[4]

The association between geology and freedom was tinged with irony; geology and the Gulag archipelago were closely linked. Geologists located precious deposits that would later be mined by prisoners, many of whom died in the process. Several of Shalamov's *Kolyma Tales* feature geologists and the search for precious minerals. Sometimes Gulag prisoners dug trenches for geologists, and former prisoners were occasional employees in geology expeditions. NKVD employees guarding prisoners helped geologists with logistics. Many geologists encountered tramps—Gulag escapees who had become hunter-fisher-gatherers.

This was the experience of a young Andrei Tarkovsky. He had started his academic career as a student of Arabic and Eastern Studies, but soon decided that he preferred to study his own country's nature and its life. His mother, meanwhile, was eager to keep him out of trouble and away from the other young men in their neighborhood. In May 1953, Tarkovsky departed on a geological expedition searching for diamonds in Turukhanskii District, in the Kureika basin, near the Yenisei River, almost as far north as Norilsk. He later claimed to have traveled a hundred kilometers on foot in the taiga—a manageable ten-day trek in a more temperate zone, but an impressive achievement in northern Siberia. In his free time, he sketched the forest, developing a visual vocabulary of towering trees, dense understory, and glittering, powerful rivers that would suffuse his cinematic work.[5]

After Stalin's death in March 1953, there was a mass amnesty of Gulag prisoners. The terms of the amnesty and Soviet sentencing standards meant that many political prisoners remained in the camps, while ordinary criminals were set free. The mighty Yenisei River was afloat with commandeered vessels carrying recently released criminals making their way back to civilization—something like pirate ships.[6] The newly free people had to rely on their wits to survive, which often meant stealing. Some committed gruesome crimes. In one case, a group raped all the women in a train car.[7] Now the greatest danger in the taiga was not frost or mosquitoes, bears or wolves, but ex-convicts. As Arsenyev had observed in *Dersu Uzala*, the most frightening encounter in the taiga is with a man, not a bear. Tarkovsky was lucky. When he ran into some ex-prisoners in the forest, he was merely robbed.

This element of danger did not detract from Tarkovsky's pleasure in his adventure. The proximity of mortality was part of the thrill of a geological expedition, a spur to the imagination of a future professional storyteller.

Tarkovsky liked to tell an anecdote about riding a horse into the taiga and getting caught in a storm. He found a cottage and lay down in some hay in the corner. As he began to fall asleep, thunder growled, lightning flashed, and a voice said: "Get out of there!" He ignored it and turned onto his other side. He heard the voice again: "Get out of there!" When the voice rang out a third time, he took his backpack and hurried out. At that moment a huge larch snapped like a match and crushed the cottage.

This was a fantasy. As his sister explained when recounting the tale in 2012, no one was allowed to go to the taiga alone. But Tarkovsky himself seemed to believe it. This was his own encounter with a benevolent forest spirit who had intervened to save his life. The three warnings mark the story as a fairytale; perhaps it was the *leshii* who saved him.

Soviet geologists spent two decades searching for diamonds in central Siberia. The first tantalizing traces were found in Yakutia in 1953 by a geologist named Larisa Popugaeva.[8] In the summer of 1955, a sunny young woman named Ekaterina Elagina was one of three geologists on a follow-up expedition in the deep reaches of the taiga. Elagina describes in her memoirs how her team was accompanied by Indigenous guides and helpers. The leader was an experienced reindeer herder and hunter in late middle age, Innokentii Ievlev. The helpers were two younger men, a Yakut named Grigory Gerasimov and a worker named Serafim Zhukov, who had served in the navy during the war. (Elagina does not specify Ievlev or Zhukov's ethnic origins.)

Elagina and her team arrived on site in June, when patches of black snow were still visible and puddles of meltwater hid the ground. Her memoir evokes the ecstatic, fleeting beauty of the taiga's fast-forward summer. Swollen buds crackle as they open, their blossoms forming ethereal clouds among unfurling leaves, but after just a few days the leaves thicken into a dense green storm, the blossoms disappear, and mosquitoes swarm. Elagina recalls how she and her fellow geologists were dizzy with the heady resin of the reawakening trees, exulting in the pure air and the white nights.

One evening in early June, Elagina's colleague Iurii Khabardin was delighted to catch a big taimen—one of the huge, delectable salmonids of the Siberian rivers—for their dinner. The third geologist on the team, the usually taciturn assistant Vladimir Avdeenko, returned late, looking "like a sparrow puffed up in the cold," with a mysterious smile. After much questioning, he explained, stuttering as he spoke, that on his walk upriver he had discovered a diamond. Though he had never seen one before, he was certain. As Elagina puts it, "These wonderful crystals have a distinctive, unmistakable oily shine." Avdeenko pulled a packet from his pocket and revealed a diamond that sparkled so intensely that Elagina felt she might go blind, awed by its perfect facets.[9]

On June 13, after the geologists had spent thirteen hours fighting with prickly bushes, they found the diamond "pipe" itself at the base of a large tree whose roots had been laid bare by a landslide. Among the gnarled coils, they saw the eerie turquoise of kimberlite, an igneous rock that often hosts diamonds, and the purple-red gleam of the mineral pyrope, which is frequently found alongside them.[10] It was as if the tree had handed them a clue. The mine established to exploit the diamond pipe soon became one of the largest manmade holes on the planet.

The USSR had the diamonds it craved for its industrial and technological development. But the geologist-heroes did not always benefit from these discoveries. Their careers often ended in disappointment or even tragedy. Khabardin received an award, but the female geologists who had been involved in the discovery of Yakutia's diamonds were written out of the story and even driven out of the profession, with men given the credit. Larisa Popugaeva, who had a dangerous illegal abortion in order to go on the expedition in which she made the initial discovery of diamonds, referred to the discovery for the rest of her life as "the fuck-up." Rival geologists kidnapped her and held her hostage until she signed doctored papers that would allow them to claim credit for discovering the first kimberlite pipe. Natalya Kind, who had helped identify the site where diamonds were found, became a dissident, sending Shalamov and Solzhenitsyn's manuscripts to the West for illicit publication.[11] The Indigenous people who assisted in the discovery were never recognized. Only Elagina's memoir even names them. Hoping to right this injustice, the son of Grigory Gerasimov, the Yakut helper, called into Putin's "open line" program in 2016 and asked that his father be recognized as the discoverer of the diamond.[12]

The "Mir" pipe became an immense wound in the planet's surface. The earth's treasure chest had been pried open at a terrible cost. The mine created a toxic lake at the bottom of an enormous funnel-like open pit, and this poisoned lake contaminated the aquifer that fed the rivers. Fish like the taimen disappeared, and locals developed stomach cancer. A Yakut village was flooded to make a hydroelectric power station for the mine. In 2017, after the open pit mine had been replaced by an underground one, the lake burst into the shafts, drowning eight workers. The earth reclaimed its riches. Diamonds worth up to $14 billion were buried in the accident.[13]

Even in the 1950s, some Soviet artists recognized the tragic fate that often awaited the geologist hero. In Mikhail Kalatozov's 1959 film *Letter Never Sent* which was based on a true story, a helicopter drops three geologists and their guide into a river valley in the central Siberian taiga. Like Elagina and her team, they are searching for diamonds. The film is prefaced by a dedication to the Soviet pioneers who have risked their lives to explore both the wilds and the cosmos. At this moment in Soviet history, geologists were almost equal in stature to cosmonauts. The death toll among geologists was higher.

The opening shot of *Letter Never Sent* is from the perspective of the helicopter. The scientists wave happily as they shrink to insignificance against the sandy ground. The cinematographer, Sergei Urusevsky, was one of the great camera-poets of the Soviet Union. The film is a hymn to the forest and river, to the play of light on diamond-bright water and the shadows cast by moving branches. As the geologists climb up a mountain, we see the beautiful, cat-eyed young scientist Tania against a skewed backdrop of endless conifers: a cipher of infinity. Diagonal camera angles capture precarious branches, reminding us that disaster is always nearby.

The geologists are intent on wresting out the taiga's secrets. But dig-

The geologists set out. Still from *Letter Never Sent*. *Mosfilm*

ging up the earth invites punishment. They discover diamonds when the summer is almost over. Their anxiety gives way to manic excitement; they seem to sense that disaster is approaching. That night they are awoken by a forest fire. The film was shot during real forest fires, with real blazing trees falling. The actors, who spent eight months in the taiga, were glad to escape from the shoot with their lives.[14]

At the end of the film, only the leader survives, his frost-rimed, unconscious body found floating down the river on a log—the dead tree that saved him. This was the Soviet equivalent of a Hollywood ending; the real-life expedition that inspired the film had no survivors.[15] The final shot, zooming away along the shining river, echoes the opening of the film. But this one is not from the perspective of a helicopter. It leaves the lone survivor and his rescuers in the distance, fading into obscurity in the taiga. The camera is nature's eye. Man has won this battle, but only barely.

Letter Never Sent was a dark look at geology with close parallels—artistic, visual, and philosophical—to Tarkovsky's terrifying account, in *Ivan's Childhood*, of World War II. Kalatozov had imagined a supernatural rescue from death in the taiga; many Soviet geologists were not so lucky. Hero-pioneers often ended up dead. Over the next decades, more Soviet writers and artists would examine the costs of exploiting Siberia's riches. They deplored the environmental and human harms caused by extraction and industry, but above all they bemoaned the harm done to Russia's national identity as the taiga was pillaged. From their work grew a new strain of Russian eco-nationalism.

In an essay celebrating his native Siberia, Valentin Rasputin describes a fire much less terrifying than the one that threatens the geologists in *Letter Never Sent*. "The forests blaze," he writes, "burning low, for a long time, inflamed with a broad scattering of fall colors that are especially pure and radiant here, filling the air to a considerable height with their iridescence." Fire words, he explains, are inevitable in any description of natural beauty in Siberia, which hurries through its brief seasons of blossoming in a conflagration of life. In July, when Siberian globe flowers—in Russian, "little fires"—bloom, "the clearings in the taiga light up with a lush, festive glow, and nothing can dispel the impression that they give off a heat you can feel."[16]

Rasputin, who was born in 1937, was one of the most famous writers of the "Village Prose" movement, which emerged in the early 1960s. Rather than celebrating industrialization and the Soviet remolding of society, these writers lamented the toll that Soviet progress had taken on rural communities and on the environment. They abhorred the man-made floods and toxic sludge of Soviet hydroelectric plants and mines.

Leonov's *The Russian Forest*, with its ecological concerns, helped break the path for them. Rasputin considered Leonov a master, calling him a giant of Russian literature. For him, the "wise and kind" *Russian Forest* placed Leonov in the ranks of Turgenev and Tolstoy. He loved the book for defending Russia's culture along with its trees.[17] Through literature and later through his involvement in politics, Rasputin protested new engineering projects that would harm forests, rivers, and lakes in his beloved Siberia. Avant-garde writers had once celebrated the subjugation of Soviet waterways to human will. Rasputin and Leonov took part in a successful campaign against the diversion of rivers, helping to bring an end to the Soviet dream of total mastery over the environment.[18]

Long before twenty-first-century Siberian wildfires that released thousands of megatons of carbon dioxide into the atmosphere, before illegal logging sent Siberian forests to Chinese mills and Swedish furniture makers, Rasputin sounded the alarm about the destruction of Siberia's forests. Using a phrase that is now more associated with the Amazon rainforest, he called the taiga "the lungs of the planet." For him, Siberia promised salvation in an age of environmental degradation—an almost sacred source of clean air, clean water, and fertile land.[19] Unchecked logging and fires signified for him the carelessness with which the Soviets had treated the earth.

As if environmental degradation was not enough, the systematic

Soviet destruction of old social structures—notably the Russian village—meant that ordinary people were left without the means to organize themselves locally to prevent disasters. In Rasputin's short story "The Fire," residents of a corrupt, slovenly logging town in Siberia rush to save the precious food in a warehouse from fire. Their efforts are hindered by rampant criminality, alcoholism, and looting—endemic in a dead-end place that exists only to despoil the taiga. The settlement has no community, no traditions, no roots in the land, no pride. For Rasputin, environmental, social, and spiritual harms were inextricably linked.

In his later years, Rasputin became notorious for his Russian chauvinism, a common vice among the Village Prose writers. But his fiction is remarkable for its distinctly Siberian blend of Russian Orthodoxy and pre-Christian animism. Earth and God are almost interchangeable. In "The Fire," a man supervising the emergency response is murdered by drunken thugs, killing one of them before he dies. Afterward, the story's elderly protagonist retreats to the forest. As he walks, he reflects that the earth "that brings forth the righteous and the guilty" will be the one to judge the two dead men. The old man finds comfort in young pine trees awoken by spring, in the thought of the "green wares" that will soon appear, waiting to be harvested. He finds a rhythm in his steps and his breath. The sound of a woodpecker seems to be his own heart beating "with gratitude and impatience." As the story ends, he wonders how long the earth will continue to be silent.[20] Earth is God, and it will surely punish man for his trespasses.

Rasputin's masterpiece, the 1976 novel *Farewell to Matyora*, concerns a Siberian village on an island that will soon be drowned by a hydroelectric dam. The story is inspired by the real-life flooding of Rasputin's home village during the construction of the Bratsk hydroelectric dam and reservoir, which were completed in 1967. This was a trauma he would never forget, the inspiration for his entire oeuvre. Many years later, he wrote, "Whenever I experience something akin to prayer, I see myself on the banks of the old Angara River, which no longer exists, alongside my native village of Atalanka, the islands across the way, and the sun setting beyond the opposite bank."[21]

Farewell to Matyora's elderly heroine, Darya, tells a young man named Andrei, "We're all like migratory birds. This land belongs to everyone—those who were here before us and those who will come after. We're only on it for a tiny time." To this, Andrei replies, "Man is king of nature." In a typical novel of the Stalinist era, Andrei would have been the hero who persuades the elderly people to accept the glory of modern machines and embrace the bright industrial future. But this is another kind of novel. Darya scoffs. "Yes, yes, king. Just reign a bit and you'll be sorry," and she is indisputably correct. In Rasputin's world, nature reigns over man, just as God does—since nature and God are interchangeable.[22] For Rasputin, Soviet modernization's disruption of cyclical time was an apocalypse, not a utopia.

Early Soviet novels and films celebrated any step taken in the name of Lenin's vaunted "electrification of the entire country." Writers like Platonov saw machines as a kind of poetry; he and many of his contemporaries depicted hydroelectric dams and similar feats of engineering as triumphs that would bring modernity, prosperity, and glory to the Soviet people. Rasputin turns this narrative upside down. In *Farewell to Matyora*, the construction of the dam means a biblical flood. At least in Genesis there was Noah's ark; in Rasputin's world, the Soviet flood means a definitive rupture in the cycles and memories that have sustained human and nonhuman existence since the beginning of time.

Like one of Shalamov's Gulag larches, the village of Matyora has survived for hundreds of years, watching the panorama of Siberian history. But while Shalamov's long-lived larch was a counterpoint to the lives lost in the Gulag, a keeper of memory, Matyora is dying like a "half-chopped tree" that has lost its roots.[23] The villagers have been offered the chance to live in modern apartment buildings in the nearest town, to have miraculous modern conveniences like faucets with cold and even hot water, toilets, and what one villager describes as a special faucet that makes fire: a gas stove. But many of them feel that, like transplanted trees, they have little hope of survival in a new location.

The novel's central metaphor is the "tsar-larch," so huge that three sets of human arms are needed to surround it. Its crown has been cut off by a storm, but its mighty branches still jut straight out. According to superstition, the tsar-larch anchors the island to the bottom of the river, and Matyora will stand as long as the tree does. This is another moment in which Rasputin embraces pre-Christian traditions. The larch is a version of the "world tree" that connects heaven, earth, and the underworld, and that appears across Indo-European traditions. In Slavic folklore the world tree is an oak, while in Siberia it is more often a larch; the presence of the anchoring tsar-larch reminds us that we are not in the Russian heartland. In his nonfiction writings on Siberia, Rasputin makes clear that he and other Siberians view Russia as a foreign country. They even have a derogatory term for it, *Raseya*, from a verb that means "scattered." While one might consider Russians in Siberia to have been scattered across an alien territory, for Rasputin it is Russian Siberians who are rooted in their land in the traditional way, while European Russians are rootless and disordered.

Over its lifetime, the tsar-larch has made its own version of the earth: "It had dropped so many needles and cones that the earth around it had risen into a light, springy mound from which rose the mighty trunk."[24] The mound evokes the *kholmy*, the burial mounds, of pre-Christian civilizations in the Slavic lands and in Siberia. Until quite recently, the villagers still brought the tsar-larch offerings of food on Easter and other spring holidays. Dogs ate the food, but the villagers continued, because they "felt that if they didn't leave the offerings the larch would be offended." Though Rasputin does not spell it out, offering food to a special tree is another obvious remnant of pre-Christian practices, the kind of paganism that Orthodox colonizers and missionaries once tried to stamp out by cutting down sacred trees.

The survival of such practices is not surprising, given the mixed backgrounds of many Siberians. The saintly Darya is half Buryat, and a character called Tunguska is Evenk—from the group formerly called the Tungus. Tunguska's daughter is the director of the state farm, but Tunguska retains some of her nomadic ways. She does not garden, unlike the other village women, and she does not sit in a chair. Elders like Darya and Tunguska are the keepers of a fragile memory, a tendril connecting them to the nature worship of the past. Food offerings to sacred trees have died out in Matyora, but "respect and fear for the important, masterful tree remained among the old people." The name "tsar-larch," meanwhile, evokes the prerevolutionary past—perhaps going back to the days before Peter the Great, Russia's first self-styled emperor.

The destruction of Matyora is contingent on the destruction of the tsar-larch, but this is no easy task. In a scene with an obvious debt to Leonov's description of the felling of the doomed forest's mightiest pine tree, workers try to chop the tsar-larch down with an axe, but the axe slips and rings on the ancient wood. They pour kerosene on the base, surrounding it with twigs, and light a fire around the trunk. But in the morning the larch still stands, "as though nothing had happened." They try again, making an even bigger fire, but to no avail: "The tree rose above them calmly and majestically, recognizing no power but its own." Like a saint, the larch can be killed again and again without dying. Unmoved, it gazes sternly out at the forest at the end of the island. Or rather at the place where the forest once stood; now there are only "a few green lonely birches and sharp, charred stumps black against the burned-out areas." The tsar-larch is the last survivor on the island, which has been stripped of trees and crops, homes and peoples. Its kingdom is empty.[25]

This is a loss not only of the present but also of the past. The trees have been cut, and so have the crosses on the village graves; the authorities don't want crosses floating down the river while tourists ride through on ships. The desecration of the cemetery is the most painful blow for the villagers, especially the elderly ones. When the flood is imminent, Darya visits her parents' grave in the deep forest. Amid the disturbed soil, the rowan tree she planted still stands. A fir tree has also grown in the days since the burial. The branches of the two trees almost meet above the graves. She finds it "terrible, and sinful, and satisfying" to imagine that the trees are feeding on the bodies of her parents—that her parents are being transubstantiated into another earthly being.[26]

She lies down beside the mound and talks to her parents, promising to see the house off and then join them. It becomes clear that she, like the tsar-larch, will go down with the island. She has a vision of herself standing with her ancestors, and she sees her son, who was killed by a falling tree. Her husband has no grave because he died in the taiga, swallowed by the earth. For Darya's family, death is inseparable from trees. Home is made of trees, too. As the day of the flood approaches, Darya leans against the house, "feeling its worn, raspy, but warm and living wood with her back," and she weeps.[27] She prepares her house for burning (required before the flooding, to prevent debris from floating up into the river) the way she would prepare a corpse for burial.

Farewell to Matyora was made into a film by Larisa Shepitko, director of *The Ascent.* After Shepitko died in a car wreck in 1979, during filming, her husband Elem Klimov finished the movie. The most powerful scene in *The Farewell* is Darya's ritual cleaning of the house, as she scrubs its floors and walls, caresses its surfaces, and garlands it in fresh fir branches—which are used, in Russian tradition, to adorn a grave. Above the house's window lintels and in its corners, Rasputin writes in the novel, the fir releases "the sorrowful aroma of final farewell."[28] The last shot Shepitko filmed before her tragic death was of a tree about to be drowned—a tree of life.

Though Rasputin was critical of damage to Siberia's forests and celebrated their bounty, he was hardly an advocate of rewilding Siberia or leaving it to the Indigenous pastoralists and hunter-fisher-gatherers. He had the settler's belief in the sanctity of agriculture. Given their harsh criticism of the consequences of Soviet policy, the Village Prose writers could easily have been subject to censorship and repression. But during the emergence of Village Prose in the 1960s, its writers were encouraged by the authorities in part because they helped to justify Brezhnev's investments in agriculture.[29] In *Farewell to Matyora*, part of the tragedy of the flood is that the Soviets are burying the black fertile soil of the island.

What matters most in Rasputin's world is the almost mystical bond with the earth and its cycles. The meaning of life is service, and one serves the land by working it. The cycles of life, too, are a kind of agriculture: Darya reflects that "death seems terrible, but it sows the most kind and useful harvest in the souls of the living, and from the seed of mystery and decay develops the seed of life and understanding."[30] The old women who refuse to leave the island dig up the last crop of potatoes even though the potatoes will be drowned with everything else. It is a sin to waste. This is the Christian colonialist aspect of Rasputin's novel.

By the early 1980s, Siberia's landscape faced a threat much more momentous than a dam flooding a few villages. Siberia's seasons were changing as global temperatures increased rapidly. Soviet scientists had contributed substantially to climate science since the 1950s, and the question of anthropogenic warming was not a foreign one in the USSR.[31] Rasputin saw that the Siberian climate had grown more "capricious" in recent decades, with snow melting on New Year's Eve and snowstorms in June. Now he used his concern about climate change, pollution, and food supplies to justify Siberia's colonization by Russia. In a 1987 essay, he wrote that Siberia promised great advantages in the era of climate change. In possession of a realm "capable of existing as a self-sufficient planet," with fertile soil, clean air and water, and abundant forests, "Russians could feel, with justification, that they had fulfilled no small part of their cleansing mission on earth."[32] Rasputin's Russian Siberians have purified the earth by possessing the north Asian land.

At the end of *Farewell to Matyora*, the tsar-larch survives underwater, waiting to be discovered, like the mythical island of Atlantis. Rasputin said in his 1999 speech celebrating Leonov that "the Russian cannot be pulled from the soil."[33] Drowning was only a temporary setback in Russia's messianic mission. A new generation of Russian eco-nationalists took up Rasputin's baton, defending the Siberian taiga and settler culture as they rallied to the cause of the new imperialism; we will meet some of them in chapter 14. But before Putin consolidated power, Russians living through the collapse of the Soviet Union fantasized, as Rasputin had, about a return to village life, deep in the Siberian taiga.

CHAPTER 13

Arks and Anarchists

In the summer of 1978, a team of geologists exploring southern Siberia found something rarer than diamonds. While searching for an appropriate helicopter landing site amid the steep hills and forested canyons of the Western Sayan mountains, their pilot caught sight of what appeared to be a garden, 250 kilometers from the nearest settlement. Hovering as low as he could, he saw a house. No people were visible, but someone was clearly tending the plot. He and his geologist passengers were shocked to find a dwelling in an area long considered too remote for human habitation.

When the four geologists set up camp fifteen kilometers away, it was the mysterious homestead that was first in their mind. Who could live here? Its inhabitants could be the last Mohicans of the Brezhnev era—the Dersus of their time. In his bestselling book about the discovery, Russian journalist Vasily Peskov again echoed Arsenyev's famous, enduring observation: "In the taiga it's less dangerous to run across a wild animal than a stranger."[1]

The geologists ventured to the settlement bearing gifts—and a pistol, just in case. They were greeted by a disheveled old man dressed in patched-up sacking cloth. This was Karp Osipovich Lykov, the patriarch of the family. Inside a tiny, dark cabin, the geologists found Karp's two adult daughters, Natalia and Agafia, weeping and praying. Six kilometers away, by the riverside, lived Karp's two middle-aged sons, Savin and Dmitry. It soon became apparent that none of the members of this aging nuclear family had interacted with outsiders in decades.

None of the Lykov children had ever seen bread. But when the geologists offered them a loaf and some jam, they refused. "We are not allowed that," they said, in a refrain that would become familiar to all their visitors. Natalia and Agafia were hard to understand, not only because of their archaic vocabulary but also because of an odd, chanting cadence that one geologist described as "a slow, blurred cooing."[2]

The Lykovs were Old Believers, members of the Orthodox Christian schismatic sect whose history is deeply bound up with that of the forest and the countryside. The Old Believers emerged in the mid-seventeenth century after Patriarch Nikon, head of the Russian Orthodox Church, amended the liturgy to bring it into harmony with the Greek Orthodox version. The reforms altered the spelling of "Jesus"—at a time when letters were understood as something close to the literal flesh of God—and changed the number of fingers to be raised when making the sign of the cross from two to three. Those who rejected these innovations became known as Old Believers. To the rebels, who soon broke into many different branches, Nikon's reforms were anathema, a betrayal of the true Christianity. Their anger fed on broader social injustices of the era and was further antagonized by the notorious lack of respect for Russian Orthodoxy shown by Peter the Great. A self-consciously Westernizing tsar, Peter preferred the gods Bacchus and Mars.

In the early days of the schism, Old Believers were burned alive, tortured, and imprisoned for their faith. Many were cast into pits in the ground. They believed that they bore a tremendous burden—the preservation of the true words of God—and their extreme ways of living reflected this sense of responsibility. As the whole world fell into sin, they maintained their purity. While they awaited the end of the world, they maintained strict rules about diet (for the Lykovs, no bread or jam), clothing, everyday practices, and the adoption of new technology. Some Old Believers and other religious dissidents resorted to self-immolation. Whole communities locked themselves in their village churches and set them aflame.

Others took refuge in the forest, the safest place to hide from the authorities and preserve their way of life without risk of contamination by the outside world. Many branches of Old Believers were "priestless," meaning that a family could worship without the help of a professional man of God. For the most radical Old Believers, holiness was directly correlated to isolation. The highest holiness was the life of the hermit. In the Bible hermits retreated to the desert; in Russia they retreated to the forest. But they called the forest a desert, deriving the names for hermits and for monasteries from the same word. The forest was the wasteland of holiness, the emptiness of God.

The enlightened Catherine the Great changed course, allowing the Old Believers to practice their faith openly. This led to a split between the Old Believers who wanted to remain "priestless" and those who decided to reenter society. Those who continued to reject the authority of both church and state told stories of a legendary place east of Russia—in Siberia, or perhaps in China—where the old ways had been preserved and the Antichrist could never enter: an Old Believer Shangri-La. Some even traveled to China in search of it.

The nineteenth century saw renewed efforts to force the sectarians into conformity. But a nostalgic fascination also arose around the Old Believers' capacity to preserve a lost past, most often in the forest. Wildly popular, acclaimed, and influential in its time, Pavel Melnikov-Pechersky's novel *In the Forests* was a literary monument to the Old Believers of the nineteenth century. It was stuffed with ethnographic detail and affectionate catalogues of local flora and fauna—for instance, plants with the poetic colloquial names "star-melting" or "white-mustache."

As in Arsenyev's paeans to Dersu Uzala and the Far Eastern forests, there was a bitter irony in the fact that Melnikov-Pechersky became the most famous fiction chronicler of the Old Believers. He was not only a writer but also a bureaucrat responsible for investigating Old Believer sectarianism in Nizhny Novgorod, on the Volga River. Just as

Arsenyev was helping to build the railroads that would destroy Dersu's home forests, Melnikov-Pechersky was studying the Old Believers with the goal of converting them. At first he was loathed by the Old Believers for inspections and raids that broke up Old Believer chapels and monasteries and resulted in arrests and forced conversions to Orthodoxy.[3] He entered their folklore as someone who made a deal with the Devil in exchange for the power to see through walls. But in the late 1850s he dramatically changed his position, eventually advocating for an end to their persecution.[4]

In Melnikov-Pechersky's fiction and in other, similar works of the period, the forest functioned as a timeless space of holy safety for Old Believers and monks in search of God. Though early Orthodox missionaries cut down the sacred trees worshipped by pagans, the trees grew back and granted their protection to persecuted Christian believers. In one scene in *In the Forests*, Melnikov-Pechersky describes how seventeenth-century monks from the besieged Solovki monastery in the Arctic Circle were guided by a floating icon into the forest. Here the taiga was the Russian analogue to the Promised Land of the Old Testament. Melnikov-Pechersky also linked the Old Believers to the Russian myth of the City of Kitezh, a tale about faithful Russians who summoned the divine drowning of their city to save it from Mongol invasion. Kitezh was preserved in Lake Svetlyi Yar, the paradoxically named "Light Ravine," awaiting the arrival of the next world. In a similar fashion, Old Believers would wait in the forest for the end of the world and the arrival of the kingdom of heaven.[5]

In the Forests influenced numerous writers, painters, and musicians, notably the composer Nikolai Rimsky-Korsakov, whose 1907 opera, *The Legend of the Invisible City of Kitezh and the Maiden Fevroniya*, was inspired in part by *In the Forests.* By then there was more sympathy for dissenters. In 1905, Tsar Nicholas II signed a law ending all religious persecution of minorities. This was a short-lived interval of total freedom for Old Believer communities, many of which retreated even farther into the remote forests when the Bolsheviks took control and imposed state atheism.

Until the 1920s, Karp's family had lived peacefully in their Old Believer village in the remote Altai region. This mountainous forested area of southern Siberia, close to the borders with China and Mongolia, was beloved by Old Believers and anyone else who hoped to avoid the authorities. The Lykovs relied on their gardens, crops, and cows, and on hunting and fishing. To avoid contact with sinful civilization, they traded via middlemen who sold their pelts and fish and brought back salt and iron in return. In this, they were not unlike the medieval forest people of Siberia, who traded their forest treasure for other goods. But the natural conditions at the settlement were not ideal—it was too wet and foggy—and there were rumors that the new government was making a list of Old Believers.

The Lykovs and four other families moved farther upriver, to an even wilder area. But this newest settlement was short-lived. In 1931, the Altai Zapovednik, or nature preserve, was created; its area included the new settlement. This made hunting and fishing there illegal. Old Believers were offered jobs on the preserve; if they refused, they were instructed to leave. For years the authorities turned a blind eye to those who refused to comply, but by 1934 the pressure was too great. The Lykovs packed up again.

Flight into the wilderness was the safest refuge from the increasingly violent authorities, who were liable to shoot Old Believers at the first provocation, made plans to wipe out their remote communities, and came looking for their children, hoping to save them from a life lived in taiga isolation. The Old Believers received treatment not unlike that experienced by the Indigenous peoples we encountered in chapter 1. As for Indigenous peoples, the best hope of maintaining a traditional way of life was to retreat to the most inaccessible terrain possible. During World War II, the authorities combed the forest for deserters. But they never found the Lykov family. The deeper in the forest the Old Believers lived, the more holy they could become.

Until the arrival of the geologists in 1978—forty-four years after they left civilization behind—the Lykovs were sighted only once, by a group of tourists floating down the river in 1958. As the tourists passed, they saw Karp fishing, his emaciated wife sitting beside him. They apparently did not call out for help, though Agafia recalled that the family had been surviving on "rowanberry leaf, roots, grass, mushrooms, potato tops, and bark. . . . Every year we held a council to decide whether to eat everything up or leave some for seed." A late hard frost in 1961 had caused a family famine. The Lykovs survived on straw, their leather shoes and ski lining, bark, and birch buds. The matriarch, Akulina, died of hunger. The family had eaten all their rye seeds in their desperation. A single spike grew the next season; they thanked God for a miracle.[6]

When the Lykovs were discovered by the geologists, they were still furious with Patriarch Nikon and Peter the Great. Karp Osipovich called Peter "the Antichrist in human form."[7] Even the recent world wars, known only vaguely to the Lykovs, were the responsibility of the vile Peter. When the geologists explained the story of the Second World War to Karp, he shook his head dolefully and said, "What is this, a second time, and always the Germans. A curse on Peter. He flirted with them."[8]

They had outdone themselves in their rejection of Peter's turn to the West. Agafia, the youngest Lykov, had never seen a wheel. The family made fire with a tinderbox. Their only light was the sun or a torch, and they wore birch bark shoes and lived without salt. The family had begun their time in the forest with carrots, but one year all the seeds were eaten by mice. (The carrot seeds provided by the geologists helped remedy their ghastly white skin, the result of carotene deficiency.) The family subsisted on dried potatoes and pine nuts, stored in birch bark containers, as well as turnips, onions, peas, and rye. Karp Osipovich thanked God for hemp, potatoes, and pine nuts every day. He had overcome the Old Believers' original hatred of potatoes, which had been introduced by Peter the Great and were denounced as "a diabolical, abundant, lecherous plant."[9] The Lykovs were proud of their ability to read their smoke-stained Bible, though it was so thoroughly blackened that the words were no longer visible. Akulina had taught her children to read and write in Old Church Slavonic, using a stick dipped in honeysuckle juice to draw blue letters on birch bark—the same medium used by the medieval people of Novgorod.

Over time, the taiga had become an increasingly important source of calories, as the Lykovs reverted from a primarily agricultural life to one closer to that of Neolithic hunter-gatherers. They drank birch juice and ate wild nettles, wild onions, mushrooms, berries, and fish. Only when they were very lucky did they manage to catch an animal in their primitive pit traps. In late August the whole family climbed Siberian pines, harvesting nuts.

Dmitry was the Dersu of the family. As if channeling Tolstoy and Arsenyev, two authors he had never read, he understood that every animal shared the human desire to live. At the same time, he recognized that he needed to kill animals to survive. He knew all the animal trails and he understood where to dig a snare pit; he was the one who got the first meat for the family, which also meant the first new leather and fur. He tracked Siberian deer and killed them with a pike. He could walk through the snow barefoot and sleep in the forest even in winter, dressed in clothes made from a burlap sack. He brought the others updates about the animals in the taiga, their only substitute for news of the outside world: the grouse whose babies had hatched, the squirrels huddled together against the cold. He made friends with a bear who took up residence nearby.

But when Dmitry came down with pneumonia, his family refused medical help even when it was offered. They were not allowed that. In autumn 1981, Dmitry, Savin, and Natalia all died. Dmitry died of pneumonia. Savin and Natalia's causes of death are obscure; they may have fallen sick because of unfamiliar illnesses introduced by the geologists' visits—another parallel with the experience of Siberia's Indigenous peoples. Now it was only Karp Osipovich and Agafia.

Karp had hoped to find a husband or another companion to live with Agafia. She spent a happy few weeks with her mother's sisters, who invited her to live permanently with them in their village, but she returned to her father in the taiga and remained there even after his death. One distant cousin came and lived with her for a while, and they were married—marriage among priestless Old Believers being an enterprise undertaken purely according to the will of the spouses. But they quarreled about whether to kill a friendly wolf who had befriended Agafia's dog. Agafia felt the wolf was no threat, but her husband disagreed. Soon he returned to town.

On a trip to visit Old Believer nuns a few hundred kilometers away, Agafia stopped in Abakan, a town with apartment buildings. She was dismayed to learn that cooking on a fire in the courtyard was not allowed, and that she had to use the gas fire indoors: a violation of her principles. She was like Dersu in town, cutting down a tree in the park when he needed firewood.

Peskov's first article about the Lykovs, published in 1982, made them celebrities—the late Soviet equivalent of reality TV stars, though far less accessible. Peskov was inundated by letters asking for more news about Karp and Agafia, or sending him gifts and money that he was to bring them on his next visit. By the time his book about them was published in 1992, he had been visiting them once or twice a year for a decade.

The Lykovs held an endless fascination for the Russian public. They were human buried treasure, a time capsule, Russian Rip van Winkles, living exemplars of a Russia that had disappeared long ago. The Lykovs had bypassed Stalin's purges and had hardly noticed the Second World War. At the same time, their experience of starvation resonated with some of the most painful episodes in Soviet history. Millions of peasants had starved to death during Stalin's collectivization of agriculture. During the wartime siege of Leningrad, a whole city had been reduced to boiling shoe leather to survive. Less dramatic forms of deprivation were familiar to almost all readers of Soviet newspapers. The Soviet government had never been good at providing a steady supply of high-quality food, and in the second half of the 1980s ration cards were reintroduced.[10]

Both stunningly exotic and remarkably relatable, the taiga family promised the possibility of living entirely outside corrupt, violent, uncertain modernity, at least for a while, and of preserving an ancient form of Russian tradition. Their story marched in step with Russia's sense of national martyrdom, which stretched back centuries, and with the idea that the more isolated Russia became, the greater its importance in world culture. The perfect emblem of endurance, faith, and self-sufficiency, the Old Believers were like an ark, preserving the essence of Russian culture through a great flood of catastrophe and modernization.

In 1906, a local Russian, when asked by Vladimir Arsenyev how far it was to the next town, replied, "Who knows? Did someone measure the taiga? The forest is what the forest is!"[11] The man was an Old Believer. In the 1980s, Agafia Lykova shared this faith in the taiga's boundlessness. At the end of one visit, when the journalist Peskov was leaving, Agafia filled his pockets with pine nuts for the journey, saying, "The taiga will bear more."[12]

But as Agafia and her father grew older, it became impossible for them to live without help. Dersu could not survive in the taiga when he lost his sight, and neither could elderly people without the assistance of the next generation. The Lykovs grew bolder in their requests of assistance from Peskov, the geologists, and by extension their many admirers throughout Russia. They relaxed their old rules, dressing in the clothes they were given (though only if they were brand-new, used clothes being against the rules because of Old Believers' fear of contamination). They traded candles for flashlights, cleaned the floor and their faces, and installed a hand-crank meat-grinder. They began using enameled pots painted with brightly colored berries.

By the 1990s, the Lykovs were like a museum exhibit, or like former dancing bears moved to a wildlife enclosure. The illusion of wildness was sustained by constant interventions from the outside world. Agafia's friends gave her an SOS button that she could use to summon a helicopter if she became ill, but she began to abuse the privilege. Someone had to explain to her how much it cost to send a helicopter into the taiga. The Russian economy was in tatters, and there was no money left to pay her bills.

As the Lykovs grew more domesticated, much of Russia was being driven back to the land by social and economic turmoil. Gorbachev's perestroika in the second half of the 1980s had been well-intentioned but poorly conceived. Criminals and entrepreneurs (there was often little distinction between the two) had exploited the glaring flaws in the government's economic policies to enrich themselves by gutting state-run enterprises. Acknowledging the failures of the government to provide food for the population, Gorbachev expanded a program that made land available for "allotment gardens," so that anyone who wished could grow their own food.[13]

By the time Yeltsin became president of Russia in 1991, a new class of immensely wealthy, ruthless entrepreneurs was emerging. Yeltsin's policies would accelerate the rise of the men who came to be known as oligarchs. When he lifted price controls, skyrocketing prices left Russians unable to afford basic goods. Every Russian received vouchers that represented their share in the state-run enterprises that were about to be privatized. But most Russians were so desperate for cash or so unaware of the potential value of the vouchers that they sold theirs for a pittance. Most vouchers ended up in the hands of the enterprises themselves. A visitor to a community of Old Believers in the 1990s remarked admiringly that not one of them had received a voucher—they had refused to accept any. After all, they still lived without electricity.[14] Independent of the state, they were invulnerable to its collapse. Here was another aspect of the Lykovs' appeal.

By 1995, the Russian government was out of money and Yeltsin needed funds for his reelection campaign. Through the "loans-for-shares" scheme, he essentially sold off Russia's largest enterprises, including its oil and gas concerns. This cemented the position of the oligarchs, whose payments to Yeltsin bought them both Russia's greatest economic assets and the support of its president. Russia was being sold for parts, the needs of ordinary people forgotten. Orphaned and abandoned children lived in sewers, heroin could be purchased for the price of a beer, and HIV rates skyrocketed among drug users and sex workers. After the 1998 economic crisis, life expectancy fell to just 58.9 years for men, an unprecedented decline for a country that was not at war. The change was due to a large increase in deaths attributable to social stress: heart attacks, strokes, suicides, homicides, overdoses, car crashes.[15] Drunk men drowned in puddles. Some Russians went so far as to say that they would die without their garden plots. In the countryside, people could bypass hard currency, which might lose its value overnight, and barter for what they needed.

When asked how they survived during this period, people often answered with one word: potatoes. Peter the Great's "lecherous," nutritious crop, imported in the seventeenth century from the Dutch Republic, was a lifeline for Russians in the hungry 1990s, just as it had been the most important protection against hunger during the Second World War. Bags of potatoes were passed between relatives, friends, and neighbors. Not even the skins were wasted. People slept at their fields near harvest time, guarding against potato thieves.[16] In 2004, an elderly man in Novgorod oblast expressed Russia's collective affection when he erected a monument to the potato. The inscription thanked Christopher Columbus and Peter the Great for bringing it to Russia.[17] The world of the Lykovs, who thanked God for potatoes every day, felt surprisingly contemporary.

With the advent of capitalism, Russia's forests faced new perils. The end of the USSR opened the door to multinational corporations eager to exploit the natural resources of the former Soviet lands. It was not only rapacious oligarchs who wanted to rifle through Russia's treasure chest; now the whole world had access. In the free-for-all of the 1990s, the state was simply unable to enforce restrictions. Those officials with the power to prevent illegal logging and other forms of environmental damage were easily bought off. And for a state so direly in need of cash, leasing the forest or selling off other resources was an appealing prospect.

Not all Russians acquiesced to the new violence being done to the land. In the Far East, Udege activists used international law and lobbying to protect the forest and their hunting and fishing rights there. Young urban radicals fought back, too. In the 1990s, anarchist eco-activists put metal spikes in trees to protest felling. The "Rainbow Keepers" abhorred the idea that the failed socialist experiment would be replaced with "brutal capitalism," transnational corporations, and consumerism. Their vision, nourished by nights spent reading Kropotkin and studying the tactics of American radical eco-activists, was one of anarchist cooperation and militant protection of nature. Like so many Russian movements, they had a writer, Sergei Fomichev, at their head. He wrote science fiction and fantasy inspired by the characters of Slavic folklore.[18]

The eco-anarchist movement was nearly stamped out in the late 1990s, thanks in large part to the increasingly organized and brutal nature of Russian law enforcement. (Draconian new punishment of "eco-terrorism" achieved similar results in the United States.) But the Rainbow Keepers continued protesting into the 2010s, when Russia was moving into a new stage of authoritarianism under Putin. They took part in one of the highest-profile Russian ecological protests in recent memory, the 2011 movement to defend the Khimki forest. These woods were not deep in Siberia, but on the outskirts of Moscow. Tsar Alexis, Peter the Great's father, had hunted wild boars among Khimki's royal oaks; for centuries, the forest nourished Muscovites with its mushrooms, nuts, and berries, lifesavers in hungry years of revolution and war.

By 2011, Khimki was Moscow's last remnant of the forested premodern past. Residents, many of them with small children, cherished the woods. They believed that the Khimki forest belt protected the capital from toxic waste produced by nearby factories and a dump. Khimki, last survivor of the mass fellings of the greater Moscow region, was a kind of *zaseka.* Now the forest barrier was imagined to protect Russians not from Mongol-Tatar invaders but from the toxins of industrial life, both real and metaphorical. As one journalist put it, "The Khimki forest, like a doctor, carefully treats the wounds of the metropolis."[19]

The leader of the Khimki protests was not an eco-activist but a businesswoman, Evgenia Chirikova. She and her husband had left Moscow to be closer to the forest, with its linden, hazel, aspen, spruce, larch, and firs, its primrose and lily of the valley. They wanted to give their children clean, healing air. In 2007, on one of her daily forest walks, Chirikova was horrified to see red paint marking many of the trees, including the two-hundred-year-old oaks that were the forest's greatest pride. She went online and learned that the forest was to be cut to build a high-speed toll road to St. Petersburg.[20]

Chirikova started a movement. Despite a string of violent attacks and police harassment—one local journalist was almost beaten to death—Chirikova's new organization attracted the support of thousands of people, including high-profile writers, artists, intellectuals, and activists, as well as international sympathizers. They held a concert featuring one of Russia's most popular bands and camped in the forest, blocking the road for construction vehicles with logs and fashioning wooden versions of anti-tank "hedgehogs."[21] A newspaper dubbed Chirikova "Joan of Arc of the Khimki Forest."[22]

"We will fight for every oak," she vowed.[23] The venerable trees had red-tinted trunks and gnarled branches. When they swayed, they emitted a melancholy groan. In a brusque 2010 article encouraging others to defend their local environments, Chirikova used the title "What the Khimki Forest Is Murmuring About,"[24] evoking Korolenko's story of rebellion against an unjust ruling class. The forest was calling Russian citizens to action. But this time it was the trees themselves who needed help.

The journalist Elena Kostyuchenko, who would later have a kill order issued against her by Russian forces in Ukraine, wrote about the forest's St. George spring, which pulsed out in a happy rhythm from a wooden frame adorned with icons. A line of people waited to collect the water, which was so much cleaner than the water that came from their pipes.[25] The pure spring under the centenarian oaks in the Russian heartland is a picture straight out of Leonov's *Russian Forest.* To cut the trees here was an act of grave self-harm. Chirikova told Kostyuchenko, "The city, like a mad beast, is gnawing out its own lungs."

The Khimki movement was protesting the corrupt status quo in contemporary Russia: crooked real estate development schemes, rigged elections, and the unsolved killings of journalists. It protested the recent changes to the Russian Forest Code, which made once-protected forests vulnerable to industry and construction, and the felling of the forest that protesters viewed as Moscow's lungs, cleansing the polluted air of the capital.[26] But it was also a cry of protest against the destruction of the past, and of a former, perhaps mythical version of Russia. It was a plea to save the oaks that symbolized strength and righteousness, the forest that still promised nourishment in times of peril. Khimki was central Russia's ark, its promise of memory and salvation.

The Moscow regional government reduced the plan for felling by a factor of thirty.[27] It pledged to pay 4 billion rubles in compensation, plant five hundred hectares of forest to replace the one hundred hectares that would be cut, and dig tunnels under the highway "for the migration of representatives of the animal world."[28] But the activists were not satisfied. The defense of Khimki was the prelude to Russia's mass protests against unfair elections in 2011–2012, the "Snow Revolution" that led to the near-complete suppression of dissent in Russia. The country was finally beginning to realize that its remaining forests would have to be conserved. But as political repressions increased, many of the country's most talented conservationists and activists left the country. Afraid that her children would be taken by the government, Evgenia Chirikova moved to Estonia in 2015.

Russia's most flamboyant environmental activist of the Putin years was Andrei Khristoforov, from Arkhangelsk, the northern city where Peter the Great first saw the sea. Khristoforov called himself the "Enlightened Drevarkh," the latter word a shortened version of "tree of Arkhangelsk." He wandered the streets in giant angel wings, their color a perfect match for the snow that so often covered the trees and rooftops. His name was tattooed on his face, along with a large tree whose foliage ensconced his eyes and forehead. One Russian journalist described him as a "holy fool," part of a grand Russian tradition.[29] His transformation began while he was collecting mushrooms and berries in the forest. He found himself on intimate terms with nature, discovering the meaning of life in the woods. His mantra became "plant your tree," and he soon began to identify as a tree himself.[30]

During 2019's six-month-long Shies protests, which managed to stop a forest being cut to make way for a toxic waste dump in Arkhangelsk region, Drevarkh was the most memorable participant. He became Arkhangelsk's folk hero and mascot, beloved for his kindness and for his willingness to risk his own liberty to protect nature. After the protests ended, he took refuge from political persecution in Ukraine for two years, but he returned to Russia in 2021 because he missed his family. A local newspaper interviewed him in 2024. He had been hospitalized for advanced liver cirrhosis, the result of hepatitis C. In a weak voice, he told the journalists that he was in severe pain, but he planned to recover. There were still so many trees he had to plant.[31] He died two weeks later.[32]

During a television interview recorded when she turned seventy, in 2013, Agafia Lykova's speech still had a lisping rasp, a cheerful lopsidedness. By this point it may have been lost teeth that were to blame rather than isolation. She has a generous mouth and a forceful, prominent nose; there is an inquisitive, childlike glint in her eyes. Despite her life of hardship and isolation, she looked no older in the interview than most seventy-year-old women, and happier than many. She still traveled on skis to collect water from a deep hole in the ice on the lake, where tall, slender conifers stood sentinel on the precipitous slopes that surrounded her homestead.[33]

But with every year that passed, it was harder for her to live as she once had. In 2021, she moved into a new cabin built with the support of Oleg Deripaska, one of Russia's highest-profile oligarchs. He first grew rich in the 1990s by buying stakes in a newly privatized aluminum plant in the same region as Agafia's settlement; he went on to expand the holding into the world's largest aluminum company, Rusal. With the help of the park ranger who is now responsible for her welfare, Agafia asked Deripaska for a new home.[34] She had never received a voucher, but she benefited more than many Russians did from privatization. In 2023, the regional news aired a video of her in her log cabin, receiving the more modest birthday gift of a gray woolen shawl from the park ranger.[35] It was again wartime for Russia, but Agafia seemed unaware of that fact.

On YouTube, Agafia, the woman who spent much of her life without bread or wheels, is a paradoxical superstar. Videos about her garner millions of views. There is even an unconvincing AI-generated account in her name that pretends to be her own video diary, as if she had a smartphone in her cabin. Her popularity testifies to the allure of self-sufficiency in the wilderness—even as the last chapters of her story show that long-term survival alone in the taiga is only a fantasy.

CHAPTER 14

Militiamen

if only he had the ark—but it was battered
by artillery from the other bank
before he'd finished and now
there's neither ark nor bank
just endless water and peeking above it
the roofs of buildings and the crowns of trees

—Iryna Shuvalova, "after the flood,"
trans. Uilleam Blacker

The Russian television show *Happy People*, which first aired in 2008, opens with a rapid, disorienting montage: grainy footage of machines, highways, and explosions. We see bored commuters going down a metro station's escalator, a woman in a hijab, and a fashion catwalk. "There is a place on earth where there are no buses, no enormous houses, no police, no salaries," a voiceover intones. "Where no one complains about the power of oligarchs—where no one complains at all. It's the center of our country, on the river Yenisei. There people rely only on themselves."

The series follows the cycle of the seasons: spring, summer, autumn, winter. It opens in a tiny taiga village called Bakhta, founded in 1745 and populated by Old Believers and runaway serfs.[1] In summer the inhabitants cut trees in the forest and then float them downriver to the town, where the logs dry. Dense coniferous hills rise from the broad blue waters of the Yenisei, the region's highway. There is no reason here to worry about the damaged roads or corrupt traffic police that plague other parts of Russia; Bakhta can only be reached by river or helicopter. The Siberian villagers live almost like hunter-fisher-gatherers. There is no apparent boundary between life and work. It is possible to live there without using money on a regular basis, though cash is necessary to buy rifles, equipment, and machines. This is a world without the disillusioning trappings of modern life. One does not have to be an Old Believer to appreciate it.

One of the show's protagonists is Mikhail Tarkovsky, who also helped conceive, script, and film the show.[2] He is the nephew of Andrei Tarkovsky; his mother, Marina, is the sister who recounted the great filmmaker's vision of salvation in the taiga. Mikhail's father was also a well-known director, and Mikhail seemed destined for life in the urban intelligentsia. But in 1981, after studying geography and biology at university, he went east to Turukhanskii District, on the Yenisei River, the same region where his uncle Andrei had gone on his geology expedition years earlier. Though Mikhail loved being in the wilderness and cataloguing animals, he had no inclination for scientific writing. In 1986, he became a professional hunter.

Mikhail's long, severe face, high forehead, and black beard make him look like a medieval Orthodox monk; he could have been cast in his uncle's *Andrei Rublev*. His cinematic flair, inherited from both sides of his family, is obvious in *Happy People*. Using just one hand, he shoots a fish with a rifle while standing in a canoe. From the boat, he shoots a capercaillie, the largest member of the grouse family, on the riverbank. His beard spackled by snowflakes, he is the movie star version of a man in the wilderness: a classic Russian type, the brave, God-fearing Siberian frontiersman. But this self-styled pioneer hero has a distinctly Russian literary flair. He is not only a hunter but also a poet, and a nature writer who advocates for the protection of Siberia's woods and waters. His 2003 novella *Give Me Back What's Mine* opens with an epigraph from his uncle Andrei about the Yenisei region: "Mighty lands. . . . We must live there!" For him, the protection of Siberian forests and rivers honors Russia's military triumphs and the promulgation of Russian Orthodoxy across Asia. Mikhail named his son, born in 2017, Yermak—the name of the Cossack conqueror of Siberia.[3]

Tarkovsky has made explicit his identification as a "patriotic" writer who opposes the liberal Russian authors admired in the West. He considers himself a "representative of a monolithic, centuries-old civilization," "a custodian of great Russian culture." For him, the Russian writer's task is the creation of stories about modern people who embody Russian spiritual ideals. The brave, self-reliant characters in his taiga novels—who resemble their author and his family and friends in Bakhta—continue the ongoing "Testament" of the Russian literary tradition.[4] The forest is a place of natural conservation, but also a place in which to safeguard Russian literature, Russian culture, and Russian faith: a Russian ark. Agafia's life of sanctified isolation in the taiga was not sustainable. Tarkovsky has found a more viable version—one that even lends itself to reality television.

The term "Russian ark" was first made famous by Alexander Sokurov's 2002 international art-house hit of the same name, a single-shot tour of the Winter Palace in St. Petersburg. In the film, a ghostly, unseen narrator follows the Marquis de Custine, the French nobleman who wrote a famous nineteenth-century travelogue about Russia, through the palace, which is now part of the Hermitage Museum. As they walk, they encounter a grand swirl of Russian aristocratic history, beginning in the days of Peter the Great, and admire the museum's magnificent collection of European paintings and sculptures. The Soviet period is represented in just a few brief moments: an allusion to the murder of the last tsar and his family, a ghastly scene of a man making his own coffin during the Siege of Leningrad, and a moment when the museum's directors whisper fearfully to one another during Stalin's purges. The post-Soviet period, meanwhile, is shown only through happy museumgoers in modern clothing.

In the eighteenth and nineteenth centuries, Russia was often accused by western Europeans like the Marquis de Custine of having no high culture of its own, of being capable of nothing but imitation. The film counters this idea with Pushkin, the great poet whose untranslatable work can never be truly appreciated by foreigners. It also suggests that amid the violent spasms of the twentieth century, Russia preserved not only its own cultural treasures but also broader European culture and values, the way Noah's ark did during the biblical flood. Russia rose to glory late, but it also became the safekeeper of all of Europe's greatest achievements, preserving them against all odds. The Hermitage becomes a metaphor for Russia itself. At the end of the film, elegant Russian aristocrats stroll out of a palace ball. Outside is a monotone vista of gray, stormy waters. "The sea is all around," the narrator concludes, "and we are destined to sail forever, to live forever."

Over the first decades of the twentieth century, the concept of a Russian ark gained purchase amid Russia's growing ranks of conservative nationalists. It was soon deprived of the artistic ambiguity and complexity of the film. A 2020 group-authored manifesto published on the website of the ultraconservative nationalist think tank the Izborsky Club elaborated on the concept of the Russian ark at exhaustive length. According to the statement, Russia's sacred mission was to preserve traditional ways of life amid the degeneracy of the rest of the world.[5] Europe and America were the flood, and Russia was the wooden ship keeping true civilization afloat and alive. In a 2017 song called "Russian Ark," the teenaged musician Monetochka—now a major star—parodied the nationalist idea of salvation through persecution, imagining a broken ark floating from the depths of the sea. "We have been sailing for so long that we've forgotten where we're from and where we're going," she sang, "what pier we left from and the prize at the end." Two years later, she released a song called "Burn, Burn, Burn," lamenting the decline of Russian culture and Russia itself. She donated proceeds to efforts to prevent forest fires.

Though the ultraconservative ideology of the Izborsky Club was nurtured largely in the urban spaces of Moscow and St. Petersburg, it fetishizes the countryside, including Russian wooden architecture of the prerevolutionary period. Above all, conservatives adore rural wooden churches. A 2014 documentary called *Ark* suggests that traditional wooden architecture can trigger ancient memories in visitors, since their ancestors were almost certainly peasants who lived in such structures. In an interview, a young, fanatically nationalist priest, a transplant from the St. Petersburg intelligentsia, explains that Peter the Great was the first Bolshevik, and that Russia must return to pre-Petrine days. Like the Old Believers, he views Peter as an antichrist. To save the country, he says, Russians must resuscitate their villages. He and others featured in the film are restoring historic wooden churches, some of which were destroyed by the Soviets. The churches are their Russian ark.[6]

Such ideas are not as eccentric as they might sound. Hatred for Peter the Great and worship of village life resonate with some of the ideas of the Village Prose writers, such as Rasputin, and echo the words of 1970 Nobel Prize winner and Orthodox Russian nationalist Alexander Solzhenitsyn, author of *The Gulag Archipelago.* In the 1990s, returned to Russia from his exile in Vermont, Solzhenitsyn denounced Peter the Great for "indiscriminately battering our customs and mores." The most famous of Russian dissidents opined that since the seventeenth century, "the original Russian character held firmly within the isolated environment of the Old Believers."[7]

One of Mikhail Tarkovsky's biggest fans is a true literary superstar and a prominent member of the Izborsky Club: the novelist Zakhar Prilepin. One of Russia's most acclaimed progovernment authors, Prilepin is a literal Village Prose writer. He lives with his wife and four children not in Moscow or St. Petersburg but in a village in the Nizhny Novgorod region—the area that was home to the Old Believers described by Melnikov-Pechersky in the nineteenth century. This is an essential part of Prilepin's identity, along with his passion for war. A 2016 article in a pro-Kremlin tabloid asked, "Where else should today's most popular and, perhaps, most Russian writer live? In the village, of course."[8] For Prilepin, as for other Russian nationalists, the countryside is a precious repository of a Russian tradition that is innately superior to modern life.

Prilepin started as a poet with a degree in philology, but he spent his postgraduate years working as a riot policeman, security guard, and gravedigger. He volunteered for two tours in Chechnya during Russia's genocidal wars of the 1990s, when the Chechens tried to break free of Russian control. These wars, which brutalized a generation of young Russian men, provided him with material for his first novel, *Pathologies* (2004). Prilepin soon established himself as one of the most popular, acclaimed writers in Russia.[9] Compact and muscular, with a disconcerting stare and obstinate jaw, he had a macho energy unusual in the Russian intelligentsia. At ease with a Kalashnikov, he celebrated the Russian canon while writing stories about tough guys who spilled semen and blood in equal measure.[10] His work titillated critics and readers alike.

Despite his voluntary military service, Prilepin did not embrace the government line. As his literary career took off, he affiliated himself with the political opposition. He worked as director of the Nizhny Novgorod office of *Novaya Gazeta*—one of Russia's most important independent journalism outlets—and joined the semi-satirical, "red-brown" National Bolshevik Party, created by the eccentric writer Eduard Limonov, post-punk rocker Yegor Letov, and the ultranationalist philosopher Alexander Dugin to unite the far left and the far right. In the 1990s, there was some overlap between the worlds of the National Bolsheviks and the eco-anarchist Rainbow Keepers; both had roots in the cultural underground. By the 2000s, the irony in the National Bolsheviks' red-brown posturing had become nearly indiscernible.

Prilepin's interest in politics was deadly serious. In 2007, he cofounded a democratic movement called "The People" with Alexei Navalny, who dabbled in nationalist rhetoric. Navalny contributed a glowing foreword to Prilepin's second novel, *Sankya*, the story of an angry young man in the provinces who joins a leftist revolutionary group similar to the National Bolsheviks. Prilepin also affiliated himself with the ultranationalist far right, contributing to the infamous journal *Zavtra*. The common thread linking his eclectic political commitments was a passionate nationalism. In one scene in *Sankya*, the hero declares, "I am Russian. That is enough. I do not need any idea." The forest plays a prominent role in the novel. In one harrowing scene, the narrator drags his father's coffin through the woods in the snow. He is returning the corpse to his family's home village, but the village is so remote that it is virtually unreachable during the long, harsh winter. When the narrator and his friends are on the run from the police after a comrade attacks the novel's Putin-like president, this arboreal isolation saves their lives. Once they retreat to the safety of the village, they know that they are unreachable. Although the villagers live in poverty, they are the guardians of the true Russian spirit.

At a time when Russian literary and cultural life was centered in Moscow and St. Petersburg, Prilepin wrote about rage and despair in the impoverished hinterlands, in dying villages or in platoons sent to the fringes of the former empire. His heroes were usually young men, not sad, saintly old villagers. But his disgust at modern life, his focus on the provinces, and his willingness to denounce the authorities while celebrating Russia's spiritual essence made him an heir to Rasputin and the other Village Prose writers. Like Rasputin, he partook of conservative, conservationist nationalist chauvinism, though he added a Stalinist twist. Prilepin's 2012 "Letter to Comrade Stalin" excoriated the (Jewish) Russian intelligentsia for their ingratitude to the great leader.[11] Much of the liberal intelligentsia denounced him; it was to their discredit that his chauvinism and bellicosity had not been enough to make them reject him earlier. In 2014, Prilepin published a massive novel, *The Monastery*, about a young parricide sent to Solovki, the early Gulag camp on the White Sea's Solovetsky Islands. Critics detected a strange sympathy for the camp's commander.

Prilepin was a prominent face in the opposition during the mass protests against Putin in 2012. At that time, nationalism was not incompatible with opposition to Putin. Many Russian ultranationalists attacked Putin for inadequate patriotism, excessive tolerance for immigrants, corruption, and mismanagement. The National Bolsheviks were among Putin's boldest critics.[12] But Prilepin, like the National Bolsheviks and other nationalists, had a dramatic change of heart in 2014, when Russia annexed Crimea and Russian-backed separatists seized Luhansk and Donetsk from Ukrainian control. This neo-imperialist land grab won his loyalty to the political regime that he had opposed for years. Perhaps his muse demanded another tour on the battlefield, this time as a famous writer. He became adviser to the head of the so-called Donetsk People's Republic (DNR) in 2015. In 2017, he formed a battalion to fight for the DNR. The pro-Kremlin media called him a "hero of our time"—a reference to Lermontov, one of the early literary practitioners of Russia's "imperial sublime" in his work about the Russian conquest of the Caucasus—and the "Byron of Donetsk." Others suggested that his military exploits were mere publicity stunts.[13] In an interview he boasted about all the Ukrainians he had killed.

In 2022, for his support of Russia's full-scale invasion of Ukraine, he was sanctioned by an array of Western countries. In 2023, he barely escaped assassination, probably by Ukrainian agents, when a bomb went off in his car, killing his driver. (The far-right ideologue Alexander Dugin's daughter was also killed, by a bomb meant for him.) The attacks only fed Prilepin's conviction. In recent interviews, there is a vacant look in his sagging, disconcerting eyes. For Russian nationalists as for Old Believers, isolation breeds faith, or fanaticism. Prilepin is no longer able to travel to Europe, but he claims he does not care. After all, Pushkin—another poet of empire—never left Russia. For Prilepin, the war in the Donbas is about defending the Russian land itself—the "good and generous land," as he called it in an interview after his assassination attempt.[14] This "Russian land" is even more valuable when it became Russian only recently.

Prilepin has a long-standing interest in the Russian tradition of adventure and isolation in the forest, evidenced by his enthusiasm for

Tarkovsky's prose. Prilepin admires the wildness of the forest even as he celebrates its conquest by the Russian empire. His admiration extends to affection for Indigenous people, at least in theory. In his introduction to a 2016 book celebrating Dersu Uzala as a central character in Russia's cultural mythology, Prilepin described Dersu as the genius loci of Ussuri Krai—the spirit of the place. Paraphrasing a comment Lenin made in 1919 about conquering Vladivostok, Prilepin wrote, "Dersu, of course, is far from us, but he is still ours!"

This is a succinct, paradoxical expression of the erratic inclusivity of Russian nationalism. In the 1990s, as Solzhenitsyn wondered, "Will we Russians continue to be?" he wrote, "Nationality need not be planted in our blood, but in the attachments of our heart and in the spiritual vector of the person." In other words, it was not necessary to be ethnically Russian to have a Russian soul.[15] As non-Russian ethnicities were subjugated, their homelands annexed, they were brought into the Russian fold through conscription into its army and its imperial endeavors. During the conquest of Siberia, Indigenous people were enlisted to help conquer the groups still resisting Russian dominion. Today, ethnic minorities are disproportionately represented in the troops Russia has conscripted for the war in Ukraine. In 2016, Prilepin proclaimed, "When we sit in a tank, we are all Russian! Buryats and Chechens alike."[16]

In July 2023, Prilepin announced on his Telegram channel that "the great Russian writer Mikhail Tarkovsky" had arrived in the Donbas and was studying life there. An accompanying photo showed Tarkovsky in a military helmet and bulletproof vest, analog camera in hand. Tarkovsky had become famous for living in the eastern forest, at a long distance from modern life. *Happy People* fascinated the public because it promised the possibility of living in nature, far from corruption, explosions, and politics. Now Tarkovsky's "patriotism" had brought him to the war zone of the eastern Ukrainian steppe. He displayed unabashed militarism and contempt for the "liberal pacifists" who protested the 2022 full-scale invasion.[17] He was no hermit, seeking holy isolation in the woods; he was a settler colonialist.

And in this version of settler colonialism, high culture was a vehicle of state power. "There is a symbolic story here," Prilepin wrote in his post. "Because Mikhail bears his great family name. One way or another, Mikhail's grandfather, the great poet and participant in the Great Patriotic War, and his uncle, the director Andrei Tarkovsky, are seeing the front through Mikhail's eyes. Thus Russian culture will absorb the pain and glory of the Donbas."[18] Prilepin fetishizes "great Russian culture," military victory, and the forest. Tarkovsky's presence in Russia's latest neo-imperial war seemed to fuse the three. Prilepin was delighted. One of his nonfiction works, *Platoon: Officers and Militiamen of Russian Literature*, provides short biographies of eleven writers and poets of the nineteenth century, rendering all of them as imperialist warriors. The term "militiamen" in the title is the approving term used to describe anti-Ukrainian separatists in the Donbas. The 2017 book was a transparent effort to justify Russia's new war in Ukraine and valorize Prilepin's own militancy via a perverse reading of Russian literary classics.[19]

Another of the writers close to Prilepin's heart—a less obvious favorite than Pushkin—is Leonid Leonov. In 2010, Prilepin released a mammoth literary biography called *Leonid Leonov: His Game Was Huge*. The book was reissued in 2012 under the new title *Leonid Leonov: Accomplice of the Epoch*; Prilepin has stimulated a minor revival of Leonov's reputation. Prilepin loves Leonov's literary style and his commitment to the Russian land, which Prilepin sees as Leonov's only unconflicted, uncompromised loyalty. Leonov, Prilepin writes in his biography, takes readers through all the versions of Russia. The reward is "pure soil open to the heavens, where a cold spring flows, unrivalled in its healing properties."[20] This is the pure spring under the felled pine in the crucial scene of *The Russian Forest*: the source not only of Russia's rivers and forests but also of its unique culture. Prilepin admires Leonov for showing that "the power of blood and soil is so great" that it can make any traitor and coward into a human again. Leonov "perceives a true Russian person as a seedling of the Russian forest—he grew here, his roots are here, and it is impossible to transplant him to another land."[21] Reinforced by this shared metaphor, the family tree of Russian eco-nationalists extends from Leonov to Rasputin to Prilepin.

Prilepin does not consider *The Russian Forest* to be one of Leonov's best works—for him, as for most contemporary readers, it is "impenetrably Soviet."[22] Leonov sacrificed great art for the defense of the forest. But Prilepin argues that from a social perspective, the novel is "more than a book." It is a "feat," a word that in Russian evokes the works of saints and heroes. The "murmuring" of *The Russian Forest* lasted for two decades, helping foresters to defend the forest's "civil rights." Prilepin regrets that the novel's obsequies to Soviet power mean that today it cannot be recruited to help "stand up for the land, for the soil, and for the unfortunate forest," which is now falling much more rapidly than it did under the Soviets.[23]

Prilepin and Mikhail Tarkovsky show how closely intertwined love of the forest can be with intense Russian nationalism and neo-imperialism. Russia's war has caused the death, injury, or displacement of millions of Ukrainians. Prilepin and Tarkovsky evidently care little for this human cost. Perhaps they might be expected to care more for the trees of the land they hope to conquer; but Russia's war has also accelerated Ukraine's loss of its own forests, which were already suffering the effects of climate change and wildfires. Between 2013 and 2023, Ukraine lost 9 percent of its forests to wildfires and loss of groundwater. Reduced humidity due to climate change is bad for the murmuring pines of eastern and northern Ukraine. In a century, much of this forest will likely be gone.[24]

The war with separatists in the east caused countless new fires, and dramatically reduced Ukraine's capacity to fight fires when they started. Since February 2022, there have been tens of thousands of fires, often close to the front, with hardly anyone left to fight them. Forest and steppe alike are riddled with land mines; Ukraine is now the world's largest mined territory.[25] Burnt woods are full of unexploded ordnance. In the Chornobyl Zone, burning forests released strontium into the air, a danger for those firefighters who remained. The danger of fire and strontium was compounded by the risk of mines, which themselves provided fuel for the fire. Firefighters in Chornobyl would ordinarily use aircraft, but after 2022 they risked being shot down by Belarusians from across the border.[26]

Yet Ukraine's forests are not only victims of war; they are also tools. Ukrainian environmentalists have noted that the forests are again functioning as *zaseki*, the forest fortresses once used in defense against steppe nomads like the Mongols. Trees help hide military equipment and provide cover for troops.[27] Dense conifer plantations have special value, since they can conceal troops year-round from the gaze of drones flying overhead. This has helped spare some old-growth forests, which are less dense and therefore not as useful in warfare. The new *zaseki* are often destroyed in the course of fighting. Wooded corridors along the front line have been reduced to charred skeletons—forests of death.

As forests vanish, the landscape of eastern Ukraine goes backward in time. The sandy forest-steppe ecosystem around the devastated eastern Ukrainian city of Severodonetsk was once a natural mosaic of Scots pines and steppe grasses. But after the 1861 emancipation of the serfs, peasants were given sandy land to farm. They cut down the pines to make room for grazing, which disturbed the sandy soil. Without trees to break the wind, the area began to turn to desert. At the beginning of the twentieth century, the Russian imperial government responded by planting willows and pines, hoping to prevent sandstorms and the migration of sand into nearby communities. The Soviets massively increased this afforestation. At least one forester, Georgii Vysotsky, warned that continuous tree cover would deplete the aquifers. But the Soviets felt that since this land was not productive for agriculture or even grazing, forest was the best way to make it useful. Never mind that it cost more to plant and maintain the dense plantations, which were described as "thick as dog hair," than could be earned with the timber that was harvested there.

The resulting pine plantations were fragrant and idyllic, with a hypnotic monotony. They produced plenty of timber and prevented sandstorms. They also displaced naturally occurring pine forests (*bory*), where trees were farther apart, better developed, and more resistant to fire thanks to clearings, wetlands, and small ponds. The pine plantations sucked up all the water, and the *bory* died of thirst. Some of the few native ecosystems that survived were conserved only because they were training grounds for Soviet tanks. After the Soviet Union fell, conservationists made them strict nature preserves.

Since 1991, the matchstick pine forests of eastern Ukraine have been fragmented by accidental fires and by those set to burn waste or revitalize pasture. More recently, war has slowly destroyed the old Soviet pine plantations. Artillery "mows" the forest, splitting the trees for thousands of acres. Unlike *bory* or deciduous forests of birch, oak, and aspen, which are wetter, the pine plantations have no defense against fire. They are planted so close together that they have thin bark—thin skin. About a quarter of Luhansk's forests burned in 2020. It is these dense, Soviet-style pine plantations that serve as the best cover for soldiers.

Ukrainian legislation still requires foresters to replant pine plantations when they burn. But the fires are usually followed by a rebound in groundwater and pocket ponds. The destruction of the pine plantations, the legacy of Russian and Soviet interference in the forest-steppe ecosystem, is beginning to create a mosaic of forest, savanna, and steppe that is closer to the original state of the landscape, restoring ecological and hydrological balance.[28] The Russian war has devastated Ukraine, but it is also severing ties between Ukraine and its former colonizer—for trees as well as for people. The Russian ark sinks as the eastern Ukrainian forest burns.

Like the forests, Ukrainian rivers have been weaponized. When Russia first launched the full-scale invasion in February 2022, Ukraine blocked the advance of Russian tanks on Kyiv by breaking a dam on the Irpin River. The tactic was successful, and now ecologists are arguing that the "Hero River" should be rewarded with its freedom. Here, emancipation would mean abandoning the dam forever, allowing the river to flow along its old course and sprawl across its former floodplain, a valuable ecosystem for many species.[29]

Where Soviet dams disappear, new forests can be born. When Ukraine's Kakhovka dam was blown up—presumably by Russian forces—in June 2023, eighty villages were flooded, one hundred people died, and forty nature preserves were swallowed up by the water. The southern reservoir that had once powered a hydroelectric plant flooded into the Black Sea, along with land mines and an array of chemicals that soon caused a toxic algae bloom. This was devastating damage. Some ecologists warned that there might be other disasters to come. The drained reservoir bed, with its sediment of heavy metals, could become a desert, and perhaps even blow storms of highly toxic dust. Invasive species would flourish.

But after a year, the reservoir was covered in native willow trees as high as three meters tall, as well as poplars: a green sea. This youthful stand is now Europe's largest floodplain forest. The river is flowing again down its former channels, and sturgeon spawn upstream, though heavy metals in the reservoir sediment still threaten to contaminate food webs.[30] After seeing how swiftly life returned to the site, Ukrainian environmentalists called for the government to abandon plans to rebuild the dam.[31] As a journalist recently wrote, they "want the newly liberated river to remain free."

Though there is a reflexive impulse to simply rebuild whatever has been destroyed by Russia, the truth is that the Kakhovka dam was never a good idea. Soviet engineers—heirs of Platonov, the writer who also supervised the construction of two hydroelectric power stations—began building the Kakhovka dam in the 1950s. Like many Soviet infrastructural projects, the dam was both environmentally harmful and inefficient. The reservoir was absurdly shallow and the hydroelectric station provided just a fifth of the energy produced by the Hoover Dam on three times as much land. It flooded the Velykyi Luh, or Great Meadow, which was an area of steppe grassland, forest, meadow, marshes, old forests, and fertile agricultural land. The region contained ninety villages, thirty-seven thousand residents (forcibly resettled to make way for the dam), and numerous archaeological remains, including relics of the former Ukrainian Cossack State.[32] Like the dam that drowns the Siberian village of Matyora in Valentin Rasputin's novel, the Kakhovka project drowned the past. And that past is especially precious to Ukrainians, many of whom feel that Cossack society represents the free origins of a subjugated people. The destruction of the dam allows that history to surface, like the lost city of Kitezh.[33]

The "war-wilding" caused by the Russians is similar to the aftermath of the 1986 Chornobyl disaster, which took place in the swampy forest region of Polesia. The 2,800 square kilometer "zone of exclusion" created around the site—larger than the country of Luxembourg or the state of Rhode Island—became a famous example of rewilding. Beavers blocked drainage canals, restoring the area's natural swamps. Fields and even villages were overgrown with forest. Tree cover in the zone has increased by almost 50 percent, and it is now Europe's third-largest nature preserve. Species like bison, lynx, black storks, and brown bears are thriving; they have reclaimed the land.[34] The forests are more biodiverse and more resilient than the Soviet pine plantations that filled the area before the disaster. Polesia long resisted imperial control with its swamps, forests, and isolated villages; Vladimir Korolenko celebrated its liberatory potential in his story "The Murmuring Forest." After the distinctly Soviet disaster at Chornobyl, the Polesian forest slipped free once more.

The Chornobyl disaster and its concealment delegitimized the Soviet government and gave rise to a burst of antinuclear activism in Ukraine that was allied with a push for national independence.[35] Eco-nationalism, along with the immense cost of the response to the disaster, helped push the USSR into its death throes. In recent years, war has devastated Ukraine—but it is also erasing some of the marks left by Russia and the Soviet Union on the land. Russian eco-nationalists see the protection of forests and rivers, rural wooden churches, and traditional village life as crucial to the preservation of Russia's soul and its culture, testaments to its "civilizing mission." For them, Russian people are trees rooted in the Russian soil; they cannot be transplanted. On the other side of the border, Ukrainians are reconsidering the presence of Russian forests on their territory. A new, ecologically grounded form of Ukrainian nationalism embraces the return of landscapes not seen for many decades.

For some Ukrainian city dwellers, war has been a reason to discover the comforts of Ukraine's native forests. In 2023, as Russian missiles flew at Ukrainian cities and villages, a forester named Andriy Sahaidak gave tours of the swampy woods north of Kyiv. Visitors from the capital admired forests carpeted in green moss and wild bilberries, cranberries, whortleberries, and hare's tail cottongrass. They marveled at the flesh-eating lustwort plant, which devours the abundant insects of the swamp. In these native forests, pine trees are joined by downy

A sign reading "Mines" on the bank of the Irpin River. Photo by Vincent Mundy. *Courtesy of the photographer*

willow and arctic dwarf birch trees, relicts of an earlier age. This is a fragment of taiga left behind by the retreat of the glaciers. Tourists were especially attracted to blossoming "broad-leafed dream," as the flower is known in Ukrainian. In English it is called the pasqueflower, and in Russian it has the oddly violent name "spreading shot." Many of Sahaidak's guests had never imagined that a swamp could be so beautiful. For a few minutes, at least, the war was forgotten.[36]

CHAPTER 15

Bears, Wolves, and Archipelagoes

For far-right nationalists, Russia's forests are an emblem of national glory, a reminder of conquest. Even Dersu Uzala is a symbol of military victory. But for others—both human and nonhuman—the woods are a precious refuge from war. The trajectory of one extended Russian family, the Pazhetnov-Bologov clan, shows how the forest nurtured a hungry, traumatized society after World War II, offered succor amid Soviet repressions, and inspired new practices of human care for orphaned animals. After Putin's invasion of Ukraine brought waves of military mobilization in Russia, the forest became an escape route for those who did not wish to fight, an eerie reminder of the days when border forests promised salvation for prisoners of the Gulag archipelago. Successful refugees mastered the art of not being seen—always an essential skill in the woods.

In recent years, escalating hostilities with Russia have caused new border fences to sprout up along the EU's eastern edges. Intended to keep Russians out, they also block the paths of animals who treat the entire forest as their own, not recognizing national boundaries. Europeans long viewed wolves as their enemies, the villains of fairytales. In truth, though wolves sometimes kill livestock, they are mostly vegetarian and terrified of humans. Now it is not only wolves, but also Russians who are imagined by western Europeans as predators emerging from the woods. It is ironic, then, that one Russian who crossed the Finnish border is a wildlife specialist who has spent his career asking humans to reconsider their animosity toward the forest's predators.

Born in 1936 in southern Russia, Valentin Pazhetnov learned to escape into the forest while still a young child. In the days of postwar hunger, the woods were one of the best places for an intrepid boy to find food. Pazhetnov rowed alone up the river and fished, a Soviet Huckleberry Finn or Tom Sawyer. Leaving home for days at a time, he slept in a hut on a bed made of branches and grass. In love with this green world of plenty, he searched the map for the most distant stretches of taiga. He was looking for a place where he might settle, a place where the memory of war was not burned into streets, buildings, bodies, and minds.[1]

While still a teenager, he became a professional hunter, like Mikhail Tarkovsky. But from the beginning he was troubled, like Tolstoy before him, by an intense sympathy and respect for wild animals that was not always compatible with his new profession. When he took part in a May wolf hunt, not yet sixteen years old, he was surprised to see the ticks that hung like peas around the wolves' necks and legs. He understood that the wolves were not all-powerful predators but vulnerable animals that had to be strong and skilled to survive.

In 1955, Pazhetnov was sent on military duty to Primorye, the land of Dersu Uzala. He followed Arsenyev's path through forests of mountain ash, birch, oaks, and bird cherry, encountering roe deer, musk deer, otters, and sable, as well as Old Believers and Chinese settlements. On one trip with foresters, he arrived at a river that was swollen with rain. Logs, boards, plants, and rubbish bobbed along in the dirty yellow water; the land was much less pristine than it had been in Arsenyev's day.

Suddenly Pazhetnov caught sight of a bear cub perched, his little ears "round as dumplings," in the gnarled roots of a giant tree that had been uprooted by the storm and was now floating down the rapids. About a hundred meters downstream the river bent, and the cub, who had fallen from the log and was doing its best to paddle, began to drift toward the shore. Pazhetnov pulled off his boots and jumped in the water. The cub clutched his savior's hand with all four paws. When the exhausted, terrified animal dried off, Pazhetnov saw that he was a Tibetan white-breasted bear, with a glossy blue-black coat and a white stripe that ran from his lower neck down his chest and belly.

Brought to the nearest village and treated as a pet, the sweet cub grew into a dangerous nuisance and had to be sent to a zoo. Pazhetnov became preoccupied with the question of how to save wild orphans so that they could be released back into the forest. In 1970, now the father of a family, he moved to a nature preserve in central Russia. He was surprised by the number of bears in the area; he had believed that bears preferred a denser, more coniferous forest. The large ursine population, he suspected, might have to do with the fact that the region was being drained of human dwelling places. Once upon a time this area had been the home of Russian villagers; now the villages were deserted, swallowed up by the forest. The old rivalry of forest and farmland, a predominant theme from the beginning of Russian history to Stalin's time, had returned. And with humans gone, bears were comfortable in the forest again.

After tracking and studying the behavior of the local bear population, Pazhetnov began working with a fellow naturalist on an experiment. Bear cubs were regularly orphaned when their hibernating mothers were killed in their dens—a cruel trick by lazy hunters. The cubs were usually sold to circuses that made them into performers. What if they were raised not to balance balls on their noses, jump through hoops, or ride tricycles, but to become free, grown-up bears?

Pazhetnov was joined at the nature preserve by an old classmate named Viktor Bologov, who had been advised to move from Moscow to the clean air of the countryside for the sake of his son, Vladimir, who had a congenital heart condition.[2] Untroubled by ethical questions, the two scientists acquired their first subjects by kidnapping three cubs from their mother in spring—they could not afford to buy orphans from hunters. Pazhetnov lived in a tent with the cubs for a week. When he left the substitute lair for milk, the cubs followed him. They had already imprinted on him, taking him for their mother. But this did not mean that they had lost their bear instincts. They proved adept at finding food; as winter approached, they searched for a place to make their den. Pazhetnov felt that his hunch was right. With minimal intervention, orphaned bears could be allowed to follow their inborn instincts.

He received permission to open a research station called Pure Forest—*Chistyi Les.* He settled in the almost-abandoned village of Bubonitsy, accessible only by an overgrown forest road that led to a rickety wooden bridge over a stream. Only two people remained in the village. One was an elderly woman, gravely ill but stoic, who survived by making linen garments and embroidered cloths from flax pilfered from the nearby collective farm. Her only company was her brother-in-law, who had fought in the Second World War. The two elderly people lived on the edge of the village, guarding its boundaries against the approach of oblivion. The whole region was being drained of anyone who had the strength to seek more promising surroundings. Between 1959 and 1989, it lost half its rural population.[3]

There were bear tracks everywhere. The dense, rustling forest yielded to meadows and fields that were like windows. A network of streams laced the land like spiderwebs. There were impenetrable spruce forests and lines of elm, maple, and ash along the valleys; this was the latitude where taiga ceded to deciduous forest. By autumn, the forest floor was covered in wild apples the size of walnuts: good food for bears and boars.

The land around Bubonitsy had been cultivated for nearly a millennium, using slash-and-burn agriculture. Some of the centenarian lindens still remembered the farms that had once dotted the landscape. Only trees had such long memories. The villages' names had already been lost to human recollection. Once upon a time, peasants had plowed the land with horse-drawn plows, sown rye and flax, and planted potatoes. Now that agricultural tradition was represented only by decrepit yards littered with rusted metal skeletons and crumbling concrete hulks. Pazhetnov took pleasure in the thought of some of these lakes and ancient settlements being enfolded into his *zapovednik*, his nature preserve.

Along with two other families, the Pazhetnovs and the Bologovs rebuilt the village's dilapidated wooden cottages, and would now live in a new symbiosis with the forest and its largest predators. The village was so remote that the only source of groceries was a van that came twice a week with a small selection of essentials. Like Old Believers, the families lived in an isolated world, a tiny village of choice in which the inhabitants were united by their affection for the forest and its inhabitants. Pazhetnov was the undisputed leader, reigning benevolently over their community and attracting visitors from all over Russia and from around the world. Volunteers arrived, eager to help, and Pazhetnov managed to get grants from several international organizations.[4]

Perestroika and the first post-Soviet years were a good time for the bear cub education project. The forest had been a relatively safe place even during the worst years of Soviet repression. During perestroika, no one was paying much attention to anything except making money. There were few regulations about the kind of research Pazhetnov was undertaking. Besides, Pazhetnov's project had many supporters—several Russian politicians came to visit, though government funding never materialized.[5] Between 1990 and 2009, the research station raised 160 bear cubs. Only 10 were from zoos. In the 1990s, den hunts grew in popularity, as more people could afford them, and the number of orphaned bears grew. There was a spike in human orphans, too, thanks to intense social stress; this lent a particular poignancy to Pazhetnov's work. He became a celebrity, featured in newspapers and on television.

Under normal circumstances Bubonitsy would have been slowly consumed by the forest. In a 2006 book, the geographers Grigory Ioffe, Tatyana Nefedova, and Ilya Zaslavsky described villages of "blackened, decrepit and sparsely situated wooden huts that are barely detached from the advancing wall of the forest" as the "aggressive forest" turned inhabited areas into an archipelago. Thirteen thousand Russian villages were entirely empty by the time of the 2002 census; 22 percent of the Russian Federation's villages had fewer than ten inhabitants. In areas like Bubonitsy, Ioffe et al. wrote, "the ruins of collective farms dot the area: frames of former animal shelters and warehouses whose remaining pieces of tin roof produce sudden noise when shaken by wind." The authors estimated that as many as twenty million hectares of farmland—comparable to all of France's arable land—were abandoned, at a moment when many Russians were living on potatoes. The rigid edges of agricultural fields were made ragged by encroaching birches, broom sedge, and aspen.[6] Maps became nearly useless, as most of the old roads and paths became too overgrown to allow passage. In 1900, 20 percent of the area around Bubonitsy had been forest and 80 percent had been farmland. Now the statistics were reversed.[7]

Vladimir Bologov, the sickly son of Pazhetnov's partner, had been born in 1965, a year after Khrushchev's Thaw gave way to Brezhnev's Era of Stagnation. He had been unhappy at his school near the nature preserve in Bubonitsy, not seeing the point of doing homework or answering questions when he was called on. The other children called him *leshii*; he was a forest creature. In retrospect, he says, the forest saved him. Life in rural Russia was a dead end, and many of the locals succumbed to alcoholism early. He too had his years of binges. Fortunately for him, the forest won out over the bottle.[8] Vladimir married one of Pazhetnov's daughters, making formal a quasi-parental relationship that had begun when Vladimir was still a small child.

In 2000, Vladimir began a project for orphaned wolves, along the same lines as Pazhetnov's program for bears. The villagers of the region, with their common stock of wolf horror stories, were sometimes a problem. When they accused wolves of aggression, Vladimir was pained but did his best to listen patiently, suggesting that wolves were not the villains they were made out to be.[9] He also experimented with lynx, who padded across his kitchen counter or hid in his attic.

During his experiments with wolves in Bubonitsy, Vladimir was most impressed by their curiosity about cause and effect, even when there was no direct link to matters of survival. The animals were delighted by the cracking sound they could make by biting dried reeds, by the wobbling of a log on an unstable foundation, or by the motion of a loose cord. Popular fear of wolves depicted them as creatures whose intelligence had the sole aim of finding prey, but in truth they were as curious as children, with a toddler's delight in uncovering the small secrets of the world.

Even the youngest wolves had a talent for discovery. After years of observation, Vladimir was convinced that much of wolf behavior was not taught but innate. That meant it could be easily brought out even in orphaned wolves, provided that they grew up free in the forest. He had learned that they could live in packs or pairs, and sometimes even on their own; wolves were flexible, intelligent creatures. But babies are hungry and trusting by nature, and the central difficulty was keeping the wolves alive and healthy without allowing them to become accustomed to people. Without fear of humans, they had no hope of survival. At the same time, they were at constant risk of being killed by other wolves who perceived them as alien.

Vladimir refined his system over the course of a decade. After bottle-feeding the wolf pups through infancy, Vladimir released them into large enclosures in the forest, where they would not see people. They were enclosed until they were ten or twelve months old. Then he opened the gates so that they could come and go freely, with access to the food he left for them. Yearling wolves from the previous cohort acted as foster parents, teaching the pups how to live in a pack.

By about 2010, Vladimir was tired of using the enclosures. He wanted the pups to be able to adapt to the environment with even less human support. What if he could find a place without predators or humans where the pups could grow up safely in the wild? He made an exploratory expedition north to Karelia in search of a suitable location, with even fewer people—the greatest enemies of wolves—fewer roads, and more islands.

In late February the Karelian taiga is comforted by fat, well-rounded drifts of snow. The tree limbs are textured with varieties of lichen: dim green snowflakes or bleached coral, ethereal tendrils the color of freshly brewed green tea. The purer the air, the longer the lichen. The Karelian air is exceedingly pure.

Karelia is located on the border of northwestern Russia and Finland, just below the Arctic Circle. The region's humidity is as low as Timbuktu's, but snow and swamps preserve water and keep the land green. Even in winter the thronging conifers enliven the white landscape. Animal burrows in the snow reveal green plants insulated under the surface. In such an extreme climate, trees grow thin and slow, but long. A Scots pine in Lapland lived for more than 810 years, and a pine that fell in 1880 had 1,029 annual rings[10]—it was a sapling when the Vikings were looting London. As pines grow older, they stop rising and spread out, rather like people. The young pines are leggy, their trunks bare to the halfway mark. Older ones are curvier, shaggier, like the recording of a voice that gradually grew louder before fading out.

These taiga trees also decompose slowly, making homes for owls, woodpeckers, flying squirrels, lichen, and other beings. Beetles etch unintelligible messages into the bark of dead larches, which can stand for a century. In the long years before they fall, the dead trees tower high over the forest floor, their snarled bare limbs exposed and angular. The pointillist rhythm of birch bark is hypnotic.

Empty of people, the forest is punctuated by bodies of water and peat, though these are invisible beneath unbroken expanses of snow. Tiny shards of ice in the crusted surface cluster around sparse bog plants, distilling the sun and making it look as if the meager, twisted flora has seeded the snow with light. The afternoon sky is a spectral turquoise.

The tracks of the forests' smallest inhabitants are barely perceptible: the tiny pawprints of ermine and vole, the V-shape left by the thumping hind feet of a hare, the squirrel's butterfly steps, the fox's jewellike trail. When it descends plumply to earth, the cloud-white willow grouse leaves tracks surprisingly large for its size. Its Latin name, *Lagopus lagopus*, or "hare's feet," comes from its dense, feathery foot covering, which helps it manage the snowy ground. The willow grouse's tracks resemble the handprints of an awkward primate. Seen from a distance, they lie in sinuous, irregular patterns on the snow, like a string of beads spilled out on a table.

The larger predators, too, are tactful with the starry crust. The wolverine's disproportionately large paws do not sink far, and the wolf's teardrop toes are discrete, never dragging. A lynx cub follows in its mother's four-toed footprints so that the line is tidy except for the blur left by the thick fur on her paws. Only the moose is too ungainly to avoid sinking deep through the crust, almost like a human. Human footsteps are unmistakable in their churning, discoloring motion.

Even when the cold makes ice into roads and snow blurs the distinction between lake and land, Karelia's islands are easy to find. They rise on the horizon, serrated and dark with miniature forests. It was on one of these islands that Vladimir Bologov decided to conduct his next experiment. In March 2011, when the snow still blanketed the ground, he found a particularly deserted area and rode a snowmobile across the icy expanse. He was searching for tracks of lynx, wolves, and wolverines as well as moose, reindeer, and hare. He needed to assess the number of rivals and the amount of prey that his wolf pups would encounter. He was pleased by what he found around Lexa, Kargi, and Tulos lakes, an area of about one thousand square kilometers: few wolves and lots of wolverines, hares, beavers, and birds, with some moose and reindeer as well. This was a place where his pups could find plenty to eat without too much risk of conflict with other wolves. Wolverines are too small to threaten wolves, and their density here showed that there was plenty of small prey suitable for a wolf pup.

In May, when night was almost forgotten and berries bejeweled the forest, Vladimir returned to the islands. He was once again pleased with what he found: not only plentiful berries but also mice, duck nests, and many kinds of birds. A one-year-old lynx named Persik, or Peach, accompanied him. They rowed out to the island together,

Persik dancing on the edge of the motorboat, his tufted ears moving in response to the sounds of the water and the rustling trees. Vladimir followed him every day to see what he found to eat. He was reassured to discover that after a week Persik was fully self-sufficient on a diet of birds and mice.

Vladimir eventually settled on a house on an island in Lake Kargi, which contains numerous islands of varying sizes. He chose the lake in part because the name of the nearest village, Kimovaara, reminded him of his little son, Joachim, called Kima in Russian. Kima was his child with his second wife, Laetitia Becker, a French wildlife biologist who had come to Bubonitsy in 2004 to study wolves and had never left. She brought baby Kima to the island. Since it was accessible only by boat, when Vladimir went to check on his wolves on the neighboring island, she had no way of leaving except by swimming. There was no electricity, running water, or cell phone signal on the island, either, and on the narrow roads of Karelia it was a four-hour drive to the nearest store. But after nearly a decade living in a dying Russian village, Laetitia did not find it hard to cope with island life. A family photo shows her introducing one-year-old Kima to a wolf. No one is frightened.

Laetitia resembles a wolf herself, with eyes that are alert but tranquil, roused to visible emotion only rarely. She has an animal's fluid confidence in her movements through the forest. In Bubonitsy she spent days perched in a tree, silent, observing the pack of wolves assigned to her. That central Russian forest pleased her: its peaceable gray before the first snowfall, winter temperatures that reached −38°C, and the nearly absolute absence of other people. Karelia pleased her, too.

On the summer solstice, Vladimir drove four wolf pups to Karelia from the Yaroslavl Zoo, more than a thousand kilometers away, releasing them from their crate onto a green summer island about twenty hectares in size. He delivered food regularly to the same spot, so that the wolves would have something to supplement their diet of plants and insects as they explored the island.

He was reassured to find that they soon behaved like wild wolves.

They avoided him, and it was hard for him to find them. When they heard or smelled him coming, they hid in the bushes or ran off. The islands were spared from logging, so deserted that no one even took fallen logs for firewood, and there were plenty of dead trees to serve as hiding places and balancing beams. He had to lurk for hours just to take their picture, catching them glimpsing out from the green bushes or sitting together on a log that jutted out onto the tranquil lake. But soon they associated the camera's click with the presence of humans and ran away when they heard it.

Now he could only imagine what they might be doing, drawing on his decades spent in the company of young wolves. Skinny, big-eyed, and innocent, the gray pups must have been nibbling leaves and bark and each other, tumbling across fallen trees, stepping gingerly down logs green with lichen, lapping at the water but not daring to dive in.[11]

In July, Vladimir introduced two more pups to the island. He noticed that they were eating mostly berries. The new pups joined the larger group without difficulty, and disappeared into the island forest with them. Vladimir had to rely on a female German shepherd to attract them so that he could confirm their survival when he came to visit. They came to greet the dog and were friendly, but they showed no interest in treating her as a foster mother, as some tamer pups did. The wolves were living their own lives.

When autumn arrived and the taiga turned golden, the adolescent wolves had already learned to swim to other islands. Vladimir relied on a boat with a silent electric motor to search for them among the islands. He began to build his own *izbushka*, a peasant's log hut, just five meters square with low ceilings, on a larger island nearby. By November the wolves hardly touched the meat he left out for them, preferring fresh kills, and he felt confident that they could survive without him.

When the first heavy snow fell, the pups dug for small animals and berries under the crackling surface of the snow. They pulled needled branches onto the ground to make nests in the shelter of the spruce, where the snow is thinner, firmer, and not so cold. Now the whole lake was frozen hard and they could run as they pleased, between islands or to the mainland, walking in each other's steps to save energy. When the thaw came, they stepped delicately over the bare branches on the ground and surveyed the receding ice on the lake. They had learned to hunt in the snow cover for prey and plants, combing the snow that landed in loose flakes on their thick, sleek winter coats.

Vladimir had to rely on his tracking skills to verify their survival. In December, he found enough prints in the snow to confirm that all six wolves were still alive. In January, he found tracks showing that his wolves were feeding on moose remains abandoned in the forest by hunters, and that they were hunting for beavers—plentiful in a place with so many lakes and rivers. They were now ranging up to thirty kilometers from their original island, but there had still been no reports of villagers encountering wolves, or of wolves attacking domestic animals.

The next summer he heard wolves howling not far from the original island. He released three more wolf pups onto the island; one of them swam to the mainland after hearing the wolves' call. He later saw the pup's tracks along with those of two yearling wolves; this was the last news he had of it. Sometimes he worried. But he knew that in this case, disappearance was a sign of success. He had trained the pups so well that they had become invisible even to him. To correct the mistakes of humans in the world of wolves, Vladimir had to teach the wolves to be unseen.

In the forest of islands it was possible to go for weeks or even months without encountering other people. Later, after he moved to Finnish Karelia, just across the Russian border, Vladimir sometimes had the sense that everyone else on earth had died, leaving behind only their neat networks of roads and electric lines as a reminder that they had once existed. But in Russian Karelia, it was possible to feel that he and his family were the only people who had ever existed at all. On long, crackling winter nights, the aurora borealis performed its green dance of the seven veils for him and Laetitia alone. When the snow cover was gone, Labrador tea suffused the air with its pungent, woody fragrance. Its juicy evergreen leaves and its corymbs of modest, sprightly white flowers obscured the ground. In the summer, the forest offered up plump crimson lingonberries, tiny, exquisite blueberries, tart cranberries, and luscious orange cloudberries. The small human family joined the wolves and bears and other animals in their berry feast. During the white nights, at midnight it was light enough to read a book outdoors. Vladimir and Laetitia were the Adam and Eve of Wolf Island. No ark was needed.

Karelia, long a disputed territory, is cut in two by the Russian-Finnish border. Vladimir, Laetitia, and their growing family—one son was named Serafim, after a hermit saint who made friends with a bear—moved to Finnish Karelia as the Russian political environment grew more hostile. They found that the forest on the other side of the EU border was surprisingly different.

Unlike Russia, which has never micromanaged its forests, tiny Finland has exploited its taiga with a tidy comprehensiveness. The Finns left very little deadwood as nests for birds and food for insects. Their cuts were more precise, eliminating unprofitable trees like aspen, which are crucial habitats for woodpeckers, flying squirrels, and other organisms. The Russian foresters were more haphazard. When Vladimir took Scandinavian researchers to visit the Russian Karelian Kostomuksha preserve, they were astonished to encounter bird and insect species that have vanished from the Finnish side, driven away by too much tree felling. There are more old-growth and mature forests left in Russian Karelia than in Finland, and more burnt areas, with their special nutrients and habitats. Vladimir's Scandinavian visitors were especially impressed by the precious silver pine they saw. Known in Russian as *sukharnik*, silver pine is a dead tree dried over time, its distinctive color a gift of beetles that spread Ceratocystis fungi. *Sukharnik* makes the best wood for building traditional log cabins, including the roof. Because the wood is so dry, it does not

Vladimir Bologov in the taiga. Photo by Lassi Rautiainen. *Courtesy of the photographer*

shrink over time, meaning that the joints fit together perfectly. The house does not need any additional insulation; the elderly tree is cozy and snug. In the forest, silver pine can take three hundred years to decompose.[12]

This region was the birthplace of the Gulag, in an unexpected place: the Solovetsky Islands, site of a self-sufficient monastic fortress complex founded in the early fifteenth century. In the late seventeenth century, the monks rebelled at Patriarch Nikon's reforms, holding out against the siege waged by Tsar Alexis, Peter the Great's father, for eight years. It was a fortress of well-armed Old Believers, assisted by peasants and rebel Cossacks. They were only defeated when one of their own betrayed them. This was the monastery that Peter the Great visited in his newly built yacht in 1694, almost dying in a storm at sea.

During the hungry, impoverished early 1920s, the Solovetsky Monastery was liquidated, its valuables and food seized.[13] The monastery complex, with its squat walls and towers, became a labor camp, used largely for political prisoners—the clergy having been subsumed into this category. The camp was run by the Soviet secret police under a mandate of economic self-sufficiency, a kind of parody of the centuries of self-sufficiency achieved by the monastery. This would become the model for the larger Gulag system as it expanded to swallow millions of people. Some of those swept away by the Gulag recalled the ancient Roman saying that "man is a wolf to man." Osip Mandelstam wrote in 1931, "The wolf-hound century pounces on my shoulders / But I am not a wolf by blood."

The new prison islands had long ago been cleared of their ancient forests, with only a few stunted trees remaining. But the land around Solovki was still covered in trees. The region was also conveniently close to Europe, with its precious hard currency. Nearby Popov Island, a part of the prison complex, had its own huge sawmill and harbor. The Gulag prisoners were sent to the mainland to fell trees, to fetch wood in knee-deep snow, to float timber along rivers, and to dig up tree stumps, work not unlike Shalamov's and Ginzburg's in Kolyma. They sometimes did this on a diet of two potatoes a day; they were so hungry that they ate the bark from the trees.[14] Prisoners sent to build barracks had to sleep under the branches of trees in the snow, like Vladimir's wolves, until construction was finished.[15]

Solovki soon became notorious throughout the Soviet Union for its harsh conditions. (It is the setting for Zakhar Prilepin's Gulag novel *The Monastery.*) But some people were happy to learn that they were to be sent there. Solovki was close to the frontier—to Europe and to anti-Communist Finland, which did not turn away desperate refugees. From Solovki it was possible to escape and survive. For centuries, the saints of the Solovetsky Monastery had retreated into the region's forest wilderness in search of enlightenment; even the monastery provided too many temptations, too many distractions and small luxuries. Now the forest held the promise of escape not only from the camp but also from the Soviet Union.

And from almost the first days of the camp's existence, people did escape. Most were captured and many shot; to attempt to escape from

Solovki was close to suicidal, even in the early days. But the lucky people who made it across wrote memoirs that were published in Europe and the United States, translated into many languages and devoured by readers. This was the first, terrifying news of the Soviet prison camps. Memoirs by Solovki prisoners resulted in a boycott of Soviet timber in the 1930s, but the Soviets soon managed to conceal much of the evidence of forced labor in timber production, allowing sales to continue.[16] Western Europe was badly in need of Russia's vast, cheap stock of wood, and it was willing to turn a blind eye to the means of its production.

Vladimir Chernavin was sent to the Gulag in 1931, during Stalin's purge of scientists. He was especially well prepared for his escape. As a youth he had explored Altai and Mongolia, the Tian Shan mountains, the Amur, Ussuri Krai, and Lapland on zoological expeditions. In the 1920s, he joined a project to improve fishing in Murmansk, not far from Solovki. For him, the region's fjords, archipelagoes, cliffs, and almost impenetrable forests and swamps were old friends. And it was only two hundred or three hundred kilometers through the forest and swamp to the border. After a train ride through the evergreens, Chernavin inhaled the pure air of Solovki with relief, moved by the familiar scent of mingled forest and salty sea air after months in prison in Leningrad.[17]

The Gulag was badly in need of scientists to help with its many projects, including the achievement of economic self-sufficiency. Eventually, it would have whole camps just for scientists. Chernavin was assigned to continue his old line of work, improving the local fishing industry. This meant trips around the region, sometimes unsupervised. He was extraordinarily fortunate compared to his fellow prisoners. He was allowed time in the forest, hours of communion with nature. He collected mushrooms and berries and admired the shining waters of the bay through the veil of trees. By this point his wife, Tatiana, had also been arrested, leaving their twelve-year-old son, Andrei, to fend for himself. As Chernavin gazed at tree trunks wrapped in the golden filigree of sunlight, he felt guilty for his pleasure, imagining Tatiana choking on putrid prison air.

Timber rafting in Karelia. Photo by Semyon Maisterman, 1969.
Courtesy of Natalia Maisterman

After Tatiana was released from prison, Chernavin's special privileges made it possible for him to spend time in the village with Tatiana and Andrei when they received permission to visit him. They were even allowed to take a rowboat out on a lake for a picnic one sunny day in early August 1932. They used this as a ruse for their plan to escape. Though Tatiana made the fateful mistake of dropping their compass and map in the water just as they were setting out, they decided to continue with their plan, hoping to navigate by the sun.

Chernavin estimated that they would have to walk about one hundred miles.

Tatiana's detailed account of their escape through Karelia, published in 1934, is a story of near death, hunger, heart attacks, and swarms of voracious mosquitoes. But it is also a story of bitter relief at being in nature, free of the fear that she and her family had suffered since the revolution. The swamps swallowed their scent and their tracks, making them harder to pursue; her husband remarked that traversing the swamp was infinitely preferable to waiting for an interrogation. The violence of the secret police and the prison guards was replaced by the silent benevolence of large conifers. The family rested—never for more than a few hours at a time—on dry needles beneath big spruces that shielded them from view. As they stepped across mossy hummocks that quivered at their steps, they found shelter under spruces that were large and thirsty enough to drain a patch of ground. When they stopped to eat after bathing in a river, Tatiana felt eyes on her. She turned to see a huge, glossy elk with chandelier antlers gazing back at her. Majestic, benevolent, and well nourished, he had never heard of the Gulag.

But even in summer, it was easy to die in the forest, lost and without supplies or equipment. Reading Tatiana's account of survival against the odds, one is tempted to say that the *leshii*, the spirit of the forest, took pity on her family, guiding them from one welcoming tree to another. The Veps, Finnic Indigenous people of Karelia known to Russians as the "forest folk," call the *leshii* the Forest Master; he sometimes appears as a bear, but most often he is an elderly man the size of a juniper bush, or a young fellow as tall as the highest tree. In the old days, this tsar of the forest was so respected and so feared that cowherds made contracts with him, recording secret lease-spells on birch bark.

The Forest Master can bestow berries, mushrooms, and game, but he demands respect. Those who litter, spit, or make a racket or a mess in the forest will be punished. So will those who venture into the forest and promise, with dangerous hubris, to come back soon. They are likely to return days later without any memory of their wanderings, or to get lost in an uncanny grove of gray aspens—the Master's favored species. This is known among the Veps as getting "caught on a bad footprint," a curse from an angry *leshii.*[18] Tatiana and her family threw themselves on the mercy of the forest, knowing they would likely die there; they were silent and tried not to leave a trace of their presence. Without knowing it, they obeyed the Forest Master's rules, and they were rewarded.

The Chernavins knew they were in Finland when they began to see signs of numbered plots of trees that were only cut at long intervals. Just as they had almost run out of food, their blistered feet hardly able to carry them, the scent of freshly cut trees indicated that they were approaching a human settlement. Tatiana admired the thoroughness with which the Finns had drained their bogs, converting them into arable land. It was the forest that had rescued her, but the signs of the forest's subjugation were a comforting sign of safety.

In those days, drained bogs still seemed like a sign of civilization. Today, the Finns are working, with their characteristic orderliness, to reestablish wetlands in their portion of the Karelian forest. They hope to attract some of the rare creatures driven out by logging and land reclamation. But they do not welcome wolves that come across the Russian border. Vladimir has been subject to fearmongering attacks on his work in the Finnish press. After the 2022 Russian invasion of Ukraine, Finland began building a long fence along its border. It may be a hindrance to bears who go to the Russian side of Karelia to hibernate, far from the noise of Finnish roads and Finnish forestry.

The border fence was built with Russian aggression in mind. But since 2022, some Russians have used the forest as a means of escape from state violence. An organization founded in 2022 to help Russians evade conscription named itself "Escape Through the Forest." According to its website, by August 2025 it had assisted 52,436 people.[19] When the administration of a Russian Karelian Veps community received a list of names for mobilization in 2022, the men listed turned off their phones and went into the taiga. For many Indigenous peoples of Russia, long trips to the forest for hunting or fishing—sometimes for months at a time—were already an ordinary part of life. Now they were the best way to avoid death in Ukraine. A defender of Saami rights, already living abroad, told the Russian opposition newspaper *Holod*, "We have lived on these lands for thousands of years. Do you know how many Putins there have been in our time? This is the tactic: go into the woods, hide, don't stick your head out, and wait."[20]

EPILOGUE

Last Stand on the Ugra

The drive from Moscow to Nikola-Lenivets Park seems endless, though on the map the park looks like it is nearby. The largest art park in Europe is on the southern fringe of the ancient, forested heartland of Muscovy. This is the region where Kropotkin once rode through the pine barrens with his family, learning reverence for the forest. It is not too far from Turgenev's hunting grounds or Tolstoy's beloved estate. The nearest city, Kaluga, takes its name from an old word for "bog," and began life as a fourteenth-century border fortress. It was often a forced residence for political exiles, including Imam Shamil, the Avar hero who nearly drove the Russians out of Chechnya in Tolstoy's day, his men reinforcing their log forts with Russian corpses.

Across a sea of meadow, the wooden skeleton of a ship rises in the distance, as if ready to sail out into the forest on the horizon. A round house consisting almost entirely of old doors in various shades of faded paint, each topped by an open window, looks like a home for a *leshii* or a homebody werewolf. The pinnacle of a wooden tower, tinted yellow with lichen, offers a vertiginous view of a sea of grass. In the distance the sparkling Ugra River cuts a path through forest that still seems infinite. In the Moscow area, Khimki Forest is an exotic treasure—half-spoiled now by the ten-lane highway. In Nikola-Lenivets, it is easier to understand why many Russians still believe that they will never run out of trees.

Rows of shingled towers topped with mysterious figures stand in ranks, the effigies of trees or soldiers praying to the wispy summer clouds. Their open tops are eyes, giving a new view of the blue sky. The expanses challenge a city dweller's sense of scale, making her feel like a field mouse. A mass looks at first like bales of hay, and then like a fortress. From close up, it becomes clear that it is constructed entirely from piles of logs: a monument to firewood. Inside is a scaffold made of trees that still wear their bark. The sunlight shining through the chinks in the walls transforms the stacks of wood into a starry fabric.

In the forest, safe from the summer sun, there is a single room on stilts, like Baba Yaga's house or the *ambari* that forest people use to protect their food from forest animals. In the filtered light, the birch trees look like buttered toast. After the forest's edge comes a riverbank covered in grass and high bushes, patrolled by stinging flies. In the cool water, listening to the laughter of strangers skipping across the surface of the river, one might be in a scene in Tarkovsky's *Andrei Rublev*. If there is anywhere to meet a modern-day *rusalka*, it must be here.

Nikola-Lenivets Park is at the site of the Great Stand (*stoyanie*) on the Ugra River, a 1480 battle between the Golden Horde and forces commanded by Ivan the Great. According to legend, on the eve of St. Nikolai Day, the settlement at Nikola-Lenivets—already inhabited by Slavs for nearly a millennium—was attacked from across the river. The inhabitants scattered immediately, too lazy to fight. *Lenivets* means "lazy person." The enemy was put off guard by the easy victory, and it was swiftly defeated by local forces that emerged from the forest.[1] In Russian historiography, this battle is imagined as the moment when Moscow cast off the so-called Tatar yoke, the centuries-long burden of subservience to the Mongols and their successors and allies.

The Great Stand on the Ugra inspired the title of an annual festival: Archstoyanie—Architectural Stand—founded by the artist Nikolay Polissky in 2006. His last name, appropriately enough, likely has the same derivation as "Polesia." He is "Nikolay of the Forested Region."

Polissky, who was born in 1957, arrived in Nikola-Lenivets village just as the Soviet Union was collapsing, invited by a young architect friend who had moved there in search of a place "lost to civilization." They built houses, and soon they were joined by other Moscow architects, designers, and artists. By then there were only three locals left in Nikola-Lenivets: two elderly women and a younger man who had remained there with his mother. This last man in the village bore the Chekhovian appellation "Uncle Vanya." This was the Moscow bohemian version of Pazhetnov's revival of the dying village of Bubonitsy.

When he arrived in Nikola-Lenivets, Polissky was a landscape painter. After a midlife artistic crisis, he conceived his first land art project, a "link between traditional local life and new artistic practices," inspired by the village Uncle Vanya.[2] The project consisted of an army of snowmen, molded with the help of the locals. In bucket helmets, the snowmen made their own stand on the Ugra. This would be the first of many works by Polissky to comment on Russia's military iconography with a playful, childlike approach. The army of snowmen was charming and ephemeral, surviving only as long as the cold did. The temporary installation rejected the commodification of art and hinted at a light-touch parody of the heroic myth of the battle on the Ugra—during which the lazy Russians famously ran away. Polissky's approach to art is the antithesis of a nationalist like Prilepin's. He represents a third way in Soviet and Russian art, an underground tradition that is humorous, ironic, and tender, allergic to bombastic ideas about "great Russian culture."

Polissky, his fellow artists, and the locals went on to construct an aqueduct from snow, a twisted tower made of live squash vines bearing fruit, and a hay ziggurat in a flooded meadow.[3] It seemed natural to create the festival, which was an instant success. In 2008, when Russia was still affluent, cosmopolitan, and deeply involved in the world of contemporary art, Polissky and his village co-authors were chosen for Russia's pavilion at the Venice Architecture Biennale. The *muzhiki*, the "peasants," as he called them, accompanied Polissky to Venice. Seeing them there felt to him like witnessing Yuri Gagarin's first flight to outer space. In a 2010 interview, Polissky expressed his anxiety about the well-being of these *muzhiki*. Some of them had started as alcoholics, paid for their artistic labor in booze. He compared them to specially educated serfs who had been groomed for a life that was out of reach. He had raised them from rural Russian poverty and hopelessness to national, even international success; it was his responsibility to make sure they did not fall back into misery, which would now seem even more intolerable.[4] His harsh choice of analogy showed how little had changed in Russia since the nineteenth century, when the Tolstoy family's serfs performed concerts among the trees and progressive landowners sent their serfs to study the latest methods in forestry.

In the words of the critic Grigory Revzin, Polissky transformed Russian land art the way Ivan Shishkin, the great nineteenth-century painter of the Russian forest, changed the landscape painting from a "respectable picture that hung above the desk in the study" into "an epic image of Russia, an object of national pride." No longer a "fringe pursuit," land art now attracted crowds of thousands.[5] Polissky invented a hybrid of conceptualism and folk art that offered a fairytale world of archetypes and myths built from trees and vines. It brought delight to everyone who saw it, whether seasoned art historians, local farmers, or children brought on holiday with their urban parents. His idea of architecture was gentler than gardening, creating structures that looked as if they had grown out of the soil and could dissolve back into it without human intervention. "I dream of building a tower," he said, "in such a way so as not to wound the earth."[6] This is the opposite of the Soviet Prometheanism that sought to reroute rivers, move mountains, and erect forest fortresses across the steppe. Stalin was born Iosif Dzhugashvili; he took his pseudonym from the Russian word for steel. Despite his late-in-life passion for forests, he would never have named himself for wood, a material too perishable to embody Soviet ambitions. Organic materials suit Polissky because he does not believe that human structures should transcend the cycles of the seasons.

Though he works mainly in wood and other organic materials, one of Polissky's permanent sculptures at Archstoyanie is made of metal: a double-headed eagle, the emblem of the Russian Empire. One head gazes west and one east, the gruesome bird's wings spreading like fingers. The creature's belly is a furnace. When the firewood inside is lit, the Russian eagle's wings reveal themselves to be pipes, shooting fire and smoke west, east, and into the sky. As the fire burns, the bird's belly begins to glow an infernal red. The two heads breathe flames, their beaks turning crimson. The sculpture is called the *Firebird*, a reference to the creature from Slavic fairytales that glows like a flame and signifies both blessing and curse. The Russian Empire is a folkloric creature transformed into a wood-burning war machine, belching smoke onto the horizon.

At the end of the summer, Archstoyanie's temporary installations are set ablaze, to the delight of onlookers. The fire recalls pre-Christian ceremonies of rebirth and renewal: summer torchlight processions to the river and burning boats, as in *Andrei Rublev*; Ivan Kupala night, the Eastern Slavic summer solstice celebration when people leap over fires; and even the *kholmy*, the mounds that accumulated after years of fire rituals in prehistoric sites. Fire once cleared the land for agriculture, fertilized the earth, and made room for the birch, the tree that became most associated with Russianness after the old oaks had been cut down for houses, furniture, and ships.

Archstoyanie has been called "the Russian Burning Man," after the notorious American festival in the Nevada desert.[7] But Burning Man assembles huge crowds in an environment that was not even entered by Europeans until the middle of the nineteenth century. It has no connection to the personal history of the great majority of the visitors. Archstoyanie, on the other hand, returns Russian visitors to the home territory of the medieval Slavs. They wander across the landscape of a folktale, through forest, fields, and river, and partake in the cleansing fires that long pre-dated the arrival of Christianity. They return to the world of Russian peasants—albeit peasants who have shown work at the Venice Biennale.

When Polissky arrived, the site of Nikola-Lenivets was something of a wasteland, a *pustosha*, in the old Russian meaning of the term as a place that has been farmed but later abandoned, often devoured by forest. Now that wasteland has been reclaimed and recivilized by contemporary artists, architects, and artisans, and by the investments of a businessman who recently expanded the park's infrastructure and monetized Polissky's bohemian dream. As the park's website puts it, "Abandoned village fields and forests gradually began to turn into an art park."[8] There are guest houses, a restaurant, a summer camp, and an eco-farm. Polissky is not pleased by these developments. After Archstoyanie's first successes, when it attracted works from many of Russia's most important architects, Polissky was horrified to realize that he had brought pop music, expensive cars, and crowds of partiers, administrators, and businesspeople to the quiet, majestic landscape. Ugra Park's director was worried about damage to the local ecosystem.[9] Polissky distanced himself from the festival. He had not intended to gentrify the wild land.

Archstoyanie was an early iteration of a trend that has now become widespread in Russian art: a return to folk traditions and fairytales, to the landscape. This is in part due to the anxiety and nostalgia provoked by accelerating technological change and environmental degradation—phenomena that are common across the globe. In some cases, it has to do with nationalist fascination with Russian folk culture, as in recent government-sponsored Russian blockbusters that turn folklore into entertainment franchises. In other cases, it is a response to the shame and fear caused to some Russians by Putin's invasion of Ukraine. Many who opposed the war left in 2022, but some find it impossible to abandon their native land. Homes, families, and professions are not easily uprooted. Writers often fear separation from the native habitat of their language, and artists sometimes dread saying goodbye to the landscape that has inspired them. The Archstoyanie festival still happens every year. The 2024 theme was "We," perhaps a covert reference to Yevgeny Zamyatin's 1921 dystopian novel, in which prisoners of a totalitarian society are isolated from nature by a "Green Wall."

Polissky's return to the beautiful, abandoned lands of central Russia, his decision to pay peasants to make art by stacking hay and firewood, had a powerful historical resonance. It evoked the nineteenth-century revolutionaries, artists, and intellectuals who "went to the people" in rural villages, searching for an authentic Russianness. By returning to the countryside, he brought Nikola-Lenivets to the center of contemporary Russian art and architecture. The project is a less sinister version, too, of post-Soviet intellectuals who sought a new national idea in the taiga or in the wooden churches of Karelia.

It was impossible for Archstoyanie to remain above the fray of twenty-first-century Russian politics. The most notorious political figure to devote attention to the high-profile art project was Vladislav Surkov. This enigmatic "political-technologist" of the Kremlin pulled the strings of Russia's "managed democracy" and rebranded Putin's authoritarianism for the twenty-first century while listening to Tupac, reciting the poetry of Allen Ginsberg, and writing postmodern fiction under a pseudonym. Surkov fascinated foreign observers in particular. The documentarian Adam Curtis featured him in a film about political manipulations in a "post-truth" era, and the French-Italian novelist Giuliano da Empoli made Surkov the basis for his prizewinning 2022 novel, *The Wizard of the Kremlin*. Surkov also dabbled in art criticism, and in 2008, he turned his attention to Archstoyanie.

The spin-doctor's essay celebrated Polissky's use of truly "national products" in his work, calling it "simple, without fuss, but not crude. . . . As if you are present at the creation of the Russian world." With his characteristic ideological dexterity, Surkov turned Polissky's use of perishable materials into a testament to Russia's eternal survival:

> And now Russia is visible—a scattering of Ryazan huts, growing into a sprawling bast* empire. . . . This fast and shaky grandeur takes your breath away. It seems that it is about to burn, rot, disappear, but no. It sways, leans, settles, crumbles at the edges—and again, creaking, rises above the continent, flaunting itself

* Bast is a fiber obtained from wood, traditionally used by Russian peasants to make shoes and other goods.

> terribly and cheerfully. Two Romes have fallen, but the third still stands, made not of iron or stone but, impossibly, of wood."[10]

In this ultranationalist logic, belatedness and vulnerability define Russia's eternal grandeur. It is because Russia has suffered, because it has nearly been destroyed on so many occasions, that Russia is the world's greatest country. For Surkov, as for many Russian nationalists, Russia is the "Third Rome," the last and thus the best. Western civilization may have begun in western Europe, but it will survive in the east. Though he does not use the term explicitly, Surkov evokes the idea of the Russian ark. And arks, of course, are made of wood.

Polissky was dismayed at Surkov's essay, which made Archstoyanie sound like a threat to western Europe, looming ominously over the rest of the continent. With Surkov's help, Russia would soon terrorize its neighbors—first Georgia, with which it fought a war in 2008, and then Ukraine. But Surkov's essay was a perverse, willful misreading of Polissky's artistic practice. Leaving aside Russia's chances at eternal life, perishability was central to the meaning of the structures at Archstoyanie. Those that did not melt were often dismantled, the materials used for other purposes. Although Polissky engaged with the concept of empire in his work, he was no glorifier of Russian imperialism. He explained in a 2016 interview that he was not in search of a single national idea; he did not believe that such an idea could be found. Instead, he propounded the idea of an individual place, and of individuals in that place who draw forth ideas and action without coercion or lies.[11]

Polissky's practice shows that not every work of art must be defined by the state. The same is true for the relationship between nature and politics. The forest can be loved and celebrated without recourse to nationalism. Empire, meanwhile, is an inferno that swallows forests and belches fire. Art has been used too frequently, in Russia and elsewhere, as an instrument to inspire and justify violence. Amid the enchantments of Archstoyanie and the woods, rivers, and meadows of Ugra Park, it is possible to imagine an alternative reality: one in which there is no nation, only landscape.

Acknowledgments

This project would not exist in its current form without the generous support of a National Endowment for the Humanities Public Scholar grant, which made possible international research as well as peaceful writing time. I am profoundly grateful for that grant, and I hope that future generations of scholars, writers, and artists will be able to benefit from federal funding. I am thankful also for the support of Cornell University and the Comparative Literature department, where Cathy Caruth and Kate Kristof provided generous support and skilled assistance that enabled the inclusion of this book's maps and illustrations.

I am deeply grateful to my editors, Tom Mayer at W. W. Norton and Arabella Pike at William Collins, whose thoughtful suggestions much improved the shape and texture of my manuscript. Zoë Pagnamenta and Carrie Plitt helped the project find a home. Chris Cumming, Cristina Florea, Niko Wojtynia, Ainsley Morse, Yana Skorobogatov, and Gillian Linden read drafts of the manuscript and offered invaluable advice and encouragement. Mari Jarris, Lori Khatchadourian, Maria C. Taylor, Leila Wilmers, and Patricia Young gave helpful feedback on an early version of chapter 1. Irina Reyfman supported the project from its inception.

I owe a special debt to Brian Milakovsky, whose adventures in Ukrainian and Russian forestry ignited my imagination many years ago when we were on a Fulbright together in Ukraine. As the years went by, I was thrilled by his stories of his conservation efforts in the Russian Far East and distressed when he was forced to leave Russia because of his support for Ukraine in 2014. I was inspired by his work helping displaced people to rebuild their lives in Ukrainian-controlled Luhansk, and then, tragically, helping eastern Ukrainians to evacuate during Russia's full-scale invasion in 2022. My conversations with him over the years have been profoundly important to this book.

At *1843*, Abigail Fielding-Smith provided skillful editing of a reported feature about the refugee crisis in Białowieża Forest; that project fertilized this one. Ludwika Włodek was a delightful and erudite traveling companion in the Polish forest. Eric Powell at *Archaeology* magazine guided me through a crash course in an unfamiliar discipline; this made possible much of chapter 1, which grew from the article I wrote for him.

My talented research assistants, Nadia Vikulina and Emily Ziffer, helped me comb through the literature of the forest—which often seemed as vast as the Russian forest itself.

Kip Hutchinson and Jessica Madison Pískatá helped me wrap my mind around Mongolia before and after my first trip there; I am grateful for their patience as I peppered them with questions about one of the most exciting places I've visited in recent years. Timmi, Chukka, and Boroo guided me across the forests, mountains, and swamps of northern Mongolia with generosity and good humor—and I didn't fall off my horse once.

Uliana Dobrova, Valzhyna Mort, Anastasiya Osipova, and Bela Shayevich provided wisdom, advice, and suggestions that enriched this project (and my life). Uliana and Noah Sneider are responsible for my glorious visit to Archstoyanie. In wintry Helsinki, Emma Vehviläinen and Hunter Dukes were gracious hosts and advisers. In Karelia, Jarkko Koivisto at Jongujoen Matkailu Oy provided invaluable connections and kind hospitality as well as exquisite dinners with abundant cloudberries. Esa Muikku generously acquainted me with the Karelian landscape, its fauna, and the joys of forest skiing. In Georgia, Tamta Khalvashi provided a warm welcome and helpful advice. Anna Kats was an expert and enthusiastic guide, and she and Alice Gorton were delightful traveling companions in magical Tusheti.

The loving grandparenthood of my mother, Judy Moore, and my parents-in-law, Denise van de Leur and Taco Mulder, made this book and its research possible.

Above all, I am eternally grateful to my husband, Nick Mulder. He read and commented on numerous drafts, enriching them with his historical and military expertise; entertained our daughter while I worked on the weekend; cooked countless dinners; and tolerated all the minor nervous breakdowns entailed in book writing—even as he was writing his own.

Notes

Introduction

1 Leonid Leonov, *Sobranie sochinenii v 10 tomakh*, vol. 9, *Russkii les: Roman* (Khudozhestvennaia literatura, 1984), 277.

2 For one take on forests in Western thought, see Robert Pogue Harrison's classic *Forests: The Shadow of Civilization* (University of Chicago Press, 1993).

3 See Aleksandr Afanasyev, "Drevo zhizni i lesnye dukhi," in *Poeticheskie vozzreniia slavian' na prirodu*, tom 2 (Izd. K. Soldatenkova, 1885).

4 Samuel Hazzard Cross and Olgerd Sherbowitz-Wetzor, trans. and eds., *The Russian Primary Chronicle: Laurentian Text* (Mediaeval Academy of America, 1953), 54.

5 Valerie Kivelson, *Cartographies of Tsardom: The Land and Its Meanings in Seventeenth-Century Russia* (Cornell University Press, 2006), 110–12.

6 James Billington, *The Icon and the Axe: An Interpretive History of Russian Culture* (Vintage, 1970), 21.

7 Cross and Sherbowitz-Wetzor, *Primary Chronicle*, 56.

8 Robert Chandler, ed., *Russian Magic Tales from Pushkin to Platonov* (Penguin, 2013), xvi.

9 Vladimir Ia. Propp, "Tainstvennyi Les," in *Istoricheskie korni volshebnoi skazki* (Izd. Leningradskogo gosudarstvennogo universiteta, 1986).

10 Igor' Podshivalov, *Anarkhiia v Sibiri* (Common Place, 2015), 36, 45–47.

11 Vladimir Nabokov, "The Wood-Sprite," in *The Stories of Vladimir Nabokov*, ed. and trans. Dmitri Nabokov (Vintage International, 1997), 3–5.

12 Data from Global Forest Watch, https://www.globalforestwatch.org/.

13 Patrick Reevell, "Siberian Wildfires Now Bigger Than All Other Fires in World Combined," ABC News, August 12, 2021.

14 Reuters, "State of Emergency Declared in Siberia Over Raging Wildfires," July 3, 2023.

15 "Smoke Over the Arctic Circle as Boreal Wildfires Intensify in Siberia and North America," Copernicus/Atmosphere Monitoring Service, July 16, 2024.

Chapter 1: A Fortress in the Taiga

1 Lennart Meri (dir.), "The Sons of Torum (Toorumin pojat)" (Eesti Telefilm, IWF, YLE-TV 2, 1989), YouTube, https://www.youtube.com/watch?v=iX7nHETRNow.

2 I am grateful to the Finno-Ugric expert Eva Toulouze for her clarification of the details of Meri's biography.

3 Elena Glavatskaya, "The Nature, History and Religion of the Khanty," in *The Man Who Sees: The World of Ivan Stepanovich Sopochin*, ed. Clive Tolley (Molnar and Kelemen, 2021), 90–93.

4 The discovery is documented in Henny Piezonka et al., "The World's Oldest-Known Promontory Fort: Amnya and the Acceleration of Hunter-Gatherer Diversity in Siberia 8000 Years Ago," *Antiquity* 97, no. 396 (December 2023): 1381–401. See also my article "Letter from Siberia: Strongholds of the Taiga," *Archaeology* (September/October 2024).

5 Wild Salmon Center, "Taimen," https://wildsalmoncenter.org/salmon-species/taimen/; "River Tigers," directed by Adam Maser and Andy Bagger (Wild Salmon Center, Maser Films, and Yonder Content, 2020).

6 See Tanja Schreiber, Henny Piezonka, Natalia Chairkina, Ekaterina Dubovtseva, and Lyubov Kosinskaya, "Towards Territoriality and Inequality? Examining Prehistoric Hunter-Gatherer Fortifications in the Siberian Taiga," in *Fortifications in Their Natural and Cultural Landscape: From Organising Space to the Creation of Power* (Habelt-Verlag, 2022), 51–68.

7 Author interview with Ekaterina Dubovtseva, December 2023.

8 Janet Martin, *Treasure of the Land of Darkness: The Fur Trade and Its Significance for Medieval Russia* (Cambridge University Press, 1986), 64.

9 Abu Khamid al-Garnati, *Puteshestvie Abu Khamida al-Garnati v vostochnuiu i tsentral'nuiu Evropu (1131–1153 gg.)*, trans. and with introduction by O. G. Bol'shakov and with commentary by A. L. Mongait (Vostochnaia literatura, 1971), 33.

10 Martin, *Treasure of the Land of Darkness*, 21–22, quoting Abu Khamid al-Garnati, *Puteshestvie*, 32.

11 Martin, *Treasure of the Land of Darkness*, 53.

12 J. G. Hather and M. A. Brisbane, "Understanding Wood Use in Its Environmental Context," 13–18, and V. I. Yanin, A. S. Khoroshev, and M. A. Brisbane, "Novgorod: An Introduction," 1, both in *Wood Use in Medieval Novgorod*, eds. Mark Bassin and Jon Hather (Oxbow, 2007).

13 See M. Alekseev, *Sibir' v izvestiiakh zapadno-evropeiskikh puteshestvennikov i pisatelei, XIII–XVII vv* (Kurkutskoe oblastnoe izdatel'stvo, 1941).

14 Martin, *Treasure of the Land of Darkness*, 80–81. The travel account is from D. N. Anuchin, "K istorii oznakomleniia s Sibiriu do Ermaka," *Drevnosti. Trudy Moskovskogo arkheologicheskogo obshchestva* 14 (1890).

15 I. A. Karapetova and L. Yu. Kitova, "Raisa Pavlovna Mitusova: Unknown Pages of Her Biography," *Archaeology, Ethnology & Anthropology of Eurasia* 25, no. 1 (2006): 153–59.

16 See Bathsheba Demuth, *Floating Coast: An Environmental History of the Bering Strait* (W. W. Norton, 2019).

17 Glavatskaya, *Man Who Sees*, 83–84.
18 Eremei Aipin, *Bozh'ia Mater' v krovavykh snegakh* (Amfora, 2010), 5–6; Glavatskaya, *Man Who Sees*, 100–101; Marjorie Mandelstam Balzer, *The Tenacity of Ethnicity: A Siberian Saga* (Princeton University Press, 2000), 110–17; Andrei Golovnev, *Govoriashchie Kul'tury: Traditsii Samodiitsev i Ugrov* (UrO RAN, 1995), 165–73.
19 Christian Vagt, "Before the Snow," YouTube, https://www.youtube.com/watch?v=OwtiINkdOTE; see also Stephan Dudeck et al., "Troubling Visits and Uncanny Encounters—Indigenous Concepts of Other Than Humans and Their Homes," *TRANSLOCAL: Culturas Contemporâneas Locais e Urbanas*, no. 5: (Un)Inhabited Spaces, Funchal: UMa-CIERL/CMF/IA, 2021).

Chapter 2: The Golden Horde and the Tree of Life

1 Igor de Rachewiltz, trans., *The Secret History of the Mongols: A Mongolian Epic Chronicle of the Thirteenth Century*, shorter version edited by John C. Street (University of Wisconsin-Madison, books and monographs, book 4, 2015), 1–18.
2 Jack Weatherford, *Genghis Khan and the Quest for God* (Viking, 2016), 19.
3 Rachewiltz, *Secret History*, 30.
4 Ata-Malik Juvayni, *Genghis Khan: The History of the World Conqueror*, trans. and ed. J. A. Boyle (University of Washington Press, 1997), 553.
5 Marie Favereau, *The Horde: How the Mongols Changed the World* (Belknap Press, 2021), 78.
6 Kivelson, *Cartographies of Tsardom*, 108–13.
7 Terence Armstrong, *Yermak's Campaign in Siberia: A Selection of Documents*, translated by Tatiana Minorsky and David Wileman, and edited with an introduction and notes by Terence Armstrong (Hakluyt Society, 1975), 64–65.
8 Armstrong, *Yermak's Campaign*, 64–65.
9 Allen J. Frank, *The Siberian Chronicles and the Taybughid Biys of Sibir'* (Indiana University Research Institute for Inner Asian Studies, 1994), 47.
10 Frank, *Siberian Chronicles*, 8–15.
11 Armstrong, *Yermak's Campaign*, 281.
12 Armstrong, *Yermak's Campaign*, 208. From the Remezov Chronicle.
13 Armstrong, *Yermak's Campaign*, 155.
14 Armstrong, *Yermak's Campaign*, 162–64.
15 Raymond H. Fisher, *The Russian Fur Trade, 1500–1700* (University of California Press, 1943), 26.
16 Armstrong, *Yermak's Campaign*, 208–23.
17 Frank, *Siberian Chronicles*, 57–59, 225.
18 Andrei V. Golovnev and Gail Osherenko, *Siberian Survival: The Nenets and Their Story* (Cornell University Press, 1999), 44–45.
19 Janet M. Hartley, *Siberia: A History of the People* (Yale University Press, 2014), 12.
20 Yuri Slezkine, *Arctic Mirrors: Russia and the Small Peoples of the North* (Cornell University Press, 1994), 16, 29.

21 S. V. Bakhrushin, "Ostiatskie i vogul'skie kniazhestva v XVI–XVII vv," in *Nauchnye trudy,* 1965, tom 3, part 2, 145, 149, 150–51; see Slezkine, *Arctic Mirrors,* 18.

22 Glafira M. Vasilievich, ed., *Istoricheskii fol'klor evenkov: Skazaniia i predaniia* (Izd. Nauka, 1966), 294.

23 The Cossacks' brutality sometimes got them in trouble; Indigenous people lodged complaints against them, and the Cossacks were whipped in turn. See Kivelson, *Cartographies of Tsardom,* 204–5.

24 Slezkine, *Arctic Mirrors,* 24–25.

25 For an overview of this history in English, see James Forsyth, *A History of the Peoples of Siberia: Russia's North Asian Colony 1581–1990* (Cambridge University Press, 1992).

26 Forsyth, *History of the Peoples of Siberia,* 64.

Chapter 3: The Emperor's Fleet

1 Tom Diserens, "The Tree Communities of Białowieża Forest" (blog), May 2, 2021.

2 Eunice Blavascunas, "Poland's Primeval Forest Has Lost Its Staunchest Defender. Obituary of Janusz Korbel," *Earth Island Journal,* August 28, 2015.

3 This paragraph and the one above it rely primarily on the author's interview with Bogdan Jarosiewicz, Białowieża Geobotanical Station, August 2022.

4 M. J. McGrath et al., "Reconstructing European Forest Management from 1600 to 2010," *Biogeosciences* 12 (2015): 4292.

5 Tomasz Samolijk et al., *Bialowieza Primeval Forest: Nature and Culture in the Nineteenth Century* (Springer, 2020).

6 William C. Fuller Jr., "The Imperial Army," in *The Cambridge History of Russia, vol. 2: Imperial Russia, 1689–1917,* ed. Dominic Lieven (Cambridge University Press, 2008), 530–31.

7 Feofan Prokopovich, "Slovo pokhval'noe o flote rossiiskom i o pobede . . ." September 8, 1720. In Prokopovich, *Sochineniia,* ed. I. Eremin (Izd. Akademii nauk SSSR, 1961), 106. Translation from Lindsey Hughes, *Russia in the Age of Peter the Great* (Yale University Press, 1998), 81.

8 Kristof Haneca et al., "Provenancing Baltic Timber from Art Historical Objects: Success and Limitations," *Journal of Archaeological Science* 32 (2005): 261–71.

9 Gilbert Burnet (Bishop of Salisbury), *History of His Own Time,* vol. 2 (William Smith, 1724), 655.

10 G. A. Grebenshchikova, "Problema sokhrannosti korabel'nogo lesa v XVIII veke," *Voprosy istorii* 12 (2007): 137.

11 Olga Ulybina, "Russian Forests: The Path of Reform," *Forest Policy and Economics* 38 (2014): 143–50.

12 Ivetta Krasnogorskaia, "Pervyi vo vsem," *LesPromInform* 35, no. 4 (2006).

13 Haneca et al., "Provenancing Baltic Timber."

14 *Istoricheskoe obozrenie piatidesiatiletnei deiatel'nosti Ministerstva Gosudarstvennykh Imushchestv, 1837–1887* (St. Petersburg, 1888), 3:173. For a full discussion of Russian steppe forestry, see David Moon, "Planting Trees in Unsuitable Places: Steppe Forestry in the Russian Empire, 1696–1850," in *Eurasian Envi-*

ronments: Nature and Ecology in Imperial Russian and Soviet History, ed. Nicholas B. Breyfogle (University of Pittsburgh Press, 2018).

15 Stephen Brain, *Song of the Forest: Russian Forestry and Stalinist Environmentalism, 1905–1953* (University of Pittsburgh Press, 2011), 13–14.

16 Brain, *Song of the Forest*, 15–16.

17 *Pamiatniki Sibirskoi istorii XVIII veka*, vol. 1 (Tipografiia Ministerstva vnutrennykh del, 1882), 413–14. Translated in Slezkine, *Arctic Mirrors*, 49.

18 Slezkine, *Arctic Mirrors*, 49–57.

19 Slezkine, *Arctic Mirrors*, 63.

20 Grebenshchikova, "Problema sokhrannosti korabel'nogo lesa v XVIII veke," 138–39.

21 *Sbornik Imperatorskogo Russkogo Istoricheskogo Obshchestva*, vol. 13 (Tipografiia Imperatorskoi akademii nauk, 1874), 254–55.

22 Ekaterina Pravilova, *"A Public Empire": Property and the Quest for the Common Good in Imperial Russia* (Princeton University Press, 2014), 9–10, 28–30.

23 Ol'ga Eliseeva, *Grigorii Potemkin* (Molodaia gvardiia, 2006), 367.

24 Moon, "Planting Trees."

25 Samolijk et al., *Bialowieza Primeval Forest*, 64.

26 Samolijk et al., *Bialowieza Primeval Forest*, 141.

27 Richard Wortman, *Scenarios of Power: From Alexander II to the Abdication of Nicholas II* (Princeton University Press, 2000), 53.

28 "Dremuchee Delo," *The Bell* 108, October 1, 1861, 905; "Eshche o dremuchem dele," *The Bell* 117, December 22, 1861, 979–80; "Eshche o dremuchem dele," *The Bell*, no. 119–120, January 15, 1862, 997–1000.

Chapter 4: Subduing the Sublime

1 Dieudonné Gnammankou, *Abraham Hanibal: L'aïeul noir de Pouchkine* (Présence africaine, 1996), 19.

2 Letter to L. S. Pushkin, 24 September 1820. In A. S. Pushkin, *Sobranie sochinenii v 10 tomakh*, tom 9: Pis'ma. 1815–1830 (Khudozhestvennaia literatura, 1959–1961), 20.

3 A. S. Pushkin, "Kavkazskii plennik: Povest'," in *Polnoe sobranie sochinenii v 16 tomakh*, tom 4: *Poemy*, 1817–1824 (Izd. Akademii nauk SSSR, 1937–1959), 89–118. On the history of the Caucasus, see Charles King's engaging history, *The Ghost of Freedom: A History of the Caucasus* (Oxford University Press, 2009). Harsha Ram's *The Imperial Sublime* (University of Wisconsin Press, 2006) is an essential study of the development of Russian poetry, including Pushkin's, in tandem with the growth of the Russian empire.

4 See Katya Hokanson, "Literary Imperialism, *Narodnost'* and Pushkin's Invention of the Caucasus," *Russian Review* 53, no. 3 (July 1994): 336–52.

5 William Tooke, *View of the Russian Empire During the Reign of Catharine the Second and to the Close of the Present Century*, vol. 1 (T. N. Longman and O. Reed, Paternoster Row, 1799), xix.

6 M. Iu. Lermontov, *Geroi nashego vremeni* (Izd. Akademii nauk SSSR, 1962), 24.

Translation from Vladimir Nabokov and Dmitri Nabokov (Everyman's Library, 1992), 39.

7 Thomas M. Barrett, *At the Edge of Empire: The Terek Cossacks and the North Caucasus Frontier, 1700–1860* (Westview Press, 1999), 59–63.

8 John F. Baddeley, *The Russian Conquest of the Caucasus* (Green and Co., 1908), 358, xxxv.

9 Barrett, *Edge of Empire*, 64.

10 Barrett, *Edge of Empire*, 64–65.

11 Quoted in Barrett, *Edge of Empire*, 65.

12 Quoted in Barrett, *Edge of Empire*, 66.

13 T. Kaznacheeva, "Cherty obshchnosti zemledel'cheskoi kul'tury i ekologicheskikh predstavlenii narodov Severnogo Kavkaza v dorevoliutsionnyi period," in *Problemy agrarnoi istorii narodov Severnogo Kavkaza v dorevoliutsionnyi period*, ed. V. Nevskaia (Stavropol'skii gosudarstvennyi pedagogicheskii institut, 1981), 84.

14 R. Sh. Sharafutdinova, "Eshche odin 'Nizam' Shamilia," *Pis'mennye pamiatniki vostoka* (1975): 168–71.

15 L. N. Tolstoi, *Polnoe sobranie sochinenii*, vol. 46: *Dnevniki* (Khudozhestvennaia literatura, 1934), 370 n405.

16 N. A. Volkonskii, "Pogrom Chechni v 1852 godu," in *Kavkazskii sbornik*, vol. 5 (1880).

17 Leo Tolstoy, *The Cossacks and Other Stories*, trans. David McDuff (Penguin Classics, 2007), 9–10. Tolstoi, *Polnoe sobranie sochinenii*, tom 6, 8–9. Ivan Turgenev wrote of Tolstoy's *The Cossacks*, "The more often I reread this story, the more convinced I become that it is the masterpiece of Tolstoy and all Russian narrative literature" (I. S. Turgenev, letter to A. A. Fet, March 4, 1874).

18 For a full discussion of the disputed origins of the Terek Cossacks, see Barrett, *Edge of Empire*, 13–19.

19 "Vospominaniia o Grebenskikh kazakakh i Kavkazskoi linii," *Kavkaz*, October 4, 1856, 313–14. Cited in Barrett, *Edge of Empire*, 14.

20 See Vladimir Hamed-Troyansky, *Empire of Refugees: North Caucasian Muslims and the Late Ottoman State* (Stanford University Press, 2024), 25–33.

21 I. Drozdov, "Posledniaia bor'ba s gortsami na zapadnom Kavkaze," *Kavkazskii sbornik* 2 (1877): 457.

Chapter 5: Clear Glade and Murmuring Forest

1 Nikolai Shipov, *Istoriia moei zhizni i moikh stranstvii* (Tipografiia V. S. Balasheva, 1881). Shipov's *The Story of My Life and Wanderings* is available in an abridged translation in John MacKay's *Four Russian Serf Narratives* (University of Wisconsin Press, 2009), 118–90. See also Daniel R. Brower and Susan Layton, "Liberation Through Captivity: Nikolai Shipov's Adventures in the Imperial Borderlands," *Kritika: Explorations in Russian and Eurasian History* 6, no. 2 (Spring 2005): 259–79.

2 Rosamund Bartlett, *Tolstoy: A Russian Life* (Profile, 2011), 26; Hilde Hoogen-

boom, "Estate Culture and Yasnaya Polyana," in *Tolstoy in Context*, ed. Anna A. Berman (Cambridge University Press, 2022), 28–30.

3 David Moon, *Abolition of Serfdom in Russia, 1762–1907* (Longman, 2001), 13, 17, 45–46; M. G. Mulhall, *The Dictionary of Statistics* (George Routledge, 1899), 541. From Hoogenboom, "Estate Culture," 30.

4 Bartlett, *Tolstoy*, 21.

5 Bartlett, *Tolstoy*, 22.

6 Viktor Shklovsky, "O parke—ostatke zaseki," in *Lev Tolstoi* (Molodaia gvardiia, 1963), 13.

7 Letter from Sergei Nikolaevich Tolstoy to Lev Nikolaevich Tolstoy, July 14, 1852. Excerpted in n. 9 to Tolstoy's letter to Tatiana Alexandrovna Ergol'skaia, July 4, 1852.

8 Letter from Tolstoy to Ergol'skaia.

9 Moon, "Planting Trees," 38. Jane Costlow, *Heart-Pine Russia: Walking and Writing the Nineteenth-Century Forest* (Cornell University Press, 2013), 103.

10 Shklovsky, "O parke—ostatke zaseki."

11 Costlow, *Heart-Pine Russia*, citing K. S. Semenov, *"Istoriia lesov Iasnoi Poliany za sto let i zadacha sokhraneniia i vosstanovleniia ikh"* (dissertation, Tula, 1954), 103–4.

12 Hoogenboom, "Estate Culture," 31.

13 Larisa Timofeeva, "Tolstoi pokupal berezy na gonorar ot 'Voiny i mira,'" *Myslo Tula*, July 19, 2013. Sof'ia Tolstaia, *Dnevniki v dvukh tomakh*, 1: 1862–1900 (Khudozhestvennaia literatura, 1978), entries for April 23, April 24, July 14, October 8, 1891; April 29, November 17, 1898; November 5, December 11, December 15, December 16, 1890; June 11, 1895.

14 Aleksandra Tolstaya, *Otets: Zhizn' L'va Tolstogo* (Direct-Media, 2016), 5.

15 L. N. Tolstoy to A. A. Tolstaya, May 1, 1858, in L. N. Tolstoi, *Sobranie sochinenii v 22 tomakh*, tom 18: *Pis'ma, 1842–1881* (Khudozhestvennaia literatura, 1984), 513–14.

16 Thomas Newlin, "The Natural World," in Berman, *Tolstoy in Context*, 217.

17 Timofeeva, "Tolstoi pokupal berezy na gonorar ot 'Voiny i mira.'"

18 Tat'iana L'vovna Sukhotina-Tolstaia, *Vospominaniia detstvo Tani Tolstoi v Iasnoi Poliane*, Section 8.

19 Maksim Gor'kii, "Lev Tolstoi," *Sobranie sochinenii v 30 tomakh*, vol. 14: *Povesti, rasskazy, ocherki* (Khudozhestvennaia literatura, 1949), 1912–23.

20 Costlow, *Heart-Pine Russia*, 101–6.

21 Newlin, "Natural World," 216.

22 Nina Nikitina, *A Tour of the Estate with Lev Tolstoy* (Izd. Dom Iasnaia Poliana, 2004), 174–82.

23 I. G. Beilin and V. A. Parnes, *Aleksandr Efimovich Teploukhov* (Izd. Nauka, 1969), 16.

24 Pravilova, *Public Empire*, 47–55.

25 I. S. Turgenev, "Khor' and Kalinych," in *Polnoe sobranie sochinenii i pisem v tridtsati tomakh*, tom 3 (Izd. Nauka, 1979), 7. See Costlow's detailed discussion of Turgenev and forests, in *Heart-Pine Russia*, chapter 1. On Turgenev as a

nature-loving hunter, see Thomas Hodge, *Hunting Nature: Ivan Turgenev and the Organic World* (Cornell University Press, 2020).

26 I. S. Turgenev, *Polnoe sobranie sochinenii i pisem v dvadtsati vos'mi tomakh*, tom. 3: *Pis'ma* (Izd. Akademii nauk SSSR, 1963), 175.

27 I. I. Panaev to L. N. Tolstoy, August 28, 1855. See also N. A. Nekrasov to L. N. Tolstoy, September 2, 1855, in L. N. Tolstoi, *Polnoe sobranie sochinenii: Pis'ma, 1844–1855* (Khudozhestvennaia literatura, 1935).

28 Pravilova, *Public Empire*, 68.

29 Brian Bonhomme, "A Revolution in the Forest? Forest Conservation in Soviet Russia, 1917–1925," *Environmental History* 7, no. 3 (July 2002): 411–34.

30 Katja Bruisch, "The State in the Swamps: Territorialization and Ecosystem Engineering in the Western Provinces of the Late Russian Empire," *Zeitschrift fur Ostmitteleuropa-Forschung* 3 (2019): 345–68.

31 David Blackbourn, *The Conquest of Nature* (W. W. Norton, 2006).

32 Bruisch, "State in the Swamps."

33 Pravilova, *Public Empire*, 76.

34 Nataliia Shakhovskaia, *V. G. Korolenko: Opyt' biograficheskoi kharakteristiki* (K. F. Nekrasov, 1912), 3.

35 Vladimir Korolenko, *Istoriia moego sovremennika* (Pravda, 1985). Korolenko's memoir is available in abridged form in English as *The History of My Contemporary* (Oxford University Press, 1972).

36 *Gr. Lev Tolstoi: Velikii pisatel' zemli russkoi v portretakh, gravyurakh, zhivopisi, skul'pturi, karikaturakh i t.d.*, ed. N. Krasnov and L. M. Vol'f (Izd. Tovarishchestva M. O. Vol'fa, 1903), 96.

37 V. G. Korolenko, *Sobranie sochinenii*, tom 1: *Povesti i rasskazy 1879–1888* (Khudozhestvennaia literatura, 1989), 369–70.

38 See note to "Les Shumit," in V. G. Korolenko, *Sobranie sochinenii*, tom 2: *Povesti i rasskazy* (Khudozhestvennaia literatura, 1954).

Chapter 6: Prince, Peasant, Tungus, Yakut

1 Peter Kropotkin, *Memoirs of a Revolutionist* (Kropotkin Collection Editions, 2018), 30. This reissue is based on the original 1899 Houghton Mifflin edition. Kropotkin's beautiful, engaging memoir was originally written in English and published serially in *The Atlantic Monthly*.

2 Kropotkin, *Memoirs*, 15–17.

3 See Mark Bassin, *Imperial Visions: Nationalist Imagination and Geographical Expansion in the Russian Far East, 1840–1865* (Cambridge University Press, 1999).

4 Kropotkin, *Memoirs*, 19–20.

5 Kropotkin, *Memoirs*, 6.

6 Kropotkin, *Memoirs*, 33.

7 Petr Kropotkin, *Sibirskie tetradi (1862–1866)* (Common Place, 2016), 25–36.

8 Kropotkin, *Sibirskie tetradi*, 61–64, 45–46.

9 Kropotkin, *Sibirskie tetradi*, 120.

10 Kropotkin, *Sibirskie tetradi*, 132.
11 Kropotkin, *Memoirs*, 130.
12 Kropotkin, *Memoirs*, 119.
13 Kropotkin, *Memoirs*, 118.
14 Hartley, *Siberia*, 19–20.
15 US Census Bureau, *1910 Census: Indian Population in the United States and Alaska*.
16 Slezkine, *Arctic Mirrors*, 97.
17 Slezkine, *Arctic Mirrors*, 70, 82.
18 I. S. Gurvich, *Etnicheskaia istoriia narodov severa* (Izd. Nauka 1982), 195.
19 Slezkine, *Arctic Mirrors*, 98.
20 Hartley, *Siberia*, 45–46.
21 James Belich, *Replenishing the Earth: The Settler Revolution and the Rise of the Anglo-World, 1783–1939* (Oxford University Press, 2009), 37.
22 Ivan Sablin and Maria Savelyeva, "Mapping Indigenous Siberia: Spatial Changes and Ethnic Realities, 1900–2010," *Settler Colonial Studies* 1, no. 1 (2011): 82.

Chapter 7: Tigers Listen to Water Talk

1 L. I. Sem and Iu. A. Sem, *Mify, skazki i predaniia Nanaitsev* (Izd. Rossiiskogo gosudarstvennogo pedagogicheskogo universiteta im. A. I. Gertzena, 2020), 93.
2 See Steven G. Marks, *Road to Power: The Trans-Siberian Railroad and the Colonization of Asian Russia, 1850–1917* (Cornell University Press, 1991).
3 *Socialist Construction in the U.S.S.R.: Statistical Abstract* (Soyuzorgouchet, 1956), table 11, 310.
4 See Jean-Baptiste Fressoz, *More and More and More: An All-Consuming History of Energy* (Allen Lane, 2024), 57–59.
5 See Slezkine, *Arctic Mirrors*, 113–27.
6 Ivan Yegorchev, "Foreword: The Unknown Arsenyev," in Vladimir K. Arsenyev, *Across the Ussuri Kray: Travels in the Sikhote-Alin Mountains*, translated and with annotations by Jonathan C. Slaght (Indiana University Press, 2016). Slaght, a champion of Arsenyev's work as a naturalist, has lovingly retranslated Arsenyev's writing with scientific precision that was lacking in earlier, abridged translations.
7 Arsenyev, *Across the Ussuri Kray*, 100, 280.
8 Arsenyev, *Across the Ussuri Kray*, 281.
9 Arsenyev, *Across the Ussuri Kray*, 285, 300.
10 Iuliia Shestakova, *Liudi-Zvezdy: Ocherki i rasskazy* (Khabarovskoe knizhnoe izdatel'stvo, 1981), 224–25.
11 Author interview with Pavel Sulyandziga, chair of the Board of the International Development Fund of Indigenous Peoples in Russia (BATANI), December 2024.
12 Arsenyev's more scientific travelogues had already been published in Ger-

many thanks to the help of explorer Fridtjof Nansen, who admired Arsenyev as a scientist. The influential Maksim Gorky (discussed in the next chapter) published a public letter in February 1928 praising Arsenyev as a "Russian Fenimore Cooper," and factographer Sergei Tretyakov (see next chapter) praised Arsenyev in a 1928 review in *Novyi LEF.* See Barbara Wurm, "On Tracks, Facts, and the Living Man: Sergei Tret'iakov's Implied Ethnographic Turn (or: Appropriating Vladimir Arsen'ev)," *Russian Literature* 103–5 (2019): 183–208.

13 Arsenyev, *Across the Ussuri Kray*, 18–19.

14 See Johanna Nichols, "Stereotyping Interethnic Communication: The Siberian Native in Soviet Literature," in *Between Heaven and Hell: The Myth of Siberia in Russian Culture*, ed. Galina Diment and Yuri Slezkine (St. Martin's Press, 1993), 185–214.

15 V. K. Arsen'ev, *Po Ussuriiskomu Kraiu*, in *Izbrannye proizvedeniia v 2 tomakh*, tom 1 (Khabarovskoe knizhoe izdatel'stvo, 1997), 220.

16 Arsen'ev, *Po Ussuriiskomu Kraiu*, 230.

17 Arsen'ev, *Po Ussuriiskomu Kraiu*, 264.

18 Arsen'ev, *Po Ussuriiskomu Kraiu*, 285–86.

19 Arsenyev, *Across the Ussuri Kray*, 332.

20 Slezkine, *Arctic Mirrors*, 74.

21 Arsenyev, *Across the Ussuri Kray*, 59–60.

22 Arsenyev, *Across the Ussuri Kray*, 63.

23 See A. V. Korovashko, *Po sledam Dersu Uzala. Tropami Ussuriiskogo kraia* (Veche, 2016).

24 For a brilliant account of the trajectory of these "small peoples" and the birth of Russian ethnography, see Slezkine, *Arctic Mirrors*.

25 B. Brunko, "Pervyi iz udege," *Literaturnaia gazeta*, no. 90 (July 27, 1963).

26 Alexander Vaschenko and Claude Clayton Smith, trans. and eds., *The Way of Kinship: An Anthology of Native Siberian Literature* (University of Minnesota Press, 2010), 195.

27 Dzhanki Kimonko, *Tam, gde bezhit Sukpai* (Molodaia gvardiia, 1951), 7.

28 Kimonko, *Tam*, 7–8.

29 Kimonko, *Tam*, 8.

Chapter 8: Cutting Orchards and Moving Mountains

1 Donald Rayfield, *Anton Chekhov: A Life* (Henry Holt, 1997), 215.

2 Rayfield, *Anton Chekhov*, 3–5.

3 Rayfield, *Anton Chekhov*, 29.

4 Letter to A. S. Suvorin, January 7, 1889.

5 Rayfield, *Anton Chekhov*, 215.

6 Anton Chekhov, "Iz Sibiri," in *Polnoe sobranie sochinenii i pisem v 30 tomakh*, tom 14 (Izd. Nauka, 1978), 5–38. I quote translations from "From Siberia," in *Sakhalin Island*, trans. Brian Reeve (Alma Classics, 2019), 33–36.

7 Rayfield, *Anton Chekhov*, 238.

8 Rayfield, *Anton Chekhov*, 238.
9 Donald Rayfield, *Chekhov's* Uncle Vania *and* The Wood Demon, Critical Studies in Russian Literature (Bristol Classical Press, 1995), 3. This study by Chekhov's biographer provides a comprehensive analysis of Chekhov's revisions to *Leshii*, along with vital historical and biographical context.
10 Anton Chekhov, *Diadia Vania*, in *Sochineniia v 2 tomakh*, tom 2: *Povesti i rasskazy, P'esy* (Khudozhestvennaia literatura, 1982), 377–78.
11 Chekhov, *Diadia Vania*, 378.
12 Quoted in Rayfield, *Chekhov's* Uncle Vania, 8–9.
13 Rayfield, *Anton Chekhov*, 498.
14 Rayfield, *Anton Chekhov*, 572.
15 Anton Chekhov, *Vishnevyi Sad*, in *Sochineniia v 2 tomakh*, tom 2: *Povesti i rasskazy, P'esy* (Khudozhestvennaia literatura, 1982), 463–64.
16 Brain, *Song of the Forest*, 20–21, 24, 56.
17 Brain, *Song of the Forest*, 61.
18 Leon Trotskii, *Literatura i revoliutsiia* (Izd. Krasnaia nov', 1923), Part 1, Section 8.
19 Sergei Tret'iakov, "Fotozametki," *Novyi LEF* 8 (1928): 41. The translation of the first paragraph is taken from Christopher Phillips, ed., *Photography in the Modern Era: European Documents and Critical Writings, 1913–1940* (Aperture, 1989), 254.
20 See Richard Stites, "Beyond the Green Wall," in *Revolutionary Dreams: Utopian Vision and Experimental Life in the Russian Revolution* (Oxford University Press, 1991), 52.
21 Sergei Tret'iakov, "Zhivoi 'zhivoi' chelovek. O knige V. K. Arsen'eva 'V debriakh ussuriiskogo kraia'," *Novyi LEF* 7 (1928): 44–46. See Wurm, "On Tracks."
22 Aglaya Glebova, "Elements of Photography: Avant-garde Aesthetics and the Reforging of Nature," *Representations* 142 (2018): 58. Glebova's brilliant, beautifully written article includes a detailed analysis of avant-garde photographic images of trees during this period. See also her book *Aleksandr Rodchenko: Photography in the Time of Stalin* (Yale University Press, 2022).
23 On early Soviet conservationism and the *zapovedniki*, see Douglas R. Weiner, *Models of Nature: Ecology, Conservation, and Cultural Revolution in Soviet Russia* (Indiana University Press, 1988).
24 Brain, *Song of the Forest*, 89–91, 77, 102–103.
25 Quoted in Vladimir Boreiko, "Sovetskaia literatura kak glashatai bor'by s prirodoi: Gody 20-e," *Belye piatna prirodookhrany* (Istoriia okhrany prirody, vypusk 31, 2003).
26 Brain, *Song of the Forest*, 96–102.
27 Brain, *Song of the Forest*, 102–4.
28 "Resoliutsiia po dokladu Soiuzlesproma i sotsialisticheskoi rekonstruktsii i ratsionalizatsii lesnoi i derevoobrabatyvaiushchei promyshlennosti," *Lesnoi spetsialist* 1 (January 1931): 49–54. Quoted in Brain, *Song of the* Forest, 117.
29 Brain, *Song of the Forest*, 117–21.
30 "Zakliuchitel'noe slovo tov. Makarova," in *Trudy Pervogo Vsesoiuznogo Siezda*

po okhrane prirody v SSSR (Moscow, 1935), 48. The term *zapovednik* is also used for cultural sites such as Yasnaya Polyana and Pushkin's estate at Mikhailovskoe, where trees as well as houses preserve the spirit of the author.

31 Mikhail Prishvin, diary entry, October 22, 1934, in M. M. Prishvin, *Dnevniki, 1932–1935*, tom 8, ed. Ia. Z. Grishina (Rostok, 2009), 528. Glebova, "Elements of Photography."

32 Brain, *Song of the Forest*, 116.

Chapter 9: Electricity and Resurrection

1 Abram Tertz [Andrei Sinyavsky], *Golos iz khora* (Stenvalley Press, 1973), 52.

2 Andrei Platonov, *Vzyskanie pogibshikh* (Shkola Press, 1995), 630. Cited in Robert Chandler and Olga Meerson's afterword to Andrey Platonov, *The Foundation Pit* (New York Review of Books, 2009), 155.

3 Andrei Platonov, *Sochineniya*, I, I (IMLI RAN, 2004), 473. Cited in Robert Chandler and Olga Meerson's afterword to *The Foundation Pit*, by Andrey Platonov, 156.

4 Chandler and Meerson, afterword to *The Foundation Pit*, by Andrey Platonov, 153–57.

5 B. Kardin, "Luchshie gody nashei zhizni," *Ogonek* 3277, no. 19 (May 1990): 19.

6 Maksim Gorky, "Prekrasnoe delo sdelano," *Pravda*, no. 243, September 3, 1933. M. Gor'kii, "Iz stat'i "O biblioteke Poeta," in *Gork'ii i nauka: Stat'i, pis'ma i vospominaniia* (Izd. Nauka, 1964), 56.

7 Robert Chandler, introduction to *Soul* by Andrei Platonov (New York Review of Books, 2008), xix–xx.

8 Andrei Platonov, "Among Animals and Plants," in *Soul*, trans. Robert and Elizabeth Chandler and Olga Meerson (New York Review of Books, 2008). I quote from this excellent, erudite translation.

9 "Platonov, Among Animals and Plants," 155–156.

10 For a full discussion, see Chandler's introduction to *Soul.*

11 Platonov, "Among Animals and Plants," 166.

12 Ralph Dutli, *Osip Mandelstam: A Biography*, trans. Ben Fowkes (Verso, 2023), 293.

13 Dutli, *Osip Mandelstam*, 291–92.

14 Evgeniia Ginzburg, *Krutoi Marshrut: Khronika vremen kul'ta lichnosti* (AST, 2015), 372–75. In English: Eugenia Semyonovna Ginzburg, *Journey into the Whirlwind*, trans. Paul Stevenson and Max Hayward (Harcourt, Brace & World, 1967), 422–30.

15 Dutli, *Osip Mandelstam*, 365.

16 V. T. Shalamov, "Iagody," in *Sobranie sochinenii v 4 tomakh*, tom 1 (Khudozhestvennaia literatura, Vagrius, 1998), 54–56. In English, "Berries," *Kolyma Tales*, translated from the Russian and with an introduction by Donald Rayfield (New York Review of Books, 2018), 60–62.

17 V. T. Shalamov, "Po lendlizu," *Sobranie sochinenii*, 350–57; and "Lend-Lease," *Kolyma Tales*, 427–34.

18 Shalamov, "Stlanik," in *Sobranie sochinenii*, 139–40, and "The Dwarf Pine,"

Kolyma Tales, 167–69. The word *stlanik* comes from the Russian word for lying down, spreading out, or getting ready for bed; it is a generic term for dwarf trees.

19 Shalamov, "Voskreshenie listvennitsy," in *Sobranie sochinenii*, tom 2, 273–76. "The Resurrection of the Larch," in *Sketches of the Criminal World*, trans. Donald Rayfield (New York Review of Books, 2020), 324–27.

20 Leonid D. Grenkevich, *The Soviet Partisan Movement, 1941–1944: A Critical Historiographical Analysis*, ed. David M. Glantz (Taylor & Francis, 1999), 262–267.

Chapter 10: Young Oaks

1 Brain, *Song of the Forest*, 85–88. Hermann Göring, "Deutsches Volk—Deutscher Wald," *Zeitschrift für Weltforstwirtschaft* 3 (1935/1936): 656. See also Michael Imort, "A Sylvan People: Wilhelmine Forestry and the Forest as a Symbol of Germandom," in *Germany's Nature: Cultural Landscapes and Environmental History*, ed. Thomas Lekan and Thomas Zeller (Rutgers University Press, 2005), 55–80; D. R. Helliwell, "Dauerwald," in *Forestry: An International Journal of Forest Research* 71, no. 4 (1997): 375–79; and Robert G. Lee and Sabine Wilke, "Forest as Volk: Ewiger Wald and the Religion of Nature in the Third Reich," *Journal of Social and Ecological Boundaries* 1, no. 1 (Spring 2005): 21–46. Since the 1990s, "continuous cover forestry" is in wide use in Europe as a sustainable approach to forestry. The history of the German and Nazi attitude to the forest is a rich and complex one beyond the scope of this book, but with fascinating overlap and differences with the Russian/Slavic case. See Jeffrey K. Wilson, *The German Forest: Nature, Identity, and the Contestation of a National Symbol, 1871–1914* (University of Toronto Press, 2016).

2 Philip W. Blood, "Securing Hitler's *Lebensraum:* The Luftwaffe and Białowieża Forest, 1942–1944," *Holocaust and Genocide Studies* 24, no. 2 (Fall 2010): 247–72.

3 Blood, "Securing Hitler's *Lebensraum*," 255.

4 Blood, "Securing Hitler's *Lebensraum*," 261.

5 David Blackbourne, *The Conquest of Nature: Water, Landscape, and the Making of Modern Germany* (W. W. Norton, 2007), 251–77.

6 Grenkevich, *Soviet Partisan Movement*, 2, 4.

7 Grenkevich, *Soviet Partisan Movement*, 249, 172.

8 Grenkevich, *Soviet Partisan Movement*, 187.

9 Ben H. Shepherd, *War in the Wild East: The German Army and Soviet Partisans* (Harvard University Press, 2004), 122–23, 204–5.

10 Grenkevich, *Soviet Partisan Movement*, 11.

11 Grenkevich, *Soviet Partisan Movement*, 200.

12 Quoted in Shepherd, *War in the Wild East*, 181.

13 Elena Sazanovich, "Boris Nikolaevich Polevoi: Povest' o nastoiashchem cheloveke," *Iunost'* 686, no. 3 (2013): 89. Quotations from "The Story of a Real Man" are my translations from Boris Polevoi, *Povest' o nastoiashchem cheloveke* (Sovetskii pisatel', 1947), 23, 28, 45.

14 Quoted in Grenkevich, *Soviet Partisan Movement*, 237.
15 Shepherd, *War in the Wild East*, 129 (photo).
16 Shepherd, *War in the Wild East*, 128.
17 Alex J. Kay, *Empire of Destruction: A History of Nazi Mass Killing* (Yale University Press, 2021).
18 Grenkevich, *Soviet Partisan Movement*, 239.
19 Quote from a 1978 interview with Shepitko, transcribed from the 1999 Bavarian TV show *Razgovor s Larisoi*, from "'I byla voina' . . . i ne tol'ko: 'Voskhozhdenie' (1976)," Vladimirskaia oblastnaia nauchnaia biblioteka.

Chapter 11: Stalin and the Wood Goblin

1 "Postavlenie Soveta narodnykh kommissarov Soiuza SSSR ob organizatsii lesnogo khoziaistva," *Lesnoi spetsialist* 7–8 (July–August 1931): 9–10. Quoted in Brain, *Song of the Forest*, 144.
2 Brain, *Song of the Forest*, 148, 140.
3 Quoted in Brain, *Song of the Forest*, 152.
4 Brain, *Song of the Forest*, 153–59, 163–65.
5 Boris Thomson, *The Art of Compromise: The Life and Work of Leonid Leonov* (University of Toronto Press, 2001), 6.
6 Thomson, *Art of Compromise*, 100–101.
7 From Weiner, *Models of Nature*, 169.
8 Leonid Leonov, *Sot'* (Eksmo, 2021), 1. See also Thomson, *Art of Compromise*, 116–18.
9 Quoted in Thomson, *Art of Compromise*, 78.
10 Thomson, *Art of Compromise*, 78.
11 Quoted in James H. Billington, *The Icon and the Axe: An Interpretive History of Russian Culture* (Vintage Books, 1970), 28. Khrushchev's remarks (addressed directly to Leonov) cited in CDSP, May 24, 1961, 6. Speech first given July 17, 1960, and reprinted in *Kommunist*.
12 Thomson, *Art of Compromise*, 237.
13 Leonov, *Russkii les*, 92.
14 Leonov, *Russkii les*, 99.
15 Leonov, *Russkii les*, 229; translation from Leonid Leonov, *The Russian Forest*, trans. Bernard Isaacs (Fredonia Books, 2003), 234.
16 Leonov, *Russkii les*, 247–48, 251. Translation adapted from Leonov, *The Russian Forest*, 252.
17 Leonov, *Russkii les*, 565.
18 Leonov, *Russkii les*, 598.
19 Leonov, *Russkii les*, 236.
20 Leonov, *Russkii les*, 278–79.
21 Leonov, *Russkii les*, 295.
22 Victor Terras, "L. M. Leonov's Novel *The Russian Forest*," *Slavic and East European Journal* 8, no. 2 (Summer 1964): 124.

23 Zakhar Prilepin, *Podel'nik epokhi: Leonid Leonov* (Astrel', 2012), 603–4. On Prilepin, see chapter 14.
24 Prilepin, *Podel'nik epokhi*, 613.

Chapter 12: The Tsar-Larch and the Flood

1 Tertz, *Golos*, 168.
2 *Istoriia vsesoiuznoi kommunisticheskoi partii (bol'shevikov), Kratkii kurs* (OGIZ-Gospolitizdat, 1948), 300.
3 Alla Bolotova, "Colonization of Nature in the Soviet Union: State Ideology, Public Discourse, and the Experience of Geologists," *Historical Social Research / Historische Sozialforschung* 29, no. 3 (109), The Frontiers of Environmental History / Umweltgeschichte in der Erweiterung (2004): 104–23.
4 Bolotova, "Colonization of Nature," 104.
5 Paola Volkova, *Nostal'gia* (AST, 2008), chapter 4.
6 *Itogi: Snimaiushchii vechnost'* (interview with Marina Tarkovskaya), Central State Museum of Film, Moscow, 2012.
7 Miriam Dobson, *Khrushchev's Cold Summer: Gulag Returnees, Crime, and the Fate of Reform After Stalin* (Cornell University Press, 2011), 39.
8 Boris Vishnevskii, "Kto i kak nashel almazy Rossii," *Novaya gazeta*, September 9, 2010.
9 Ekaterina Elagina, *Almaznye ekspeditsii*, vol. 2 (Izd. dom "Poliarnyi krug," 2003), 298–305.
10 Elagina, *Almaznye ekspeditsii*, 324; Natal'ia Taran, "Intrigi pervootkryvatelei almazov, ili kto pervyim nashel 'Mir,' *Forpost*, February 13, 2021.
11 Kirill Rukov, "Kak my poteriali 'Mir': Istoriia samoi dorogoi tekhnogennoi avarii Rossii"/ "Losing 'Mir': The Story of Russia's Most Expensive Industrial Disaster," *Baza*, September 20, 2023.
12 Taran, "Intrigi pervootkryvatelei almazov."
13 Rukov, "Kak my poteriali 'Mir.'"
14 Ol'ga Shablinskaia, "S'emki na grani. Kak Kalatozov sozdaval 'Neotpravlennoe pis'mo,'" *Argumenty i fakty*, January 15, 2023.
15 V. Osipov, "Neotpravlennoe pis'mo," *Iunost'*, no. 8 (1957).
16 Valentin Rasputin, "Siberia Without the Romance," in *Siberia, Siberia*, translated and with an introduction by Margaret Winchell and Gerald Mikkelson (Northwestern University Press, 1996), 66.
17 Andrei Rumiantsev, *Valentin Rasputin* (Molodaia gvardiia, 2016), 350–53. Valentin Rasputin, "Imeet silu natsional'nogo parolia. K 100-letiiu L. M. Leonova," in "U nas ostaetsia Rossii" (Institut russkoi tsivilizatsii, 2015), 126–28.
18 Prilepin, *Podel'nik epokhi*, 605–6. The campaign took place in 1985.
19 Rasputin, "Siberia Without the Romance," 35.
20 Valentin Rasputin, "The Fire," in *Siberia on Fire*, selected, translated, and with an introduction by Gerald Mikkelson and Margaret Winchell (Northern Illinois University Press, 1989), 159.

21 Quoted in the translators' introduction to *Siberia, Siberia*, by Rasputin, 13.
22 Valentin Rasputin, *Farewell to Matyora*, translated by Antonina W. Bouis, with a foreword by Kathleen Parthe (Northwestern University Press, 1991), 120.
23 Rasputin, *Farewell to Matyora*, 2.
24 Rasputin, *Farewell to Matyora*, 183.
25 Rasputin, *Farewell to Matyora*, 186–89.
26 Rasputin, *Farewell to Matyora*, 177.
27 Rasputin, *Farewell to Matyora*, 194.
28 Rasputin, *Farewell to Matyora*, 197.
29 Yitzhak Brudny, *Reinventing Russia: Russian Nationalism and the Soviet State, 1953–1991* (Harvard University Press, 2000), 24.
30 Rasputin, *Farewell to Matyora*, 116.
31 See Jonathan D. Oldfield, "Imagining Climates Past, Present and Future: Soviet Contributions to the Science of Anthropogenic Climate Change, 1953–1991," *Journal of Historical Geography* 60 (2018): 41–51.
32 Rasputin, "Siberia Without the Romance," 51, 35.
33 Rasputin, "Imeet silu."

Chapter 13: Arks and Anarchists

1 Vasily Peskov, *Lost in the Taiga: One Russian Family's Fifty-Year Struggle for Survival and Religious Freedom in the Siberian Wilderness* (Doubleday, 1994), 3.
2 Peskov, *Lost in the Taiga*, 6.
3 Thomas H. Hoisington, "Melnikov-Pechersky: Romancer of Provincial and Old Believer Life," *Slavic Review* 33, no. 4 (December 1974): 681–82.
4 Hoisington, "Melnikov-Pechersky," 687–88.
5 See discussion in Costlow, *Heart-Pine Russia*, 41–80.
6 Peskov, *Lost in the Taiga*, 46.
7 Peskov, *Lost in the Taiga*, 34.
8 Peskov, *Lost in the Taiga*, 86.
9 Peskov, *Lost in the Taiga*, 50.
10 Louiza M. Boukharaeva and Marcel Marloie, *Family Urban Agriculture in Russia: Lessons and Prospects* (Springer, 2015), 75.
11 Arsenyev, *Across the Ussuri Kray*, 101.
12 Peskov, *Lost in the Taiga*, 92.
13 Boukharaeva and Marloie, *Family Urban Agriculture in Russia*, 78.
14 Nikolai Muravin, "K staroveram na Biriusu, ili puteshestvie raionnogo masshtaba," *Vokrug sveta* 1 (1996).
15 Tamara Men et al., "Russian Mortality Trends for 1991–2001: Analysis by Cause and Region," *British Medical Journal* 327, no. 7421 (October 25, 2003).
16 Nancy Ries, "Potato Ontology," *Cultural Anthropology* 24, no. 2 (2009): 181–212.
17 Polina Moroz, "Society: Eccentric Monuments Replace Overturned Lenin Busts," *Moscow News*, no. 42, November 3, 2004.
18 "Radikal'nye ekoaktivisti: Kratkaia istoriia nasil'stvennoi bor'by za chistuiu pla-

netu," *Furfur*, October 6, 2015. I benefited from Ania Aizman's presentation on Russian eco-anarchism at the panel "Sprouts of Freedom Under the Crown of the Russian Woods: Arboreal Power and Arboreal Resistance" at ASEEES, December 2023, as well as from presentations by Jonathan Flatley (on Shalamov) and Artemy Magun (on Vladimir Bibikhin).

19 Nadezhda Kostina, " . . . Nam liubye dorogi dorogi," *Sovershenno sekretno*, January 10, 2010.

20 Elena Kostyuchenko, "Vzbesivshiisia zver' vygryzaet svoi legkie," *Novaya gazeta*, February 4, 2008.

21 Andrei Kozenko, "Khimkinskii les ogorodili brevnami," *Kommersant*, no. 129 (4429), July 20, 2010.

22 Zoia Svetova, "Zhanna d'Ark iz Khimkinskogo lesa," *Novoe vremia*, no. 24, August 9, 2010.

23 Svetova, "Zhanna d'Ark iz Khimkinskogo lesa."

24 Evgeniia Chirikova, "O chem shumit Khimkinskii les," *Forbes.ru*, July 26, 2010.

25 Kostyuchenko, "Vzbesivshiisia zver' vygryzaet svoi legkie."

26 Kostina, ". . . Nam liubye dorogi dorogi."

27 "Lesnaia sestra: Evgeniia Chirikova, lider dvizheniia v zashchitu Khimkinskogo lesa," *Ogonyok*, no. 9, July 13, 2009, 4.

28 Andrei Kozenko, Khalil' Aminov, and Alisa Ivanitskaia, "Khimkinskii les otshumel," *Kommersant* no. 232 (4532), December 15, 2010.

29 Tat'iana Britskaia, "'Oni radovat'sia dolzhny, chto menia vydavili': Kak zhivet v ukrainskoi emigratsii russkoi iurodivyi Drevarkh," *Novaia gazeta*, January 31, 2020.

30 Danil Zakharov (dir.), *Drevarkh* (short film), Kinolaboratoriia "Arkticheskaia zhara," 2023, YouTube, https://www.youtube.com/watch?v=_VmUUq4AEH8.

31 Anton Danilov, "'Mne ochen' bol'no.' Drevarkhu Prosvetlennomu sdelali neskol'ko operatsii v Arkhangelske," *29.ru.*, April 25, 2024.

32 "Umer odin iz samykh znamenitykh arkhangelogorodtsev Andrei Khristoforov, izvestnyi pod imenem Drevarx," *Ekho severa*, May 3, 2024.

33 Vice News, "Surviving in the Siberian Wilderness for 70 Years," 2013, YouTube, https://www.youtube.com/watch?v=tt2AYafET68&t=930s.

34 "Sibirskaia otshel'nitsa Agaf'ia Lykova pereekhala v novyi dom," *Blagovest*, March 11, 2021.

35 GTRK Khakasiia, "Agaf'e Lykovoi ispolnilos' 79 let!" April 17, 2023, YouTube, https://www.youtube.com/watch?v=dtibE9M_C9U.

Chapter 14: Militiamen

1 "Poselok Bakhta," *Entsiklopediia Krasnoiarskogo kraiia*, https://web.archive.org/web/20160414042340/http://my.krskstate.ru/docs/villages/poselok-bakhta/.

2 Tatyana Trufanova, "Schastlivye liudi Sibiri: Mikhail Tarkovskii rasskazal o pravde i lzhi," Amic.ru, February 7, 2013.

3 Iurii Belikov, "Tarkovskii rodil Ermaka," Park istorii reki Chusovoi, June 27, 2017.

4 Mikhail Tarkovsky, "U kazhdogo pisatelia est' vybor—s kem ty i vo imia chego," *Argumenty i fakty*, February 26, 2020.

5 V. Aver'ianov et al., "Russkii Kovcheg: Al'ternativnaia strategiia mirovogo razvitiia," February 18, 2020, https://izborsk-club.ru/18825.

6 Aleksandr Pasechnik (dir.), *Kovcheg*, Obshchee delo, 2014, YouTube, https://www.youtube.com/watch?v=Em4EJcZeDmk. See also Alexey Golubev, "'A Wonderful Song of Wood': Heritage Architecture and the Search for Historical Authenticity in North Russia," *Rethinking Marxism* 29, no. 1 (2017): 142–72.

7 Alexander Solzhenitsyn, "Russia in Collapse," *The Solzhenitsyn Reader: New and Essential Writings, 1947–2005*, ed. Edward E. Ericson Jr. and Daniel J. Mahoney (ISI Books, 2006), 475–76.

8 Egor Aref'ev, "Zakhar Prilepin: Kogda sidim v tanke, my vse—russkie! I buriat, i chechenets," *Komsomol'skaia pravda*, November 22, 2016.

9 On Prilepin's contradictory biography and oeuvre, and on the fascist aspects of his politics, see Mark Lipovetsky, "Politicheskaia motorika Zakhara Prilepina," *Znamia* 10 (2012).

10 See Lipovetsky, "Politicheskaia motorika Zakhara Prilepina."

11 Zakhar Prilepin, "Pis'mo Tovarishchu Stalinu," *Svobodnaia pressa*, July 30, 2012.

12 On the strange story of the National Bolsheviks, see Fabrizio Fenghi, *It Will Be Fun and Terrifying: Nationalism and Protest in Post-Soviet Russia* (University of Wisconsin Press, 2020).

13 For a summary of Prilepin's career and role as a militarist propagandist, see Julie Fedor, "Spinning Russia's 21st Century Wars: Zakhar Prilepin and His 'Literary *Spetsnaz*,'" *RUSI Journal* 163, no. 6 (2018): 18–27.

14 Ksenia Sobchak, *Ostorozhno: Sobchak*, "Zakhar Prilepin: Pervoe bol'shoe interv'iu posle pokusheniia," YouTube, https://www.youtube.com/watch?v=uU-zrcBuX2E.

15 Solzhenitsyn, "Russia in Collapse," 479.

16 Aref'ev, "Zakhar Prilepin."

17 Aleksei Shorokhov and Mikhail Tarkovsky, "Otvechu stikhami Arseniia Tarkovskogo, moego deda . . ." *Zavtra*, March 5, 2022.

18 "Na Donbass priekhal i vovsiu izuchaet byt, front i vzhivaetsia v etu zhizn' russkii pisatel' Mikhail Tarkovskii," July 6, 2023, Telegram post, reposted at https://dzen.ru/b/ZKZm4SOBQRw77Y9P.

19 Galina Iuzefovich dissects and debunks the book's claims in "Chto ne tak s knigoi Zakhara Prilepina *Vzvod*," *Meduza*, February 20, 2017.

20 Prilepin, *Podel'nik epokhi*, 10.

21 Prilepin, *Podel'nik epokhi*, 575.

22 Prilepin, *Podel'nik epokhi*, 12.

23 Prilepin, *Podel'nik epokhi*, 561–65.

24 Anatoly Shvidenko et al., "Vulnerability of Ukrainian Forests to Climate Change," *Sustainability* 9, no. 7 (2017): 1152.

25 Ukraine and Eastern Europe Programme, "Walking on Fire: Demining in Ukraine," GLOBSEC, 2023.

26 Sergiy Zibtsev, Professor of Silviculture at National University of Life and Envi-

ronmental Sciences of Ukraine, Presentation for the Yale School of Forestry, April 10, 2023.

27 Stanislav Viter and Viktoria Hubareva, "Reforestation in Ukraine: During and After Wartime," Ukraine War Environmental Consequences Work Group, September 11, 2024.

28 Brian Milakovsky, presentation for the Yale School of Forestry, April 10, 2023, and interview with author, March 21, 2023.

29 Oleksii Vasyliuk and Eugene A. Simonov, "Plans to Rebuild Ukraine Shaped by Solutions for Irpin," Ukraine War Environmental Consequences Work Group, September 2022.

30 On the damage caused by the flood and ongoing threats posed by heavy metals, see O. Shumilova et al., "Environmental Effects of the Kakhovka Dam Destruction by Warfare in Ukraine," *Science* 387 (2025): 1181–86. The article is dedicated to Lyudmyla Shevtsova, a Ukrainian ecologist and river specialist killed in a Russian missile attack on her Kyiv apartment building in 2024.

31 Viktoria Hubareva, "One Year After the Terrorist Attack at Kakhovka Hydropower Plant: 1B Trees Instead of Desert and Willow Forests Unique to the Continent," Ukraine War Environmental Consequences Work Group, July 4, 2024.

32 Oleksiy Vasilyuk et al., "Is It Time to Restore Velykyi Luh?," Ukraine War Environmental Consequences Work Group, September 25, 2023.

33 Fred Pearce, "Ukraine Rewilding: Will Nature Be Allowed to Revive When War Ends?," *Yale Environment 360*, October 21, 2024.

34 Oleksiy Vasyliuk, "Restoring Ukraine's Nature Post-War: Hopes and Risks," Ukraine War Environmental Consequences Work Group, November 10, 2023.

35 See Jane I. Dawson, *Eco-Nationalism: Anti-Nuclear Activism and National Identity in Russia, Lithuania, and Ukraine* (Duke University Press, 1996).

36 Author's correspondence with Andriy Sahaidak, April 2023.

Chapter 15: Bears, Wolves, and Archipelagoes

1 Unless otherwise noted, all details of Pazhetnov's life come from his memoir, *Moia zhizn' v lesu i doma* (Veche, 2014), which I obtained in manuscript form. I am grateful to Yves Gauthier for sharing the file. The book is available in French translation under the title *L'ours est mon maître*, trans. Yves Gauthier (Editions Transboreal, 2016).

2 Author interviews with Vladimir Bologov, February 2023.

3 Grigory Ioffe, Tatyana Nefedova, and Ilya Zaslavsky, *The End of Peasantry? The Disintegration of Rural Russia* (University of Pittsburgh Press, 2006), 80. I am grateful to Tony Wood for pointing me to this material.

4 Author interviews with Vladimir Bologov, February 2023.

5 Author interviews with Vladimir Bologov, February 2023.

6 Ioffe et al., *End of Peasantry?*, 80–81, 166.

7 Jean-Luc Nachbauer (dir.), *Laetitia et ses loups* (360 GEO-Report/Arte, 2010).

8 Author interview with Vladimir Bologov, February 2023.

9 Author interview with Vladimir Bologov, February 2023.

10 C.-A. Haeggström, "The Oldest Known Scots Pine Tree in the Nordic Countries," *Svensk Botanisk Tidskrift* 99, no. 3 (2005).

11 Kseniia Kirsanova (dir.), *Volchii Ostrov* (Chistyi Les, 2016), YouTube, https://www.youtube.com/watch?v=U_xULWChZoA.

12 Outi Isokaanta, *Enchanted by Nature: Getting Acquainted with the Border Area Nature* (Kainuu Regional Environment Centre/Friendship Park Research Centre, 2007), 64–65.

13 On the history of Solovki, see Roy R. Robson, *Solovki: The Story of Russia Told Through Its Most Remarkable Islands* (Yale University Press, 2004).

14 S. A. Malsagoff, *An Island Hell: A Soviet Prison in the Far North*, trans. F. H. Lyon (A. M. Philpot, 1926), 44, 153–54.

15 Vladimir Viacheslavovich Chernavin, *Zapiski vreditelia* (Kanon, 1999), 233. The Chernavins both wrote their memoirs, and both were published in English: Vladimir V. Tchernavin, *I Speak for the Silent: Prisoners of the Soviets*, trans. Nicholas M. Oushakoff (Hale, Cushman & Flint, 1935), and Tatiana Tchernavin, *Escape from the Soviets*, trans. N. Alexander (E. Dutton, 1934). Unfortunately, the English texts diverge substantially from the Russian ones. See Tat'iana Vasil'evna Chernavina, *Pobeg iz GULAGa* (Kanon, 1999).

16 Nick Baron, *Soviet Karelia: Politics, Planning and Terror in Stalin's Russia, 1920–1939* (Routledge, 2007), 127–28.

17 Vladimir Chernavin, *Zapiski vreditelia*, 225–41.

18 Veronica Davidov, *Long Night at the Vepsian Museum: The Forest Folk of Northern Russia and the Struggle for Cultural Survival* (University of Toronto Press, 2017), 39–48.

19 Escape Through the Forest, https://iditelesom.org/ru/. The organization's current English name is Get Lost.

20 "Idi cherez les," *Kholod*, October 13, 2022.

Epilogue: Last Stand on the Ugra

1 Nikola-Lenivets Park official website, "History," https://nikola-lenivets.ru/history.

2 Nikola-Lenivets Park official website, "History," https://nikola-lenivets.ru/history.

3 Irina Kulik, "Oblako, ozero, bashniia," *Proekt klassika*, April 29, 2004.

4 Elena Fedotova, "Nikolai Polisskii: 'Nuzhno byt' tiranom, a ne khochetsia'," *Art khronika*, February 1, 2010.

5 Grigory Revzin, "Nikolay Polissky and Russian Architecture," Archi.ru, July 21, 2008.

6 Quoted in Revzin, "Nikolay Polissky."

7 Vadim Smyslov, "Moi lichnyi stat Nikola-Lenivets," *The Blueprint*, July 23, 2021.

8 Nikola-Lenivets Park official website, "History," https://nikola-lenivets.ru/history.

9 Fedotova, "Nikolai Polisskii."

10 Vladislav Surkov, "Polisskii v"ezzhaet," *Art khronika* no. 6 (2008).

11 "Interv'iu Nikolaia Polisskogo o Nikola-Lenivtse, biznese i tvorchestve," *PoproscheTV*, September 5, 2016, YouTube, https://www.youtube.com/watch?v=9KucL-41Jvo.

Index

Page numbers in italics refer to illustrations. Page numbers after 251 refer to endnotes.

afforestation projects, 52, 55–56, 75–76, 155–59, *157*, 171, 213
Africa, 18, 19, 60
agrarian socialism, 96, 161
agriculture, 6, 14, 84–85
  agricultural labor and the family unit, 98
  complex societies without, 14–18, 25
  deforestation of western Europe, 3, 19, 49, 234
  on "empty" lands, 39, 42–43
  the end of the traditional village, 222–24
  forced collectivization of, 14, 23–24, 127, 130, 162, 193
  investments in agriculture under Brezhnev, 184
  the ruins of collective farms, 224
  slash-and-burn agriculture, 6, 222
  Soviet "allotment gardens," 195
  See also peasantry; serfdom
Ainu people, 116
Aipin, Eremei, 24
Akhmatova, Anna, 135
alcoholism, 97, 106, 180, 224, 242
Alexander I, 57
Alexander II, 90, 94–95, 97
Alexander III, 97
Alexis of Russia, 52, 197, 232
All-Union Congress on the Protection of Nature, 128
Altai Zapovednik nature preserve, 190
Amnya Neolithic site, 15–18, 24–25, *26*, 36, 40
"Among Animals and Plants" (Platonov), 131–33, 162
Amur cork, 103
Amur River, *91*, 91–92, 105, 113, 234
Amur tiger, 108
anarchism, 88, 89, 127
  Christian, 95–96
  eco-anarchism of the 1990s, 197, 207
Andrei Rublev (A. Tarkovsky), 32–34, *33*, 149, 203, 240, 243
animism, 32–34, 35, 97, 180
Anna Karenina (Tolstoy), 79
anthropology. *See* ethnography
antinuclear activism, 216
Archstoyanie festival, 240–46
aristocracy, 56, 83, 90, 97, 204–5
  after the emancipation of the serfs, 83–84
  forest management and the, 42, 55, 56
  inclusion of non-Slavic peoples in the, 42, 60
  indebtedness of the, 66, 67, 75, 79, 83
  progressive-minded landowners and early conservation, 80–85, 117, 242
  serfs and the, 7, 92
  Stroganov family, 37–39, 80–81
  See also serfdom
Ark (documentary), 205–6
Arkhangelsk, *44*, 49, 161, 165, 200
Arsenyev, Vladimir, 101–13, 116, 124, 129, 174, 188, 194, 210, 219, 259–60
Ascent, The (film), 151–54, 184
Astrakhan, 36, 90
avant-garde, 123–24, 162, 179
Avars, 2–3, 63–66, 70–71, 73, 145, 239
Avdeenko, Vladimir, 175
Azov Sea, 50

Ba'atur, Yesugei, 28
Baba Yaga, 5–6, 9, 240
Badgers (Leonov), 161–62
Bakhta village, *172*, 202–4
Bakunin, Mikhail, 95
Baltic oaks, 51
banditry, 6, 73, 92, 113, 143, 162
bandura (Ukrainian stringed instrument), 87, 88
Bashman of the Kipchak, 30–31
Bazykina, Aksinya, 73
bears
  cubs orphaned by hunting, 220–23
  as dangerous enemy, 5, 16, 20, 47, 174
  Khanty bear ceremony, 13–14, 22–23
Becker, Laetitia, 228, 230–31
beech trees, 64
beehives and honey, 5, 20, 47
Belarus, 2, 3, 9, 45–46, 48, 84, 142–46, 150, 152, 153, 213
Bell, The (journal), 57
"Berries" (Platonov), 137–38
Białowieża Forest, *44*, 45–48, 56–57, 141–43, 154
birch bark, 17, 90, 99, 161, 191, 192, 236
birch trees, 35, 41, 76, 101, 156, 191, 243
bison (wisent), 48, 57, 216
Black Sea, *44*, 71, 215
Bologov, Viktor, 221–23
Bologov, Vladimir, 221, 224–33, *232*, 237
Bolsheviks, 7–8, 122–23, 132–33, 161, 189
Borodino, Battle of, 154
Bratsk hydroelectric dam, *172*, 180
Brezhnev, Leonid, 170, 184, 186, 224
Bubonitsy village, *44*, 222–25, 228, 249
Bukhara (now Uzbekistan), *26*, 37
Burkhan Khaldun mountain, *27*, 28–29, 32
Buryats, 41, 93, 113, 182, 210
"Buryga" (Leonov), 161
Bykaŭ, Vasil, 152

cannibalism, 22
capercaillie grouse, 203
capitalism, 9, 84, 158–59, 167–68, 196–96
Catherine the Great, 54–57, 58–63, 188
Caucasian wars, 59–62. *See also* North Caucasus
Caucasus Mountains, 58–60
Central Asia, 1, 2. *See also* steppes
Chechen people, 2, 63–71, 201, 207, 210
Chechnya, 63–71, 72–80, 207, 239
Chekhov, Anton, 11, 50, 86, 116–22, 123, 127
  The Cherry Orchard, 11, 121–22, 123
  on Sakhalin Island, *91*, 116–22, 130, 134
  Uncle Vanya, 118–19, 123, 130
  The Wood Demon (*Leshii*), 116, 118, 120–21, 130
Chekhov, Egor, 116, 117
Chepyzh oak forest, 75, *77*
Cheremis (Mari) people, 37
Chernavin, Tatiana, 234–37
Chernavin, Vladimir, 234–37
Chernyshevsky, Nikolai, 86
"Cherry Brandy" (Platonov), 137
Cherry Orchard, The (Chekhov), 11, 121–22, 123
Chertkov, Vladimir, 116–17
Childhood (Tolstoy), 74
China
  borders with Russia, 93, 98, 220
  in legend, 188
  legends from, 16
  Qing Empire, 91, 98, 106
  trade, 18, 19, 109–10
Chinggis Khan, 1, 2, 29–30. *See also* Mongol Empire
Chirikova, Evgenia, 198, 199
Chita, 93–94, *172*
Chornobyl, *44*, 184, 213, 216
Christianity. *See* Russian Orthodox Christianity
Chukchi people, 99
Circassians, 61–62, 67, 69, 70, 110
citizenship to nonhuman entities, 166
civil war. *See* Russian Civil War
civilization, 14–18, 54, 96, 204
  the "civilizing mission" of colonialism, 23–24, 53, 67
  as corrupt, 9, 112, 190
  notions of progress, 14–18, 25, 82, 95, 107, 132, 164, 179
  See also modernization
climate change, 8, 17, 120, 157, 185, 212
coal mining, 101–2
Colbert, Jean-Baptiste, 52
collectivization of agriculture, 14, 23–24, 127, 130, 162, 193
colonialism. *See* settler colonialism
Columbus, Christopher, 196
Come and See (film), 153
common lands, 55, 83
Communist Party, 124. *See also* Bolsheviks; Revolution of 1917; Soviet Union
Congress of Siberian Writers (1926), 126

coniferous forests, 92, 93, 135
conscription, evading, 9–10, 210–11, 237
conservationism
 the progressive landowners of imperial Russia, 80–85, 117, 242
 in the Russian Federation, 199, 208, 214
 sacred groves, a form of forest preservation, 65
 in the Soviet Union, 124–28, 159, 160, 164
 Soviet *zapovedniki* (nature preserves), 124, 128, 190, 223, 262
conservative nationalism, 205–6, 208
convicts, 6–7, 61–62, 94, 97, 98, 174. *See also* Gulags
Cooper, James Fenimore, 70, 105–9, 110, 113–14, 186
Cossacks, 39–43, 63, 65
 along the Amur and the Chinese border, *91*, 91–92, 98, 103
 artifacts of the Ukrainian Cossack State, 216
 ethnic intermixing, 68–69
 myths of the, 69
 Old Believers, 68, 232
 in Russian literature, 66–70, 86–88
 of the Terek River, North Caucasus, 63–69
 the Zaporizhian Host, 48
Cossacks: A Caucasus Tale of 1852, The (Tolstoy), 66–71, 256
Crimea, *44*, 55, 209
Crimean Tatars, 50
Crimean War, 57, 70, 90
culture. *See* Russian culture
currency, 9, 196, 233
Curtis, Adam, 245
Custine, Marquis de, 204
"Cutting Down the Forest" (Tolstoy), 82

dachas, 125
Dagestan, 61, 63–64
dams, hydroelectric, 128, 176, 179, 180–81, 215–16
Dauerwald model ("continuous" or "eternal" forest), 141–42
Daurian people, 103
Dead Souls (Gogol), 80
Decembrist uprising, 60
deciduous forests, 2, 51, 132, 214
deforestation
 droughts and, 80, 124, 128, 124, 154–55, *157*, 157, 165
 erosion and, 65–66, 68, 76, 81
 famine, 80, 94, 130, 135, 157, 165
 flooding and, 65–66, 80
 from land reform after emancipation, 7, 83–84, 213
 of western Europe, 3, 19, 49, 234
Deripaska, Oleg, 201
Dersu Uzala (Arsenyev), 101–13, 116, 124, 129, 174, 188, 194, 210, 219
desertification, 155
de-Stalinization, 160
development. *See* civilization; modernization
diamonds, 171–77, *172*
dissidents and dissent
 in exile, 7–8, 13, 22–23, 43, 60, 92, 96–97, 239
 religious dissidents, 6, 187–88
 Soviet censorship and political prisoners, 130–35, 173, 176
 See also Gulags; Old Believers; resistance
Dnieper River, *26*, 31, *44*, 169
Don River, *44*, 50, 169
Donetsk People's Republic (DNR), 209
Dovzhenko, Oleksandr, 124
droit du seigneur, 87
droughts, 80, 124, 128, 124, 154–55, *157*, 157, 165
Drozdov, I., 70–71
Dugin, Alexander, 207, 209
Dutch East Indies Company, 50
Dutch Republic of the United Provinces, 49–52, 53, 196
"Dwarf Pine, The" (Shalamov), 139
Dzhugashvili, Iosif. *See* Stalin, Joseph

Earth (film), 124
Eastern Slavs, 4, 20, 243. *See also* Slavic people
eco-anarchism of the 1990s, 197, 207
eco-nationalism, 155, 178–85
ecosystems
 permafrost, 10, 136, 138, 139
 temperate zones, 173
 tundra, 14–15, 23–24, 41–43, 99, 136, 139, 161
 See also rivers; steppes; taiga
Edward I of England, 19
Elagina, Ekaterina, 174–77
electricity, 116, 124, 129, 176, 179, 180–81, 195, 215–16
Elizabeth of Russia, 60

emancipation of the serfs, 7, 73, 80–84, 97
dual emancipation of forest and serf, 82, 112, 121–22
social transformation after the, 102, 116–17, 122
Empoli, Giuliano da, 245
engineering, 130–34, 179, 181, 215
England, 19, 49–51, 57, 74
environmentalism
climate change, 8, 17, 120, 157, 185, 212
desertification, 155
eco-anarchism of the 1990s, 197, 207
eco-nationalism, 155, 178–85
See also conservationism; deforestation
ermine, 19
erosion, 65–66, 68, 76, 81
"Escape Through the Forest" (organization), 237
Estonia, 13–14
Estonian language, 21, 37
ethnicities of Russia
chauvinism, 86, 160, 180, 205, 208, 211
ethnic intermixing in the Russian Empire, 54, 68–69, 98–99, 182
"small peoples," 113
xenophobia, 160, 169
See also Cossacks; Indigenous peoples of Russia; Slavic people
ethnography, 14, 22–24, 61, 188
Europe. *See* western Europe
European bison (wisent), 48, 57, 216
"European Russia," 2, 8, 80, 84, 85, 93, 112, 118, 182
European Union (EU), 46, 219, 231
Evenki (Tungus) people, 42, 89, 90, 99, 105, 110, 112–13, 182–83
expansionism. *See* Russian Empire
expeditions/exploration, 21–22, 102–3, 171–78, 186–87, 191–92
extinction, 99, 109–10, 134

fairytales. *See* folk culture
famine, 80, 94, 130, 135, 157, 165
Farewell to Matyora (novel), 180–85, 216
far-right ultranationalism, 202–4, 207–9, 21, 246
federalism, 95
fermented mare's milk, 61
films, 110, 142n, 147–54, 176–78, 205–6
avant-garde, 124
depicting Indigenous people, 13–14, 16
documentary films, 24–25, 205
Finland
forest management in, 231–33, 237
Karelia, 17, 226–38, *235*
prehistoric, 17
reintroducing wolves in, 230–33, *232*, 237
White Sea Canal, 131, 133
Finnish language, 13, 14
fir trees, 79, 135, 184
fire
forest fires, 10, 93–94, 109, 123, 165, 178–79, 205, 212–14
sacred fires of the pagan Slavs, 17, 243
"Fire, The" (V. Rasputin), 180
Firebird (sculpture), 243
fishing, 15–18, 22, 43
collectivization of, 23–24, 113
taimen fish, 16, 114, 175, 176
Flaubert, Gustave, 82
flax, 49
flooding
biblical flood, 181, 205
to build hydroelectric plants, 176, 179, 180–81, 215–16
deforestation and, 65–66, 80
from draining swamps and wetlands, 84–85
folk culture/folklore, 1–2, 4–5, 9, 11, 53, 59
Baba Yaga, 5–6, 9, 240
the City of Kitezh, 189, 216
in contemporary art, 242–44
Cossack origin story, 68–69, 87, 88
creation myths, 4, 101
myths and sacred trees, 1–2, 182
of Old Believers, 189
proverbs and sayings, 4, 122, 151, 171
rusalka (forest mermaid), 32
Russian fairytales, 1–2, 4–5, 9, 11, 243–44
in Soviet culture, 159, 166–67
"world tree," 182
See also leshii (wood goblins)
Fomichev, Sergei, 197
"For Future Use" (Platonov), 130
forced (re)settlement, 23–24, 70–71, 144, 216
"Forest Day" holiday, 125, 127
forest fires, 10, 93–94, 109, 123, 165, 178, 205
"forest question, the," 118, 128, 171
forest sabotage, 145
forestry and forest management, 52, 55–56, 80–86
afforestation projects, 52, 55–56, 75–76, 155–59, *157*, 171, 213
"continuous cover forestry," 263

Dauerwald model ("continuous" or "eternal" forest), 141–42
German expertise in land reclamation and, 52–56, 75–76, 80–81, 85, 122–23, 141–42
of the Soviet Union, 124–25, 160–64, 168
pollarding, 74, 78
Soviet Prometheanism, 125, 157, 160, 242
"sustainable yield" technique, 126–28
union of forest workers, 124
forests of Russia, 1–4
Białowieża Forest, 45–48, 56–57, 141–43, 154
biodiversity of, 52, 216
Chepyzh oak forest, 75, *77*
coniferous, 92, 93, 135
deciduous forests, 2, 51, 132, 214
"emancipation" of the, 81, 83–85, 112
as enemy combatant, 70–71
as escape, 6, 9–10, 22–23, 155, 172, 173, 219, 233–37
forest fires, 10, 93–94, 109, 123, 165, 178, 205
Khimki Forest, *44*, 196–200
as places of exile, 7–8, 13, 22–23, 43, 60, 92, 96–97, 239
the primeval forest, 46, 56–57, 142
See also deforestation; taiga; timber; trees
Four Winters (film), 142n
French and Indian War, 105
French Revolution, 92
frontier literature, 70, 105–6, 112–13
fur, 2, 6, 18–25, 35–43, 49, 53
Fyodorov, Ivan Alekseyevich, 131–34

Ganibal, Abram Petrovich, 60
gardening
English-style parks, 74
home gardens, 9, 195, 196
"hunting gardens," 47–48, 52
in literature, 59
pollarding, 74, 78
trees in orderly rows, 52–53, 56, 123–24
gas stoves, 81, 193
genetics, the study of, 158
geology, 171–78, 186–87, 191–92
Georgia, independent, 246
Georgia, kingdom of, 58–59
Gerasimov, Grigory, 175, 176
Germany
forestry and land reclamation, 52–56, 75–76, 80–81, 85, 122–23, 141–42
influence at imperial court, 49, 52–56
intellectual influences from, 81–82
Nazi Germany, 141–54, 155, 166
Ginzburg, Yevgenia, 135–37, 233
Give Me Back What's Mine (M. Tarkovsky), 203
Gmelin, Samuel, 61
Gogol, Nikolai, 80
"going to the people," 96, 161, 245
Gold (Nanai) people, 101, 105, 112, 116
gold, 99, 136, 171
Golden Horde, 1, 2, *26–27*, 28–31, 35–37, 40, 240. *See also* Mongol Empire
"Golden Jungle of Russia," 51
Gorbachev, Mikhail, 9, 195, 223
Göring, Hermann, 141–42, 154
Gorky, Maksim, 79, 130–31, 163, 259–60
Great Britain, 19, 49–51, 57, 74
"Great Embassy" to western Europe, 50
Great Northern War of 1700– 1721, 51
"Great Stalin Plan for the Transformation of Nature," 155–60, *157*, 168
Great Stand (*stoyanie*) on the Ugra River, 240
guerrilla warfare, 2–3, 64, 66, 142–45
Gulag Archipelago (Solzhenitsyn), 206
Gulags
censorship and political prisoners, 130–35, 173, 176
economic self-sufficiency of each camp, 233, 234
escaping, 137–38
mass amnesty for Gulag prisoners, 173–74
memoirs of survivors, 135–37, 235
prison labor, 131, 133, 136, 172–73
Solovetsky Monastery (Solovki), 50, 189, 208, 232–34

Habsburg Empire, 56
Hadji Murat (Tolstoy), 71, 73
Hāmid, Abū, 20
Happy People (TV show), 202–3, 210
Henry III of England, 19
Hermitage Museum, 204–5
Hero of Our Time, A (Lermontov), 62, 209
Herzen, Alexander, 57
Himmler, Heinrich, 144
Hitler, Adolf, 141, 151, 153
Holod (newspaper), 238
"holy fools," 200
horses in warfare, 5, 29–30, 39, 58–59

hostage-taking, 24, 42, 61, 137
Hungarian language, 13, 14, 21, 37
Hungary, kingdom of, 31
Hunter's Sketches, A (Turgenev), 82–83, 110
hunter-gatherers, 14–18, 23, 25, 95
hunting, 43, 46–47, 52, 57, 70, 75, 77, 190
  British style, 57
  "hunting commandos," 143
  hunting grounds and preserves, 46–47, 52
  as literary trope, 131
  professional hunters, 203, 220
  rehabilitating bear and wolf cubs orphaned by, 220–23
hydroelectric power plants, 128, 176, 179, 180–81, 215–16

"I have built myself a monument . . ." (Pushkin), 89
icons, 4, 32–34, 165, 199
idols, 35, 53–54
Ievlev, Innokentii, 174–75
immigration, 45–46, 169, 209
imperial Russia, 72–88
  forces of revolutionary change, 7–8, 81, 86, 89, 92, 95, 119–23
  state reform, 55, 62, 81–84, 122
  the merchant class of, 19–22, 117
  See also aristocracy; peasantry; Russian Empire
"imperial sublime," 62, 209
In the Forests (Melnikov-Pechersky), 188–89, 206
Indigenous peoples
  affinities with the Russian peasant, 10, 102
  the Ainu, 116
  the Avars, 2–3, 63–66, 70–71, 73, 145, 239
  the Buryats, 41, 93, 113, 182, 210
  the Chechens, 2, 63–71, 201, 207, 210
  the Cheremis (Mari), 37
  the Chukchi, 99
  the Daurians, 103
  the Evenki (Tungus), 42, 89, 90, 99, 105, 110, 112–13, 182–83
  films depicting, 13–14, 16
  the Iura/Iugra, 20–21
  the Kabardians, 65
  the Komi, 21, 35, 41
  the Mansi, 13, 18, 25, 35, 37, 40, 41, 53–54
  the Nanai, 101, 105, 112, 116
  the Nenets, 18, 23–24, 25, 41
  the Nivkh, 116
  Russians' dependence on, 99, 102, 112, 172, 174
  the Saami, 238
  the Selkup, 16, 18, 23, 25, 37
  "small peoples," 113
  smallpox introduced to, 43, 106
  the Udege, 105, 112, 113–14, 197
  women, 43, 98–99
  the Yakuts, 97–100, 105, 112, 113, 175, 176
  See also Khanty people
Indo-European culture, 32–33, 182
Industrial Revolution, 57
Ingush language, 65
intelligentsia, 10
  anarchism, 88, 89, 127
  "going to the people," 96, 161, 245
  liberalism, 10, 57, 60, 82, 86
  nihilism, 78
  of today, 203–4, 206, 208, 210
  See also socialism
Irpin River, *44*, 214, *217*
Italy, 53
Iura/Iugra people, 20–21
Ivan III of Muscovy (Ivan the Great), 35, 240
Ivan IV (Ivan the Terrible), 36, 41, 68
Ivan Kupala night (Eastern Slavic summer solstice), 243
Ivan's Childhood (film by A. Tarkovsky), 149–51, *149*, 153, 178
Izborsky Club, 205, 206

Jagdkommandos (hunting commandos), 143
Jewish people, 86, 142–44, 150–51, 208
Journey into the Whirlwind (Ginzburg), 136
Juvayni, 30–31

Kabardian people, 65
Kalatozov, Mikhail, 176–79
Kaluga province and city, 89, 92, 239–46
Kama River, *26*, 36, *44*, 39, 93, 135, 136
Kaplan, Fanny, 161
Karakorum, *27*, 31
Karelia, 17, 226–38, *235*
Kavkaz (newspaper), 64–65
Kazan, 35–37
Khabardin, Iurii, 175, 176
Khanate of Sibir, *26*, 36–42
Khanty people, 13–14, 15–16, 22–24, 41, 53–54, 60
  bear ceremony of the, 13–14, 22
  in the medieval fur trade, 18, 35, 36

in Siberia, 40
silent and trackless, 24–25
Khimki Forest, *44*, 196–200
Khiva (now Uzbekistan), *26*, 37
kholmy (burial mounds), 182, 243
Khor River, 113
Khristoforov, Andrei, 200
Khrushchev, Nikita, 160, 164, 170, 224
kimberlite, 175–76
Kimonko, Dzhansi, 113–15
Kind, Natalya, 176
Kipchak people, 30–31
Kitezh, mythical city of, 189, 216
Klimentov, Andrei. *See* Platonov, Andrei
Klimov, Elem, 153, 184
Kolomna city, 26, 31
Kolyma River basin, 136–40
Kolyma Tales (Shalamov), 137–39, 173, 263
Komi people, 21, 35, 41
Korean people, 95
Korolenko, Vladimir, 86–88, 96–100, 102, 105, 116–17, 127, 132, 216
Kostomuksha preserve, 231
Kostyuchenko, Elena, 199
Kotoko people of Africa, 60
Kozlova Zaseka (line of tree barricades), 74–75
Kravchuk, Leonid, 9
Kropotkin, Peter, 89–96, 98, 99, 102, 127, 158, 168, 197, 239
Kuchum, Khan of Sibir, 39–41
"kulaks," 127
Kumyk language, 73
Kurosawa, Akira, 110–11
Kyiv, 4, 26, 31, 214, 217–18, *217*
Kyivan Rus, 2, 4–5, 26, 31

Lake Baikal, *27*, 28, 93, 99, *172*
Lake Chad, 60
Lake Kargi, 227, 228
"land art," 240–46
land mines, 212–13, 215
land reform after emancipation, 7, 83–84
landscape painting, 241–42
language
Mongolic languages, 22, 103
Old Church Slavonic, 192
Paleo-Siberian languages, 22
reform of the Russian language, 53
toponyms, 19, 46, 65
Tungusic languages, 22, 105, 113
Turkic languages, 19, 22, 30, 37
Uralic (Finno-Ugric) languages, 13, 22, 35, 36
vernacular language in literature, 59
larches, 2, 51, 76, 94, 101, 136, 139–40, 181–84, 185
Last of the Mohicans, The (Cooper), 105–9, 113–14, 186
Latvia, 142
Legend of the Invisible City of Kitezh, The (Rimsky-Korsakov), 189
Lena River, *27*, 41, 43, *172*
"Lend-Lease" (Shalamov), 138
Lenin Prize, 163, 169
Lenin, Vladimir, 129, 161, 181, 210
Leningrad, siege of, 146, 193, 204, 234
Leonov, Leonid, 160–70, 179, 183, 185, 199
"A Note on Birchbark," 161
biography by Zakhar Prilepin, 211–12
The Russian Forest, 160–70, 179, 211–12
Lermontov, Mikhail, 62, 66–68, 110, 209
leshii (wood demons), 5–9, 88
becoming one, 224
in Chekhov's play *The Wood Demon* (*Leshii*), 116, 118, 120–21, 130
possible encounters with, 174, 236
as a socialist patriot, 167
to the Veps of Karelia, 236–37
in the works of Leonid Leonov, 161–66
Letter Never Sent (Kalatozov), 176–79, *177*
"Letter to Comrade Stalin" (Prilepin), 208
liberalism, 10, 57, 60, 82, 86
Limonov, Eduard, 207
linden trees, 76, 147
"Literature and Revolution" (Trotsky), 123
Lithuania, 48, 142
Lithuanian grand dukes, 46–47
"loans-for-shares" scheme, 195–96
Logone city, of the Kotoko people of Africa, 60
Louis XIV of France, 52
lumber. *See* timber
Lykov family of Old Believers, *172*, 186–96, 200–201
lynx, 57, 216, 224, 227–28
Lysenko, Trofim, 158–59, 167

"Makar's Dream" (Korolenko), 97
Manchuria, 102–3
Mandelstam, Nadezhda, 135, 140
Mandelstam, Osip, 134–40, 163, 233
Manichean sense of good and evil, 25
Mansi people, 13, 18, 25, 35, 37, 40, 41, 53–54

maps, 34, *38*, 61, 99, 120, 224
Maresyev, Aleksei, 146–48
Mari (Cheremis) people, 37
Mayakovsky, Vladimir, 116
medieval Russia, 18–22
  fur trade, 2, 6, 18–22, 35–43, 49, 53
  Muscovy, 2, 4–5, 34–43, 49, 59, 92
  Novgorod, 20–24, 26, 31, 35, 53, 192
  wooden churches of, 205–6, 216–17, 245
Melnikov-Pechersky, Pavel, 188–89, 206
Memoirs of a Revolutionist (Kropotkin), 89–90
merchant class, 19–22, 117
Meri, Lennart, 13–14
Merkit people of Mongolia, 28, 29
Meyer, Franz, 75–76
Mickiewicz, Adam, 56–57, 142
Mikhailovskoe, Pushkin's estate, 60, 62, 262
Mineral Resources Institute, Saint Petersburg, 96
"minever" fur, 19
mining, 101–2, 145
  coal, 101–2
  diamonds, 171–77, *172*
  geology and, 171–78, 186–87, 191–92
  gold, 99, 136, 171
  open pit mining, 176
"Mir" diamond mine, *172*, 174–77
Mitusova, Raisa, 23
modernity
  destructiveness of both Western and Soviet visions of, 167
  mapping space, 34, *38*, 61, 99, 120, 224
  modern notions of time, 3, 4, 8, 168, 168
  zones of anti-modernity, 84
modernization, 126–28, 167–68
  engineering, 130–34, 179, 181, 215
  gas stoves, 81, 193
  railroads, 101–10, 126, 132–33, 145, 189
  surplus economies, 18
Monastery, The (Prilepin), 208, 233
Monetochka (musician), 205
Mongol Empire, *26–27*, 28–34, 189
  Burkhan Khaldun mountain, 28–29, 32
  fall of Kyiv, 4
  fall of Ryazan, 31
  Great Stand (*stoyanie*) on the Ugra River, 240
  the legacy of "the Mongol-Tatar yoke," 31–32, 42, 62, 240
  in the Russian chronicles, 31–34
  siege engines of the, 30
Mongolian folklore, 16
Mongolic language group, 22, 103
Moscow, 31, 197
  as the center of Muscovite Russia, 2, 4–5, 34–36, 49, 59, 92
  College of Agriculture and Forestry, 96
  the "German Suburb," 49
  as a "Third Rome," 35, 246
"mountain dwellers," 21, 63
Mozdok city, 63
Muravyov, Nikolai, 91, 94, 95
Murmansk, 52, 234
"Murmuring Forest: A Polesian Legend, The" (Korolenko), 86–88, 96, 216
Muscovy, 2, 4–5, 34–43, 49, 59, 92
mushroom picking, 79, 125
mutual aid, 95, 107, 158, 168

Nabokov, Vladimir, 7–8
Nadym River, 23
Nanai people, 101, 105, 112, 116
Nansen, Fridtjof, 259–60
Napoleonic Wars, 51, 62, 142, 144, 154, 155
Narodniks, 96–97, 161
National Bolshevik Party, 207, 209
"national products," 245–46
nationalism
  eco-nationalism, 155, 178–85
  erratic inclusivity of Russian nationalism, 210
  eternal forest, eternal nation, 142
  far-right ultranationalism, 202–4, 207–9, 21, 246
  Romantic nationalism, 59, 62, 90
  Russia's sense of national martyrdom, 31–32, 168, 194
nationalization of Russia's forests, 122
Native Americans, 43, 99, 105–6
nature
  as aesthetic object, 59, 62, 70
  as culture, 120
  cycles of, 8, 132, 171, 184–85, 202, 242
  as eternal, inexhaustible, 78–79, 134
  Indigenous views of, 25
  as place of freedom, 172–73
  Russian ambivalence to nature, 1, 129–30, 161
  as a "senseless emptiness," 172
  subjugation of, 8–10, 25, 118, 123–28, 130–32, 143–44
  unspoilt by man, 106, 118–20
  See also Slavic paganism

nature preserves, 124, 128, 190, 223, 262
Naturphilosophie, 82
Navalny, Alexei, 207
Nazi Germany, 141–54, 155, 166. *See also* World War II
Nenets people, 18, 23–24, 25, 41
Neolithic site at Amnya, 15–18, 24–25, *26*, 36, 40
Nevsky, Alexander, 31
New Economic Policy, 124, 126
new forests. *See* afforestation projects; rewilding
New Russia (Novorossiya), 55–56
Nicholas I, 90
Nicholas II, 189
nihilism, 78
Nikola-Lenivets Park, Kaluga region, 239–46
Nikon, Patriarch of Moscow, 187, 191, 232
1917 revolution, 7–8, 45, 83, 122–23, 160
Nivkh people, 116
Nizhny Novgorod, 72, 92, 188, 206
NKVD (Soviet secret police), 173
"noble savage," 70, 118
North Africa, 18, 19
North Caucasus, 2–3, 58–69, 71
  the Avars, 2–3, 63–66, 70–71, 73, 145, 239
  the Caucasian wars, 59–62
  the Chechens, 2, 63–71, 201, 207, 210
  the Kabardians, 65
  the Kipchaks, 30–31
  Terek River, 63–69
"Note on Birchbark, A" (Leonov), 161
Novaya Gazeta (newspaper), 207
Novgorod (medieval city-state), 20–24, 26, 31, 35, 53, 192
Novgorod (modern city), 31, 146

oak trees, 1–2, 4, 21, 45, 51–56, 65, 76, 92–94, 182, 199, 243
Ob River, 15–16, 18, *26*, 36
October Revolution, 122. *See also* Bolsheviks; Revolution of 1917
Oka River, 31, *44*
Okhotsk fort, 42
Old Believers, 6, 206, 209
  Cossacks, 68–69, 232
  the Lykov family, *172*, 186–96, 200–201
  "priestless," 188, 193
  on television, 202–3
Old Church Slavonic, 192
oligarchs, 195–97, 201, 202
Onon River, 28, 29
Operation Bagration, 153–54
orangeries, 74
Order of the Red Star, 131
Orientalism, 67, 70
Oroch peoples, 116
Oryol, 81, 110, 150
Ossetians, 65
Ottoman Empire, 52, 54, 58, 70
outer space, 171–72

Paleo-Siberian language group, 22
Pan Tadeusz (Mickiewicz), 56–57, 142
partisans of the Second World War, 3, 142–54
pasqueflower, 218
Pasternak, Boris, 135
Pathfinder (Cooper), 70
Pathologies (Prilepin), 207
Pazhetnov, Valentin, 220–25, 241
peasantry, 1, 6–7, 43, 47, 53
  affinities with Indigenous peoples, 10, 102
  agrarian socialism, 95, 96–97
  alcoholism among the, 97, 106, 180, 224, 242
  after emancipation, 83–84, 102, 116–17, 122
  the Green Armies, 7
  idealization of, 74, 96–98
  "kulaks," 127
  "peasant" as nationality, 98
  "state peasants," 73
  See also Russian village, the; serfdom
peat, 143
penal colonies. *See* Gulags
People of the Railway Kingdom, 131
"The People" movement, 207
People's Will, 97
perestroika, 195, 223
Perm, *26*, 35, 41, 96
permafrost, 10, 136, 138, 139
Persian Empire, 18, 30–31, 58
Pesikova, Agrafena, 24–25
Peskov, Vasily, 186, 193, 194
Peter and Paul Fortress, St. Petersburg, 86, 96
Peter the Great, 48–57, 191–93
  as "the first Bolshevik," 206
  the navy under, 2, 46, 48, 49–51, 54–55, 63
  "Russia's first forester," 52
  Westernization under, 50–53, 59, 74, 187

Piezonka, Henny, 16
pine trees, 2, 4, 13–15, 139, 213–14, 231–32
plane trees, 65, 68, 69
Platonov, Andrei, 129–34, 135, 181, 215
Platoon: Officers and Militiamen of Russian Literature (Prilepin), 211
"Pogrom in Chechnya, A," 66
Poland
  Białowieża Forest, 45–48, 56–57, 141–43, 154
  third partition of, 56
  during WWII, 141–42
Polesia, 84–87, 143–46, 216
Polevoi, Boris, 147, 147n
Polish-Lithuanian Commonwealth, 48
Polissky, Nikolay, 239–46
poplar trees, 9, 69, 103
Popov Island, 233
Popugaeva, Larisa, 174–76
post-Soviet Russia. *See* Russian Federation
potatoes, 191, 196
Potemkin, Grigorii, 55, 58
"Potemkin villages," 55
pre-Christian Russia. *See* Mongol Empire; Slavic paganism
prehistoric Russia, 4–6, 13–18, 24–25, *26*, 36, 40
preservationism. *See* conservationism; environmentalism
Prilepin, Zakhar, 206–10, 212–18, 233
Primary Chronicle of 1096, 20
Primorskyi Krai (Primorye), *91*, 102–5, 108, 220
Pripet marshes in Ukraine and Belarus, 143–44
Prishvin, Mikhail, 128
"Prisoner of the Caucasus, The" (Pushkin), 61
privatization of Russian forests, 55, 56
privatization vouchers, 195, 201
"production novels," 162
progress, notions of, 14–18, 25, 82, 95, 107, 132, 164, 179
Prokofiev, Sergei, 147
proletariat, the, 1, 122–23
Prometheanism, 125, 157, 160, 242
property ownership, 7, 15, 17–18
  common lands, 55, 83
  forestry and calls for reform, 85–88
  land reform after emancipation, 7, 83–84
  nationalization of Russia's forests, 122
  the parallel bondage of serf and forest, 81, 83–85, 112
  privatization of the forests, 55, 56
protest. *See* environmentalism; resistance
Prussia, 56
Pure Forest research station (*Chistyi Les*), 222. *See also* Pazhetnov, Valentin
pushcha ("thick forest"), 46
Pushkin, Alexander, 59–63, 66–67, 110, 205, 209
  "I have built myself a monument . . . ," 89
  Mikhailovskoe estate, 60, 62, 262
  "The Prisoner of the Caucasus," 61
Putin, Vladimir, 3, 9, 176, 208–9, 238, 238, 245
Pyatigorsk spa town, 60, 72
pyrope, 175

race. *See* ethnicities of Russia
railroads, 101–10, 126, 132–33, 145, 189
Rainbow Keepers, 197, 207
Rasputin, Valentin, 178–85, 206, 208, 212, 216
realism, in literature, 66
Red Army, 113, 141, 151, 153–54
red ochre, 17
"red-brown" political position, 207
Reds and Whites. *See* Russian Civil War
reforestation, 7. *See* conservationism; rewilding
reindeer, 14, 23–24, 28, 41–42, 43, 99, 227
Remezov Chronicle, *38*, 39, 41
Repin, Ilya, 79
resistance, 2, 53, 59, 85, 144–45
  antinuclear activism, 216
  assassination attempts, 97, 161, 209
  to the Bolsheviks, 7, 113–15, 123, 127, 144–45, 161
  Decembrist uprising, 60
  eco-anarchism of the 1990s, 197, 207
  led by shamans, 24, 97
  to Mongol conquest, 30
  to the Nazis, 3, 142–54
  to Putin, 208–9
  "Snow Revolution" of 2011–2012, 199
  See also intelligentsia
"Resurrection of the Larch, The" (Shalamov), 139–40
revolution, 7–8, 81, 86, 89, 92, 95, 119–23. *See also* Bolsheviks; Revolution of 1917
Revolution of 1905, 81
Revzin, Grigory, 242
rewilding, at Chornobyl, 184, 213, 216

Rimsky-Korsakov, Nikolai, 189
Riurik of Kyivan Rus, 74
rivers
  deforestation and, 125, 128
  drying up, 83, 120
  impact of emancipation on, 7
  as a kind of noble savage, 118
  piracy on the, 39, 68, 173
  rerouting and diversion of, 85, 123–24, 179, 242
  Siberian rivers in early Russian chronicles, 37
  weaponized, 214–15
Rodchenko, Alexander, 124
Rogovich, Giuriata, of Novgorod, 20–21
Romanov dynasty, 6–7
Romantic nationalism, 59, 62, 90
Romanticism, 123–24
Rostov, *26*, 31
Rublev, Andrei, 34. *See also Andrei Rublev* (film)
Rumiantsev, Piotr Aleksandrovich, 56
Rusal state aluminum company, 201
rusalka (forest mermaid), 32
Russia, 1–11, *26*, *44*
  Arkhangelsk, 49, 161, 165, 200
  borders with China, 93, 98, 220
  Bubonitsy village, 222–25, 228, 249
  demographics, 48, 54, 73, 92, 196
  Don River, 50, 169
  immigration in, 45–46, 169, 209
  Kaluga province and city, 89, 92, 239–46
  Kama River, 36, 39, 93, 135, 136
  Karelia, 17, 226–38, *235*
  Kazan, 35–37
  Khimki Forest, 196–200
  Novgorod, 31, 146
  Oka River, 31
  Perm, 35, 41, 96
  Pyatigorsk spa town, 60, 72
  Rostov, 31
  Saint Petersburg, 53, 86, 96, 204–8
  Taganrog harbor, 50, 52, 117
  temperate zones, 173
  Tver, 31
  Ugra River, *44*, 239–41
  Vladimir city, *26*, 31, 32, 237
  Volga River, 4, 13, 30–31, 36, 39, 117–19, 130
  Yaroslavl, 31, 228
  See also ecosystems; Moscow
Russian Ark (film), 204–5
"Russian ark" as metaphor, 181, 194, 199, 202, 204–6, 214, 231, 246
Russian Civil War, 7, 113–15, 123, 127, 144–45, 161
Russian Empire, 58–71
  closing of the eastern frontier, 113
  Decembrist uprising, 60
  double-headed eagle, 242
  ethnic intermixing, 54, 68–69, 98–99, 182
  Forestry Department, 86
  the "imperial sublime," 62, 209
  in maps, *26–27*, *38*, *44*, *91*, *172*
  New Russia (Novorossiya), 55–56
  in the North Caucasus, 2–3, 58–69, 71
  parallels with America's westward expansion, 99
  railroads of the, 101–10, 126, 132–33, 145, 189
  smallpox among Indigenous peoples, 43, 106
  the Stroganov family, 37–39, 80–81
  See also settler colonialism
Russian Far East, *91*
  the Ainu, 116
  Amur River, 91–92, 105, 113, 234
  the Daurians, 103
  the Evenki (Tungus), 42, 89, 90, 99, 105, 110, 112–13, 182–83
  the Koreans, 95
  the Nanai, 101, 105, 112, 116
  the Nivkh, 116
  Primorye (Primorskyi Krai), 102–5, 108, 220
  Sakhalin Island, 116–22, 130, 134
  the Udege, 105, 112, 113–14, 197
  Ussuri River, 94, 113, 210, 234
  Vladivostok, 102, 210
Russian Federation
  capitalism in the, 194–96
  conservationism in the, 199, 208, 214
  economic crisis of 1998, 196
  the intelligentsia of today, 203–4, 206, 208, 210
  "managed democracy," 245
  neo-imperialism of, 209, 211, 212
  politics of immigration in the, 169, 209
  privatization vouchers, 195, 201
  resistance in the, 196–200
  "Snow Revolution" of 2011–2012, 199
  war on Ukraine, 3, 9–11, 208–15, 216–18, *217*, 237–38, 244, 246
Russian Forest Code, 199

Russian Forest, The (Leonov), 160–70, 179, 211–12
Russian Imperial Army, 102
Russian invasion of Ukraine, 3, 9–11, 208–15, 216–18, *217*, 237–38, 244, 246
Russian Navy (imperial Russia), 2, 46, 48, 49–51, 54–55, 63
Russian Navy (Russian Federation), 9
Russian Orthodox Christianity
anarchism, 95–96
animism, 32–34, 35, 97, 180
conquest of Siberia, 36–42
conquest of the Caucasus, 58
conversion of non-Russians, 14, 35, 41, 46, 68, 182, 189
conversion of the Slavs, 5–6
distinctly Siberian blend of pre-Christian animism and, 180
excommunication, 79
"holy fools," 200
icons, 4, 32–34, 165, 199
last Europeans to convert to, 46
man's subjugation of nature, 10, 32, 41
Manichean sense of good and evil, 25
Moscow as a "Third Rome," 35, 246
Peter the Great and, 53–54, 187
reversing Christian colonialism, 182, 185
See also Old Believers
Russian society. *See* aristocracy; peasantry; serfdom
Russian village, the, 180
end of the traditional village, 222–24
"Potemkin villages," 55
as proto-socialist model, 95, 96–97
ultranationalism and, 206–8
the "Village Prose" movement, 179–80, 184, 206, 208
See also peasantry; serfdom

Saami people, 238
sable, 18–20, 22, 36, 40, 43, 114
Sahaidak, Andriy, 217–18
Saint Petersburg, 53, 86, 96, 204–8
Sakhalin Island, *91*, 116–22, 130, 134
Sankya (Prilepin), 207–8
science, 3, 82
backwardness of peasants, 122
engineering, 130–34, 179, 181, 215
scientists sent to the Gulag, 234–35
in the Soviet Union, 128, 134, 158–59, 167, 171–78, 185, 186–87, 191–92
See also forestry and forest management
scorched-earth policy, 150–51
Scythian warrior-nomads of Siberia, 17
Secret History of the Mongols, 29
secret police, 24, 95, 96, 135, 202, 233, 236
Selkup people, 16, 18, 23, 25, 37
serfdom, 7, 60, 73–74, 80–88, 92
droit du seigneur, 87
escaped, 6, 202
forbidden the use of guns, 143
household serfs, 83
notable serfs, 72, 80–81, 92, 242
parallel bondage of serf and forest as property, 81, 83–85, 112
serf women and noble marriages, 73, 82
See also emancipation of the serfs
settler colonialism, 42–43, 56, 63, 92–99, 184–85
contemporary, 210–11
forced (re)settlement, 23–24, 70–71, 144, 216
German and Mennonite settlers, 56
Severodonetsk, 213
Shakhovskoi, Miron, 41
Shalamov, Varlam, 136–40, 173, 176, 263
shamans, 24, 97
Shamil (imam of Chechnya), 2–3, 63–66, 70–71, 73, 145, 239
shaving of men's beards, 53, 54
Shelgunov, Nikolai, 86
Shepitko, Larisa, 151–54, 184
Shevchenko, Taras, 88
Shies protests of 2019, 200
Shipov, Nikolai, 72–73, 80, 100
Shipov, the grove, 51, 166
Shishkin, Ivan, 242
Shklovsky, Viktor, 75
Shostakovich, Dmitrii, 159
Shushkevich, Stanislav, 9
Siberia, 2, 6–7, 14–25, *26–27*, *38*, *172*
Bakhta village, 202–4
Bratsk hydroelectric dam, 180
the Buryats, 41, 93, 113, 182, 210
Chita, 93–94
conquest of, 36–42
Irtysh River, 36, 39–41
the Iura/Iugra, 20–21
Kama River, 36, 39, 93, 135, 136
Khanate of Sibir, 36–42
the Komi, 21, 35, 41
Lake Baikal, 28, 93, 99

Lena River, 41, 43
Lykov family of Old Believers, *172*, 186–96, 200–201
the Mansi, 13, 18, 25, 35, 37, 40, 41, 53–54
"Mir" diamond mine, 174–77
Ob River, 15–16, 18, 36
the Selkup, 16, 18, 23, 25, 37
the taiga, 6, 22, 43, 47, 102–10, 176–78, 185
Taz River, 41
Tobol River, 39
Trans-Siberian Railroad, 101–10
the Yakuts, 97–100, 105, 112, 113, 175, 176
Yakutsk, *27*, 43, 98, 99
Yenisei River, 41, 42, 117–19, 173, 195, 202–3
See also Khanty people
Siberian globe flowers, 179
Siberian tigers, 10
Silk Road, 18
silviculture. *See* forestry and forest management
Simard, Suzanne, 158
Sinyavsky, Andrei ("Abram Tertz"), 8–9, 105n, 129, 171
slash-and-burn agriculture, 6, 222
"Slavic flood," 144
Slavic paganism, 4–5, 182
in film, 32–33
fire in, 17
sacred trees and groves, 3, 6, 41, 65, 182–83, 189
suppression of, 14, 182, 189
Slavic people, 20–21, 34–35, 59
conversion to Christianity, 5–6
during WWII, 143–44, 150
Eastern Slavs, 4, 20, 243
"small peoples," 113
smallpox, 43, 106
"Snow Revolution" of 2011–2012, Russia, 199
"social complexity," 95
socialism, 86–88, 167–68
agrarian socialism, 96, 161
the proletariat, 1, 122–23
the proto-socialism of the village commune, 95, 96–97
Socialist Revolutionaries (SR), 161
Sokurov, Alexander, 204
Solovetsky Monastery (Solovki Gulag camp), 50, 189, 208, 232–34
Solzhenitsyn, Alexander, 176, 206, 210
Song of the Forests, The (Shostakovich), 159
Sons of Torum (Meri), 13–14, 16
Sot, The (Leonov), 162
Soviet Union, 1, 3–4, 7–9, 122–26
"allotment gardens," 195
approach to time and nature, 8, 132, 131, 181
Brezhnev's Era of Stagnation, 224
censorship and political prisoners, 130–35, 173, 176
Chornobyl disaster, 213, 216
conservationism in the, 124–28, 159, 160, 164
electrification, 116, 124, 129, 176, 179, 180–81, 195, 215–16
end of the, 9, 195–97, 216
"Forest Day" holiday, 125, 127
Ministry of Agriculture and Food, 124–25
nature preserves (*zapovedniki*) of the, 124, 128, 190, 223, 262
New Economic Policy, 124, 126
the new Soviet man, 114–15, 133
Prometheanism, 125, 157, 160, 242
propaganda, 130, 158–59
rationing in the, 136, 194
science in the, 128, 134, 158–59, 167, 171–78, 185, 186–87, 191–92
secret police, 24, 173, 233
"sustainable yield" technique, 126–28
war against the "kulaks," 127
War Communism, 124
See also Gulags; Stalin, Joseph
spruce trees, 21, 76, 147–48, 236
Stalin, Joseph, 8, 126–28, 162–63
annexation of Estonia, 13
collectivization of agriculture, 14, 23–24, 127, 130, 162, 193
construction of the White Sea Canal, 131, 133
in contemporary Russia, 208
death of, 159, 160, 173
industry under, 126–28, 134, 171–72
literature under, 129–40, 148, 162–63, 181, 193, 234
purges, 23, 126, 134–40, 162–63, 193, 234
the "Great Plan" to forest the steppes, 155–60, *157*, 168
"Stalin Epigram" (Mandelstam), 134–35
Stalin Prize, 159
"state peasants," 73

Stefan, Bishop of Perm, 35, 41
steppes, 1, 2, 4, 8, 28–31, 38–39, 56
  afforestation of the, 52, 55–56, 75–76, 155–59, *157*, 171, 213
  in literature, 61, 67–68, 88, 89
  See also Ukraine
Story of a Real Man (Polevoi), 146–49, 147n
Streltsy, the tsar's infantry, 49
Stroganov family, 37–39, 80–81
Stroganov, Grigory, 38–39
sublime, 34, 59–62, 66, 209
sukharnik (silver pine), 231–32
supply chain collapse, 9
Surkov, Vladimir, 245–46
surplus economies, 18
"sustainable yield" technique, 126–28
swamps. *See* wetlands
Sweden, 51

Taganrog harbor, 50, 52, 117
taiga, 2, 6–7, 19–20
  as devoid of artistry, 120
  in Indigenous myth, 101
  in Karelia, 17, 226–38, *235*
  in prehistory, 13–25
  in Siberia, 6, 22, 43, 47, 102–10, 176–78, 185
taimen fish, 16, 114, 175, 176
Tarkovsky, Andrei, 32–34, 149, 173–74, 203, 211
  Ivan's Childhood, 149–51, *149*, 153, 178
  Andrei Rublev, 32–34, *33*, 149, 203, 240, 243
Tarkovsky, Mikhail, 202–4, 206, 209–11, 212
Tatars, 32–33, 37–42, 50, 60, 76, 99, 113, 240
taxes, 21, 30, 31, 85
Taz River, *27*, 41
temperate zone, 173
Temujin, 28–29. *See also* Chinggis Khan; Mongol Empire
"Tenants" (Sinyavsky), 8–9, 105n
Teploukhov, Alexander, 80–81
Terek River, *44*, 63–69
Tertz, Abram (Andrei Sinyavsky), 8–9, 105n, 129, 171
tigers, 10, 108
timber, 7, 46, 63, 101–2, 126–27, *235*
  forest management and, 52, 54–55, 142
  international trade in, 49, 234
  pine plantations, 213–14
  poaching, 51, 83
  prison labor and, 136, 138, 233
  strategic value in war of, 145
  tumbling price of, 84
  union of timber workers, 127
  See also deforestation
Timmerman, Franz, 49
Timofeevich, Yermak, 39–41, 68, 98, 203
Tobol River, *26*, 39
Tobolsky province, 93
Tolstoy, Lev, 7, 66–71, 73–85
  Anna Karenina, 79
  The Cossacks, 66–71, 256
  excommunication of, 79
  Hadji Murat, 71, 73
  military service in Chechnya, 66, 72–80
  War and Peace, 7, 78–79, 108, 139
  Yasnaya Polyana estate, *44*, 73–80, *77*, 262
Tolstoy, Sophia (Tolstoy's wife), 73, 76, *77*
Tolstoy, Tatiana (Tolstoy's daughter), 79
toponyms, 19, 46, 65
Torum, the Khanty father god of bears, 13, 22
trade
  fur, 2, 6, 18–25, 35–43, 49, 53
  through Indigenous middlemen, 20–21
  international demand for timber, 49, 234
Trans-Siberian Railroad, 101–10
trees
  beech, 64
  birch trees, 35, 41, 76, 101, 156, 191, 243
  fir, 79, 135, 184
  imported North American trees, 76
  larch, 2, 51, 76, 94, 101, 136, 139–40, 181–84, 185
  linden, 76, 147
  oak, 1–2, 4, 21, 45, 51–56, 65, 76, 92–94, 182, 199, 243
  orderly rows of, 52–53, 56, 123–24
  pine, 2, 4, 13–15, 139, 213–14, 231–32
  plane, 65, 68, 69
  poplar, 9, 69, 103
  spruce, 21, 76, 147–48, 236
  See also forests
Tretyakov, Sergei, 123–24, 259–60
Trotsky, Leon, 123
tsarist Russia. *See* imperial Russia
tundra, 14–15, 23–24, 41–43, 99, 136, 139, 161
Tungus (Evenki) people, 42, 89, 90, 99, 105, 110, 112–13, 182–83
Tungusic language group, 22, 105, 113
Turgenev, Ivan, 7, 81–82, 86, 110, 150, 179, 256

Turkic language group, 19, 22, 30, 37
Turkmenistan, 130–31
Turukhanskii District on the Yenisei, *172*, 173, 203
Tver, *26*, 31

Udege people, 105, 112, 113–14, 197
Ugra River, *44*, 239–41
Ukraine, 2–3, 9–11, *44*, 88
  Azov Sea, 50
  bandura (stringed instrument), 87, 88
  Black Sea, 71, 215
  Chornobyl, *44*, 184, 213, 216
  Crimea, 55, 209
  Dnieper River, 31, 169
  famine in, 157
  imperial Russia and, 48, 55–56, 58
  Irpin River, *44*, 214, *217*
  Kakhovka dam, 215–16
  Kyiv, 4, 26, 31, 214, 217–18
  Kyivan Rus, 2, 4–5, 26, 31
  Polesia, 84–87, 143–46, 216
  Pripet marshes, 3, 143–44
  Russian war in, 3, 9–11, 208–15, 216–18, *217*, 237–38, 244, 246
  Severodonetsk, *44*, 213
  Zhytomyr, 86
  See also Cossacks
ultranationalism, 202–4, 207–9, 21, 246
Uncle Vanya (Chekhov), 118–19, 123, 130
union of forest workers, 124
Union of Soviet Writers, 162
union of timber workers, 127
United States, 95, 97–99
  eco-activism in the, 197
  the experience of Native Americans, 43, 99, 105–6
  French and Indian War, 105–6
  frontier literature of, 70, 105–9, 112–13
  Khrushchev's visit to the, 160
  lend-lease aid during WWII, 138
  railroads in, 101
  Soviet memoirs published in the, 234
"United States of Siberia," 95
Untermenschen, 143
Ural Mountains, 2, 17, 31, 36
Uralic (Finno-Ugric) language group, 13, 22, 35, 36
urban culture, 96–97, 126. *See also* intelligentsia
Urusevsky, Sergei, 177
USSR. *See* Soviet Union
Ussuri River, *91*, 94, 113, 210, 234
Uzala, Dersu, 101–13, 116, 124, 129, 174, 188, 194, 210, 219

"vair" fur, 19
Velykyi Luh (Great Meadow), Ukraine, 215
Venice Architecture Biennale, 241, 243
Vep people of Karelia, 236–38
Viardot, Pauline, 82
"village communes," 95, 96–97
"Village Prose" movement, 179–80, 184, 206, 208
villages. *See* peasantry; Russian village, the
Vladimir city, *26*, 31, 32, 237
Vladivostok, *91*, 102, 210
"Voice from the Chorus, A" (Sinyavsky), 1, 129
Volga River, 4, 13, *26*, 30–31, 36, 39, 117–19, 130
Voronezh, 50, 51, 116
Vorontsov, Mikhail, 64, 73

War and Peace (Tolstoy), 7, 78–79, 108, 139
War Communism, 124
warfare
  arboreal fortifications (*zaseki*), 4–5, 8, 74–76, 156, 166, 198, 213
  ethnic minorities in Russian troops, 210
  evading conscription in the forest, 9–10, 210–11, 237
  forest sabotage, 145
  German hunting tactics in, 143
  guerrilla warfare, 2–3, 64, 66, 142–45
  horses in, 5, 29–30, 39, 58–59
  hostage-taking in, 24, 42, 61, 137
  in prehistory, 15, 17–18
  land mines, 212–13, 215
  memories of war, 148, 220
  scorched-earth policy, 150–51
  See also specific conflicts
"war-wilding," 216
wasteland (*pustosha*), 243
We (Zamyatin), 244
Wehrmacht, 143, 154
weirs for fishing, 16
western Europe
  deforestation for agriculture, 3, 19, 49, 234
  and "European Russia," 2, 8, 80, 84, 85, 93, 112, 118, 182
  first Russian writers famous in, 81
  gardens and estates in the style of, 74

western Europe (*continued*)
"Great Embassy" of Russia to, 50
Moscow as a "Third Rome," 35, 246
Peter the Great's love of, 50–53, 59, 187
publication of Russian censored works, 176
technical and cultural advances of early modern, 48, 82
views of Russians, 204–5, 219–20
Western Sayan mountains, 186
wetlands
draining of, 84–85, 130, 143–44, 237
near Kyiv, 217–18, *217*
mud and warfare, 30, 40
of Polesia, 84–87, 143–44, 216
swamps in literature, 124
Where the Sukpai Flows (Kimonko), 114
White Army, 7, 113, 161
White Sea. *See* Arkhangelsk; Solovetsky Monastery
White Sea Canal, 131, 133
Winter Palace, Saint Petersburg, 204
wisent (bison), 48, 57, 216
Wizard of the Kremlin, The (Empoli), 245
wolves, 57
in folklore, 28
"man is a wolf to man," 233
rehabilitation/reintroduction of, 221, 224–33, *232*, 237
women
Circassian slave girls in Russian literature, 61–62, 67, 110
in ethnography, 23
in geology, 174–77
illegal abortions, 176
as partisans in WWII, 151
scarcity in Siberia, 43, 94
serf women, 73
Siberian convict wives, 94, 98–99
Wood Demon, The (Chekhov), 116, 118, 120–21, 130
wood demons. *See leshii* (wood demons)
"wood wide web," 158
wooden churches, 205–6, 216–17, 245
"Wood-Sprite, The" (Nabokov), 7–8
"world tree," 182
World War I, 84
World War II, 8, 141–44
collaboration with the Nazis, 142n, 151–53
Operation Bagration, 153–54
partisans of the Second World War, 3, 142–54
scorched-earth policy, 150–51
siege of Leningrad, 146, 193, 204, 234
"writers' brigade" trip to Turkmenistan, 130–31
Writers' Congress in Moscow, 135

Yakutia, 97–100, 174–76
Yakutsk, *27*, 43, 98, 99
Yaroslavl, *26*, 31, 228
Yasnaya Polyana estate, *44*, 73–80, *77*, 262
Yeltsin, Boris, 9, 195–96
Yenisei River, *27*, 41, 42, 117–19, 173, 195, 202–3
Yermolov, Alexei, 62
Yesipov Chronicle, 36–37
YouTube, 201

Zaandam shipyards, Netherlands, 50
Zamyatin, Yevgeny, 244
Zaporizhian Host, 48
zapovedniki (nature preserves), 124, 128, 190, 223, 262
zaseki (arboreal fortifications), 4–5, 8, 74–76, 156, 166, 198, 213
Zavtra (journal), 207–8
Zazubrin, Vladimir, 126
Zhukov, Serafim, 175
Zhytomyr, *44*, 86
"zone of exclusion," *44*, 213, 216